Economic Development
And Regional Cooperation
KUWAIT

Publications of the Center for Middle Eastern Studies, Number 3
The University of Chicago

WILLIAM R. POLK, GENERAL EDITOR

Economic Development
And Regional Cooperation
KUWAIT

RAGAEI EL MALLAKH

THE UNIVERSITY OF CHICAGO PRESS

CHICAGO · LONDON

To the memory of my parents

PUBLICATIONS OF THE CENTER FOR MIDDLE EASTERN STUDIES

Number 1: *Beginnings of Modernization in the Middle East:*
The Nineteenth Century
Edited by William R. Polk and Richard L. Chambers

Number 2: *The Mosque in Early Ottoman Architecture*
By Aptullah Kuran

Number 3: *Economic Development and Regional*
Cooperation: Kuwait
By Ragaei El Mallakh

Library of Congress Catalog Card Number: 68-20512

THE UNIVERSITY OF CHICAGO PRESS, CHICAGO 60637
THE UNIVERSITY OF CHICAGO PRESS, LTD., LONDON W.C.1

General Editor's Preface

The Center for Middle Eastern Studies at The University of Chicago was founded in October, 1965. The more than two dozen members of its faculty offer courses on subjects ranging from the geography of Morocco to the literature of Iran, and from the beginnings of the Muslim state in the time of Muhammad to contemporary political problems. The Center and the Oriental Institute, which deals with the more ancient periods of the Near East, enable the University to offer perhaps the most complete program on the Middle East available anywhere in the world.

It is the purpose of the Center to encourage and disseminate scholarly work on the Middle East. To this end, the Center provides fellowships and research funds and brings to the University visiting scholars.

Professor Ragaei El Mallakh, now of the University of Colorado, has had a long and distinguished career dealing with the economies of the Middle Eastern countries. In this volume, the third of a series of works published by The University of Chicago Press for the Center for Middle Eastern Studies, Professor El Mallakh deals with the economy of one of the most interesting countries of the Middle East. As he shows, his work is relevant to those interested in wider and different fields: Kuwait embodies aspects of "under-development" and "overdevelopment" as measured by contemporary experience and is the economic generator for development over much of the Middle East and Africa.

This and forthcoming volumes in the series will illustrate the extent and diversity of the interests of the members at the Center for Middle Eastern Studies at The University of Chicago.

WILLIAM R. POLK

Director of the Center for Middle Eastern Studies

v

Foreword

This volume treats a subject which is of vast import to the Middle East and an undeniable factor in international finance. The Kuwaiti experience in the economics of rapid development and the regional implications of its aid-investment policies have long needed a serious study. Although articles and fragmentary comments exist dealing with the various domestic aspects of Kuwait's economic stance, this work offers social scientists, development and finance specialists as well as students of Middle Eastern affairs the first critical examination of that nation's economy within a larger, regional framework. It complements the World Bank report, which was a comprehensive compilation based largely upon domestic issues and demands, by combining pragmatic and theoretical interpretations with recent data and an assessment of the accelerated trend toward external investment.

In recent years the economic situation of Kuwait has been characterized by increasing capital surplus, and the country has joined the limited list of major aid-extenders. Yet the tendency is to dismiss Kuwait as something rather freakish and to explain it away on the basis that it is merely an oil producer of great magnitude. While the vastness of the Kuwaiti reserves, estimated the largest in the world, distinguishes it, other developing countries find themselves dependent upon this resource in varying degrees. Over 25 per cent of the export earnings of the less-developed nations is attributable to oil, making it the most important single source of foreign exchange. It should be pointed out that the oil investment of the United States and Great Britain is a net gainer and a positive factor in the balance of payments. Not only do two American companies and one British firm participate in the operation of the concessions in the country, the United States is also the largest single supplier of Kuwaiti imports. Kuwait's role as an international development financer illuminates the potential of intra-help among developing nations, and the relative stability of that state both economically and politically lends a note of optimism to regional cooperation and promotes greater international mobility of capital.

There are numerous facets of Kuwaiti development elucidated here which should interest economists and planners in the West. For example, the usual measurements employed in classifying an economy as "developed" or "developing" could be misleading when applied to Kuwait. It has the highest per capita income in the world and one of the highest savings rates, and it can claim an extremely favorable balance of payments. Yet the economy still reflects symptoms of underdevelopment including sectoral imbalance and overdependence on a single product. The savings-investment relationship is intriguing. The former has reached a high level, but the latter represents a bottleneck. What incentives can be applied to lessen this obstacle? Private and public investment abroad is sizeable, and in those countries which have become heavy recipients the sudden and/or mass movement of Kuwaiti funds can be critical, e.g., in Great Britain and Lebanon. Another relationship, that between effort and reward, bears observation. Can the hardy, trade-oriented entrepreneurial ability of the indigenous population survive such sudden wealth, and can it be redirected from commerce into other sectors?

In his opening discussions of the economics of rapid development, Professor El Mallakh points out that not all features accompanying swift capital accumulation are instantly positive. The condition of surplus capital in a developing economy causes great socioeconomic stresses, with the most potentially damaging that of waste and wasteful attitudes in human endeavor and productivity of total resources. Factoral imbalance, in addition to the accepted categorization of balance by sectors, is represented by the disproportionate relationship between capital and the other three factors of land, labor, and management; availability of capital is not a simple answer to the question of balanced development unless there is concurrent efficiency in utilization. This examination is not merely a case study; it has wider implications because of the regional ramifications and the existence of economies which share certain of the same characteristics with Kuwait, such as Libya, Saudi Arabia, and Venezuela.

The section dealing with the economics of oil is a careful treatment, attempting to draw out and clarify the major economic
issues without championing either the producing countries or the
companies. The point is made that petroleum cannot be compared
with many other primary commodities, particularly agricultural
ones, as it is a wasting asset which, with the present lines of utilization, must compete with other forms of energy. Questions of
elasticity and projection of demand for crude oil are considered,
but for reasons of clarification rather than in support of a point of
view. A major contribution is the author's presentation of multilateralism in oil, specifically the Organization of the Petroleum
Exporting Countries.

Having discussed the source of Kuwaiti affluence, oil, El Mallakh
turns to the problems of financing domestic development, identifying the characteristics of a capital-surplus economy, and analyzing
the role of the public sector. This surplus is described and measured
in terms of the gap between government revenues and expenditures,
in a comparison between the total savings and the total amount
invested in the economy, and finally, in the balance of payments.
Although Kuwait has been tabbed a "welfare state" because of
its level of social services, there is a clear distinction between
government participation and government control in business.
This portion also includes a critical study of the Kuwaiti government
policy vis-à-vis overreliance on the land purchase program and
overstaffing as related to efficiency.

Chapter 4 pertains to planning and balanced growth, with a
comparison drawn between the exigencies of development planning,
in the conventional sense of capital shortages, and the differing
requirements in a capital-surplus economy. Diversification is studied
within this context, and it is stressed that capital itself does not
eliminate the need of choice although it can widen the range of
choice. The book contains the first description and examination
of Kuwait's initial Five Year Plan (1967/68—1971/72). One
principal limitation in planning for balanced growth is the narrowness of the domestic market and the restricted absorptive capacity.
Therefore, external economic relations are of paramount importance, leading to the scrutiny of regionalism in the Middle East.
Here the reader is offered a frank and objective evaluation of the
collective measures and attempts to affect economic cooperation.
The "implementation gap" as drawn by El Mallakh goes a long

way toward correcting the impression fondly held by many that Arab economic unity is inevitable. Instead, it discerns the advantages and restrictions in certain stages of economic cooperation.

Finally, the first comprehensive and detailed exposure of the Kuwaiti aid programs is given, differentiating between those fulfilling economy and investment goals and those where political content is pronounced. These assistance activities place Kuwait in a position of economic power in the area which is far greater than its population and size would ordinarily command and which is vastly underestimated and unstudied in the West, particularly in the United States. The newly established institutions include the Kuwait Fund for Arab Economic Development, the General Authority for South Arabian and Arabian Gulf States, and the Arab-African Bank. In contrast is the assistance which has been extended for program and general support rather than project lending through credits from the state reserves. The operations of the Kuwait Fund have been singled out for special discussion because of the internationally accepted procedures followed and the businesslike demand for creditworthiness and feasibility of the projects seeking financial participation. The transfer of funds in a capital-deficit region has international overtones which, again, should not be overlooked. The author has done a valuable service by placing Kuwaiti aid within the total picture of all donor nations and multilateral agencies in terms of quality, relative magnitude, and impact. These are but a few aspects of this penetrating inquiry into the economics of development and regionalism.

El Mallakh's background has served him well in this study. He is by birth a Middle Easterner, in higher education a product of American universities. He has spent the last seventeen years in the United States, which gives objectivity to his analysis of economic affairs in the Middle East. His experience is both academic and practical, including his work as an economic consultant to the World Bank. The author's research and publications pertaining to Kuwaiti and Middle Eastern economic development mark him an expert in this area. His work on economic aid in general, international economics, resource development, and planning gives added breadth to the basic understanding underlying this volume.

EUGENE R. BLACK
Former President, The World Bank

Preface

My first research experience with Kuwait came in 1961 when I visited that country in connection with a study on regional economic cooperation in the Middle East supported by the Rockefeller Foundation. In the four years which elapsed between the initial and second trips to Kuwait, development had raced ahead. The nation had moved to full independence, the economy had witnessed an increasing capital surplus, and the country had become an aid-extender with all the attendant problems an assistance program encompasses. Despite such occurrences, no scholarly study has appeared on the Kuwaiti economic experience and the regional and international implications of its activities.

The objectives of this book are twofold. The first and main goal is to clarify and analyze the Kuwaiti example for development economists, other social scientists, those concerned with international finance, and students of Middle Eastern and African affairs. The second objective is to give Middle Eastern readers a study of the development taking place in one small but influential nation in their midst. One of the greatest difficulties in the area is that the countries know too little about each other's nonpolitical facets.

In the course of collecting data and materials, I discovered little-known aspects of economic affairs in Kuwait; hence at times this study is descriptive. Moreover, this description is valid as such data do not exist in any single comprehensive work. Additionally, as a first study this work is heir to the errors and omissions which mark a primary research effort. I have tried to keep the treatment understandable and clear, free from unnecessary jargon. Within the following pages I have also attempted to raise some questions pertaining to rapid economic development and the obstacles to Middle Eastern economic regionalism. Some cannot be answered at this point, but their presentation serves to illuminate the issues involved. The Kuwaiti experiment (and experience) is so recent, and the process of identifying its goals and limits so incomplete, that my purpose has been not so much to pass judgment as to analyze and pinpoint the trends and potentialities and to offer a few tentative projections.

The persons to whom my appreciation is due are numerous. Among those giving encouragement and support have been Eugene R. Black; Professors Morroe Berger and Philip Hitti of Princeton University, Charles Micaud and Josef Korbel of the University of Denver, Max Gideonse of Rutgers, and William R. Polk of Chicago; Mr. Claude Loombe of the Bank of England; and the late Lord Piercy. In gathering documentation and data I have received assistance from Yousef El Mallakh; Professor Y. Sayegh of the American University of Beirut (former advisor to the Planning Board); H. E. Jabir al-Ahmad al-Jabir, Prime Minister and former Minister of Finance and Oil, H. E. Jabir al-'Ali al-Salim, Minister of Guidance and Information, and their respective staffs; Abdulatif Al-Hamad, Director of the Kuwait Fund for Arab Economic Development; Ahmed Duaij and Fuoad Hussain of the Planning Board and its Statistical Office; Lucio Corradini of the European Coal and Steel Community; Edward Symonds with the Petroleum Department of the First National City Bank of New York; Haytham Malluhi, the Kuwait Chamber of Commerce and Industry; Miss Jamileh Fadel Khoury of the Ministry of Health; Dr. M. El-Shafie, Director of the Kuwait Institute of Economic and Social Planning in the Middle East; Hamzah Abbas Hussain of the Kuwait Currency Board; Saba George Shiber; Faisal al-Mazidi, Managing Director of the Kuwait Chemical Fertilizers Company; A. Abdul Wahab; S. Al-Jasem; M. Al-Sharekh; Dr. B. Chatti; and the staff of the Kuwait National Petroleum Company, particularly Mr. Ahmed Sayyid Omar and Dr. Rajai Abu-Khadra.

Among those who have been willing to scan all or part of the manuscript have been Professors Charles Issawi of Columbia University and E. S. Mason, Wassily Leontief, and A. J. Meyer of Harvard. My debt to them is great. The discussions of this study with, and comments by, my colleagues John Cassels, Carl McGuire, and John Powelson have been a source of stimulation, help, and enjoyment. Any errors, oversights, and shortcomings are my own. Teaching associates Faika Selim, Hassan Selim, and Said Dohia have assisted in the statistical compilation and tabulation. Eloise Pearson capably typed the manuscript and Teressa Hendry reviewed it. Finally, as a trained historian my wife Dorothea has given valuable criticism, and her contributions in every step to the manuscript's completion have been considerable.

I should like to acknowledge the support, facilities, and assistance I have received during the two years of research on Kuwaiti economic development from the Social Science Foundation of the University of Denver, the Center for Middle Eastern Studies of Harvard University, the Council on Creative Research of the University of Colorado Graduate School, and the Social Science Research Council.

R. EL MALLAKH

University of Colorado
Boulder, Colorado

Contents

List of Tables   xix

1. AN INTRODUCTION TO THE ECONOMICS OF
   RAPID DEVELOPMENT   1

   Resources and Growth   1
   The Rate of Development   6
   Backdrop to Development   8
      The Social and Political Setting   8
      Population and Labor   13
   Sectoral Development   17
   Trade and the International Outlook   22

2. THE ECONOMICS OF OIL   28

   Production and Reserves   30
   Utilization of Natural Gas   34
   Refining   37
   The Structure of the Kuwaiti Concession and the
      Royalty Issue   39
      Royalty Expensing   42
   Elasticity and Projection of Demand for Crude Oil   46
      Demand Projection for Oil   49
   Price Stabilization   53
   Production Programming   62
   Multilateralism in Oil   69

3. FINANCING DOMESTIC DEVELOPMENT   74

   The Capital-Surplus Economy   74
   Government Participation in Mixed Ventures   84
   Banking and the Capital Market   89

4. BALANCED GROWTH AND PLANNING   96

   Planning in a Capital-Surplus Economy   96
   Problems of Balanced Growth   100
   Industrialization: Stimulating a Sector   104
   Agriculturalization: Creating a Sector   116
   Human Resource Development   120
   The First Five Year Plan, 1967/68—1971/72   124

5. REGIONAL ECONOMIC COOPERATION:
   MOTIVES, PATTERNS, AND SHORTCOMINGS   133

   Some Economic Implications of Size   133
   Economies of Scale   140
   Balanced Development   142
   Regional Sectoral Planning   146
   Collective Measures   150
   The Implementation Gap   154
   Bilateralism   158
   Regionalism and Trade   161
   The Arab Common Market   166
   Interdependence   172
      Population   172
      Waterways and Water   174
   Conclusions   178

6. FOREIGN AID: A NEW FACTOR   181

   Kuwait's Entry into the Donor List   181
   The Kuwait Fund for Arab Economic Development   184
      Development Lending and Creditworthiness   184
      The Quality of Aid   186
      KFAED Operations   193
      Assessing the Fund's Impact   203
   Economic Aid through Grants   208
   The Arab-African Bank   210
   Credits from the State Reserves   212
   The Level of Economic Assistance   216
   Aid, Trade, and Development   220
      Tying Aid   220
      Kuwaiti Aid in Perspective   222
      A New Dimension for Economic Aid   224

7. MAINTAINING DEVELOPMENT: A SUMMING-UP 227

    The Economics and Constraints of a Wasting Asset 227
    Development through Cooperation: Regional
      Linkages 232
    Affluence versus Development 237

Selected Bibliography 240

Index 246

List of Tables

CHAPTER 1

Table 1: GNP and Net National Product of Kuwait, 1962/63—1965/66   7

Table 2: Expenditure on Gross National Product, 1962/63— 1965/66   9

Table 3: Population of Kuwait—Census of 1957, 1961, 1965   13

Table 4: Population by Age Group, Nationality, and Sex, 1965   15

Table 5: Distribution of the Labor Force, 1965   16

Table 6: Population by Economic Activity in 1965 Census   17

Table 7: Annual Increment in Trade, Percentage of Exports to Imports, 1952–65   23

Table 8: The Share of Oil in Kuwaiti Exports, 1958–65   24

CHAPTER 2

Table 1: Major Producers and Their Share of Total Oil Reserves and Production in 1965   31

Table 2: Crude Oil Production in Kuwait and the Neutral Zone   32

Table 3: Oil Production as Per Cent of Reserves of Major Producers, 1965   33

Table 4: Energy Consumption in Developed Countries   51

Table 5: Production of Crude Petroleum in the Middle East by Countries, 1913–65   63

Table 6: OPEC Oil Output Growth Rates   65

CHAPTER 3

> *Table 1:* Oil Revenues and Companies' Currency Purchases, 1958—1964/65   75

> *Table 2:* Government Budget and Surplus, 1961/62—1963/64   77

> *Table 3:* The Share of Current and Development Expenditures in Total Budgetary Outlays, 1961/62—1966/67   80

> *Table 4:* Summary of Balance-of-Payments Estimates, 1965/66   82

> *Table 5:* Government Participation in Joint-Stock Companies as of January 1, 1966   86

> *Table 6:* Yearly Stock Market Fluctuations, 1960–65   91

CHAPTER 4

> *Table 1:* Countries Ranked by Per Cent of Exports in the Three Commodities of Highest Value   99

> *Table 2:* Number of Enterprises and Workers (Excluding Oil Production), 1963   107

> *Table 3:* Wages as Percentage of National Income, 1964   109

> *Table 4:* Shares of Sectoral Contribution in the GDP for Base Year and Final Year and Investment Goals of Plan   127

> *Table 5:* Savings and Investment in Base Year and Final Year of Plan (at Base Year Prices)   129

> *Table 6:* Public Receipts during the Plan Period by Origin   131

CHAPTER 5

> *Table 1:* Distribution of Production Among Major Sectors in Selected Arab Countries   143

> *Table 2:* Regional Summary of Kuwaiti Imports, 1960–65   162

> *Table 3:* Share of Individual Countries in Total Arab Imports to Kuwait, 1960–65   163

> *Table 4:* Regional Summary of Kuwaiti Non-Oil Exports, 1960–65   164

> *Table 5:* Share of Individual Countries in Total Kuwaiti Exports to the Arab World, 1960–65   165

Table 6: Kuwait's Trade with Arab Common Market
  Members, 1965   166

Table 7: Non-Kuwaiti Arab Population, 1961, 1965   173

CHAPTER 6

Table 1: Ratio of International Liquidity to Imports
  (Selected Arab Countries, 1963)   188

Table 2: Terms of Official Bilateral Loan Commitments
  of D.A.C. Countries, 1964   190

Table 3: Major KFAED Loans Classified by Purpose and
  Country as of August 1966   204

Table 4: State Reserves Loans to Arab Countries Ranked
  by Amount Borrowed to August 1966   213

Table 5: Disbursements of Assistance as Percentage of
  National Income of Major Contributors, 1964   217

Table 6: Ranking of Official Bilateral Lending Commitments, 1964   218

Table 7: Net Flow of Lending from the OECD and Kuwait
  to Selected Arab Countries, 1963   219

Chart 1: Decline in Net Flow of Resources if Gross Lending
  Is Maintained at an Annual Fixed Level   192

An Introduction to the Economics of Rapid Development

1

RESOURCES AND GROWTH

Rapid development, so eagerly sought by most countries, has a set of economic and related social problems of its own. A study of the changes undergone by the Kuwaiti economy offers the development economist and other social scientists a rare opportunity to discern and analyze the economic consequences of highly accelerated growth. While the experience of Kuwait may have implications for general developmental economics and the less-developed nations as a whole, it has still wider ramifications for the Middle East and Africa, encompassing the impact of surplus capital on a regional basis and assuming further implications through the occurrence of similar economic expansion in the neighboring Gulf states and North Africa, specifically Libya.

The economy of Kuwait defies classification in the traditional academic categorizations of either "developed" or "underdeveloped." The rapidity of change has contributed to the blurring of the distinction; the Kuwaiti economy combines extreme features of both classifications. The highest per capita income, one of the highest savings rates—44 per cent of the GNP—a strong annual growth rate, and a consistently favorable balance-of-payments situation are all indicators of a developed economic status. Yet, on the debit side of the development ledger there are equally striking examples of underdevelopment, such as the near-total reliance of the economy on a single product, an inadequate indigenous supply of technical skills and labor, and overdependence on imports of capital goods and consumer products. Another symptom of under-development is the narrowness of the domestic market that does not emanate in this instance from a low per capita income but

1

rather from the sophisticated tastes affluence brings and the actual numerical size of the population. More critical, the effectiveness of the high rate of capital savings is largely offset by the limitations of the economy in offering ample productive investment opportunities, resulting in domestic absorption of but a minor portion of total Kuwaiti savings.

The assessment of how other factors of production respond to the growth of a single factor, capital, is a problem facing those less-developed countries experiencing rapid capital growth, whether that capital is derived from internal sources or through international transfer in the form of economic assistance. Yet another question: is capital the key to the process of economic development? For developing nations suffering from capital shortage, an increment in this factor can appear the panacea for underdevelopment itself. While capital could substitute for labor and resources, it remains a matter of the degree to which this substitution takes place. It would seem, however, that the efficient use of capital is every bit as important as its availability. In most developing nations there are elements which negate the availability of capital, such as hoarding, distortions through inflation, conspicuous consumption, bidding up prices of land, the lack or inefficiency of lending institutions, and finally, the most damaging—capital flight. Additionally, the existence of capital does not guarantee the existence of suitable or efficient banking mechanism or capital market so that savings might be loaned in an orderly fashion for productive internal and external financing. Assuming that investment does materialize, then the crux of the problem is ensuring that it is in the most productive lines for spurring further economic growth.[1] An examination of the Kuwaiti case may shed some light on the vagaries of capital.

The base of Kuwait's capital accumulation is oil, a primary commodity which is also a wasting asset. Of the estimated 80 developing nations Kuwait therefore belongs to that group of 30 countries which depend for more than half of their foreign exchange earnings on exports of a single crop or commodity.[2] The case of

---

[1] See Charles P. Kindleberger, *Economic Development*, 2d ed. (New York: McGraw-Hill Book Co., 1965), pp. 101–3.

[2] George D. Woods, "The Development Decade in the Balance," *Foreign Affairs*, January, 1965, p. 208, discusses the implications of a one-product economy. Oil accounts for over 90 per cent of Kuwait's foreign exchange earnings.

Kuwait, however, is more extreme than that of most of the economies falling in this category. Over 94 per cent of the budgetary revenue is attributable to its single product, oil, and it accounts for 61 per cent of the gross domestic product. The extent of this dependence and the limitations in non-oil resources of the country have dictated a single-product economy, rather than an economic choice of specialization or selected means of development through unbalanced growth.

The rapidity of Kuwaiti economic development mirrors to a great extent the smooth and unparalleled exploitation of its vast reserves. In 1946 Kuwait produced 800,000 tons of crude oil, 17 million in 1950, rising threefold in the next five years to 54 million and by 1964 to a staggering output of 105 million tons. Kuwait is now the world's second largest exporter of oil, the fourth largest producer, and holder of about one-quarter of the world's total proven reserves; one field alone, the Greater Burgan, is estimated to contain reserves equal to those of the United States. The speedy growth of the oil industry in Kuwait is without comparison in resource development.

The availability of capital alone did not make inevitable the path of development adopted by Kuwait; rather it resulted from a combination of a moderate attitude and specific policy decisions. The 8 per cent annual growth rate was, in the past, a direct result of the expansion of the oil industry. Resource exploitation will continue as the major contributor to the rate of growth, but ultimately the growth rate will depend upon the success with which other factors are met. W. Arthur Lewis has pointed out the following relationship between economic growth and resources.

> The extent of a country's resources is quite obviously a limit on the amount and type of development which it can undergo. It is not the only limit, or even the primary limit. For most countries could make better use of their existing resources than they do. Given the country's resources, its rate of growth is determined by human behaviour and human institutions; by such things as energy of mind, the attitude towards material things, willingness to save and invest productively, or the freedom and flexibility of institutions.[3]

Having met most of its social overhead requirements and still having a surplus of capital, Kuwait's stance vis-à-vis productive

[3] W. Arthur Lewis, *The Theory of Economic Growth* (Homewood, Ill.: Richard D. Irwin, Inc., 1955), p. 52.

investment assumes a position of paramount importance. The shortage of resources that has not impeded the unprecedented growth of Kuwait in turn limits the possibility of diversification and, by extension, domestic investment. Thus, regional and international investment are supplementary alternatives.

Besides the traditional avenues of investment, Kuwait has pursued a substantial but little-known investment-oriented assistance program on a regional basis.[4] Almost 10 per cent of the national income is being disbursed annually; this puts Kuwait in the forefront among world donors in the relative share of aid in the national wealth. In amount-value of bilateral lending commitments, Kuwaiti foreign aid ranks seventh internationally and sixth in comparison with the members of the Development Assistance Committee of the Organization for Economic Co-operation and Development, surpassed only by the United States, the United Kingdom, Germany, Japan, and France. This is an experiment in intra-help among developing countries in an area where capital deficit rather than shortages in skills and labor is the primary bottleneck in accelerating the rate of economic development. The validity of this experience lies in its applicability where similar conditions of accumulated capital occur within a regional framework—Libya in Africa, Venezuela in Latin America, and Saudi Arabia in the Middle East.

In planning, Kuwait has been spared the necessity of a rigid system of "either-or" choices, so often imposed by capital limitations, in selecting priorities. Conversely, capital surplus has widened the range of economic choice but has not diminished the need for choice. Wherever a surplus exists the possibilities of waste run high. There may be, as well, a weakening of the relationship between effort and reward. With its capital based upon the depletion of an asset, slow though this process may be, Kuwait must make its capital as productive as possible to offset and replace the nonrenewable resource. Where capital-deficit countries could not leave the development of their resources to accident or chance, the

[4] In two recent publications, I. M. D. Little and J. M. Clifford, *International Aid* (Chicago: Aldine Publishing Co., 1966), and Raymond F. Mikesell, *Public International Lending for Development* (New York: Random House, 1966), which cover the full scope of development lending and other forms of assistance, both bilateral and multilateral, there was no mention whatsoever of Kuwait or its position as an aid-extender. This demonstrates how little-known and hence undervalued the Kuwaiti assistance efforts have been by Western scholars.

capital of a rich, developing nation cannot be left to idleness. For a country like Kuwait, which is small in size and economically trade-directed, planning cannot be inflexible or regimented, as the most efficient use of capital requires adaptability to the changes in the profitability of investment at home and abroad.

The question in developmental economics, whether an increase in productivity comes through large, discontinuous steps or with a multiplicity of small incremental improvements, might be clarified by a study of the Kuwaiti experience.[5] Yet the issue is not only how but where in the economy the change takes place. Economic development occurring at a highly accelerated pace and beginning at a low base more likely than not is premised upon an imbalance. Three types of imbalance either exist or lie latent in the Kuwaiti economy: one, the deficiency in sectoral balance; another, factoral imbalance; and third, the possible imbalance in the investment mix. The sectoral structure of Kuwait indicates a severity of imbalance; while one form of primary production has been developed extensively (oil) another (agriculture) remains, for all practical purposes, nonexistent. Trade is highly developed in both oil and non-oil products, the latter largely of a transit nature. Industry, although still accountable for only a minor share of the GNP, is receiving substantial public and private attention.

In the factoral makeup, capital has left the other factors far behind, with entrepreneurial ability ranking second. Generally the emphasis in private entrepreneurship has been of a Middle Eastern sort, that is, Levantine, in trade and in real estate development. The latter concern has been reflected in a third factor of production, land. The urbanization of the country, particularly in the capital of Kuwait, has been phenomenal. In less than two decades this center moved from a typical Arabian peninsula town, modest and traditional, to an air-conditioned ultramodern city, one of the largest on the Gulf. The absence of agriculture has given a unique twist to traditional land reform; for income distribution purposes Kuwait utilizes its urban core. Kuwait also found itself deficit in labor to meet the demands of rapid development. The response to the needs for a larger labor force came through a stream of immigration, for the most part of regional origin. The hundreds of

[5] See the discussion of this aspect of economic development in Edward S. Mason, *Economic Planning in Underdeveloped Areas* (New York: Fordham University Press, 1961), pp. 44–51.

thousands of non-Kuwaitis furnished both the skilled and unskilled human resource requirements.

Third, in the initial flush of capital inundation, the surplus was mainly banked abroad. As oil production continued and increased, and as capital surplus became the expected rather than unexpected condition, the population grew acclimated to their wealth and a new element of stability brought about the need for domestic investment. Thus, the second phase was one of financing local construction. The government's land purchase scheme was instrumental in encouraging this trend. The imbalance lay in the preponderant share of real estate and construction in total investment. Having met most of the internal investment requirements, which were narrow because of both factoral and sectoral imbalance, the Kuwaiti investors then turned to international as well as regional opportunities. The drive toward diversification and balance has been dualistic, on the one hand in sources of income and on the other in the investment of accumulated reserves. The regional assistance programs, particularly the Kuwait Fund for Arab Economic Development, has been in the forefront of this diversification trend. Simultaneously Kuwait continues to take advantage of productive international investment opportunities in other developed and developing nations.

THE RATE OF DEVELOPMENT

In no country in the world has development proceeded with such speed as in Kuwait. Two decades ago at the close of World War II, the per capita income was estimated at only $21; in 1965/66 the per capita income could be computed at almost $3,215.[6] Even if the 1945/46 per capita income has been grossly underestimated and, say, for illustration, was as high as $100, the increase is still unparalleled elsewhere in developmental economics. The population of Kuwait rose almost fivefold in the same span of time. In this aspect, the Kuwaiti performance was not quite so phenomenal as the figure would indicate; immigration has been the key factor in this growth rather than natural increment. The history of population expansion in the Western United States is possibly the only similar

[6] The Planning Board, *Kuwait—Economic Survey 1965/66* (mimeographed, July, 1966), pp. 1, 5.

occurrence of this type; immigration and population movement were stimulated by gold fever and a boom-town mentality which bears a striking resemblance to the oil fever abounding in Kuwait.

The rate of economic growth since the mid-1950's has been high and relatively stable. Compilation of official time series estimates of the national product and national income have been carried out only in recent years. An average annual growth rate of 7.7 per cent has been ascribed to the period from 1959 to 1962/63.[7] This increment was a direct reflection of the growth in the oil sector and the substantial influx in the labor force. From 1963/64 through 1965/66 the average annual growth in the GNP was some 8.3 per cent, although since 1963/64 there has been a slight decline, as seen in Table 1. While the last three years have shown a greater rate of

TABLE 1

GNP AND NET NATIONAL PRODUCT IN KUWAIT, 1962/63—1965/66
(IN MILLION DOLLARS)

	1962/63	1963/64	1964/65	1965/66
Gross National Product	1,288.0	1,400.0	1,517.6	1,629.6
— Capital Depreciation	53.2	70.0	78.4	89.6
= NNP (national income)	1,234.8	1,330.0	1,439.2	1,540.0
Per cent change in GNP	...	9.1	8.4	7.4

SOURCES: Computed from The Planning Board, *Annual Statistical Yearbook 1965* (Kuwait: Government Printing Press, 1965), pp. 108–10; The Planning Board, *Kuwait—Economic Survey 1965/66* (mimeographed, July, 1966), p. 4.

growth than the earlier corresponding period, still the former has witnessed a gradual decline since 1963/64, a year of substantial oil production increase. In the following years the relative rise in crude oil output has been less, thus indicating the heavy reliance of the economy on its single product, a dependence as yet unchanged in two decades.

Generally speaking, during the 1959—1965/66 period the increase witnessed in the GNP was accompanied by a hike in investment outlays in Kuwait but with a magnitude of less than half the percentage increase in the GNP. Such a discrepancy between the investment and gross national product growth rates is explainable in the shortage of domestic competitive investment opportunities.

[7] The International Bank for Reconstruction and Development, *The Economic Development of Kuwait* (Baltimore: Johns Hopkins Press, 1965), p. 52. (Hereafter cited as *IBRD Report*.)

Using the first available official figures which cover the period from April 1, 1962, through March 31, 1966, Table 2 offers a breakdown of the major GNP components. From this we can note that the latest figures show the exceptionally high savings rate of 44 per cent of the gross national product. Yet only 45 per cent of these savings are invested locally. From 1962/63 to 1965/66 there was a rise of over 27 per cent in total consumption, the bulk of this increment attributable to public rather than private consumption. This might also be explained as a condition of near-saturation of consumer demand, particularly in 1963/64, offset by government purchases and development programs. Conversely, there has been a greater private influence in capital formation, a 60 per cent rise from 1962/63 to 1965/66, with more than two-thirds of this increase occurring in the latter year. Apparently government participation in mixed enterprises was largely responsible for the upward trend. Monetary investment increased 25 per cent in the four-year period although the 1965/66 level is down slightly from the preceding year. Income on total foreign investment has shown, then, the most spectacular rise—over 50 per cent in the period since 1962/63—thereby strengthening the international outlook of the country.

BACKDROP TO DEVELOPMENT

The Social and Political Setting

Kuwait is not a large country in area or population. Its 6,000 or so square miles (excluding the Neutral Zone) make it approximately equal in size to the combination of Connecticut and Rhode Island, while its population size is about that of Wyoming's. It is located on the northwestern shore of the Arab Gulf (Persian Gulf) between Saudi Arabia and Iraq. The 2,000-square-mile Neutral Zone has been administered jointly by Saudi Arabia and Kuwait since 1922. The climate and terrain are extreme and inhospitable, to say the least. The land is, for the most part, a barren, riverless desert with intensely hot temperatures and less than five inches of rainfall annually.[8] Of the islands belonging to Kuwait in the Gulf,

---

[8] The flatness of the land is broken only by a 400-foot ridge at Ahmadi, the oil center 25 miles south of the city of Kuwait, and a 900-foot prominence in the interior. An unexpected boon of this landscape has been the ability to skid entire oil rigs from one site to another because of the evenness of the surface.

TABLE 2

Expenditure on Gross National Product, 1962/63—1965/66
(In Million Dollars)

	1962/63	1963/64	1964/65	1965/66
Private consumption expenditure	526.4	537.6	560.0	588.0
General government consumption expenditure	224.0	249.2	285.6	322.0
Gross fixed capital formation of semi-public and private enterprises	126.0	131.6	137.2	201.6
Gross fixed capital formation of government enterprises	92.1	126.0	131.6	100.8
Increase in stocks	19.6	8.4	8.4	19.6
Estimated expenditure on consumption and gross capital formation	988.4	1,052.8	1,122.8	1,232.0
Exports excluding oil and oil products	22.4	28.0	33.6	36.4
Estimated exports of oil and oil products	1,159.2	1,215.2	1,310.4	1,380.4
Estimated expenditure on gross domestic products and imports	2,170.0	2,296.0	2,466.8	2,648.8
Less imports of goods and services:				
(i) imports of goods	−285.6	−324.8	−322.0	−378.0
(ii) net payments for non-factor services	−61.6	−70.0	−72.8	−86.8
Expenditure on gross domestic product	1,828.4	1,901.2	2,072.0	2,184.0
Net factor income payments from the rest of the world:				
(i) factor income transfers by oil companies	−627.2	−602.2	−674.8	−686.0
(ii) income on government foreign assets	33.6	33.6	42.0	47.6
(iii) income on private foreign assets	33.6	47.6	56.0	84.0
(iv) banks' income on foreign investments	19.6	19.6	22.4	...[a]
Expenditure on Gross National Product	1,288.0	1,400.0	1,517.6	1,629.6
Less depreciation	−53.2	−70.0	−78.4	−89.6
Net National Product (NNP) or National Income	1,234.8	1,330.0	1,439.2	1,540.0

Sources: The Planning Board, *Annual Statistical Yearbook 1965*, pp. 108–10; The Planning Board, *Kuwait—Economic Survey 1965/66*, p. 4.

[a] Not given separately in 1965/66 but included in (iii).

several are uninhabited; Failakah, the most populous, has about 3,000 persons.[9] Remains of an ancient Greek outpost used by Alexander's army have been located on Failakah. Yet despite such an accumulation of difficult conditions, Kuwait was fortunate in its accessibility—its geographical location at the head of the Gulf, which services the city of Kuwait, one of the finest natural harbors on that body of water. The Kuwaiti experience offers an excellent example of what Arthur Lewis considers the human element in the will to economize.

> Accessibility plays a decisive part in stimulating economic growth. It stimulates trade, therefore widening the range of demand, encouraging effort, and furthering specialization. It also results in a mingling of peoples, with different customs and ideas; and this keeps the mind active, stimulates the growth of knowledge, and helps to keep institutions free and flexible. Degree of accessibility must play a large role in explaining the economic vigour of any people.[10]

While historically Kuwait may have lacked resources, it never lacked contacts. As early as 1775 Kuwait served as the starting point of a desert mail route to Aleppo and the Mediterranean. Just before the opening of the nineteenth century, the British East India Company moved its trade headquarters for the northern Gulf from Basrah to Kuwait. Kuwait was once envisaged as the possible terminus of the Berlin–Baghdad railway. The English traveler-author William Palgrave recorded the conditions of Kuwait in the early 1860's in the following manner:

> ... the import duties are low, the climate healthy, the inhabitants friendly, and these circumstances, joined to a tolerable roadstead and a better anchorage than most in the neighborhood, draw to Koweyt hundreds of small craft which else would enter the ports of Aboo-Shah [Bushire] or Basrah. ... In its mercantile and political aspect, the town forms a sea outlet, the only one, for Djebel Shomer [Jabal Shammar] and in this respect is like Trieste for Austria.[11]

In 1899 Kuwait concluded a treaty of protection with Great Britain, which was eager to forestall Russian and German railroad schemes, the former seeking a line from the Gulf to the Mediterranean and the latter hoping to extend the Baghdad line. The interests of British shipping were intimately involved in such transport

[9] The main islands include Bubiyan, Warbah, Failakah, Kuber, and Auha.
[10] Lewis, *Economic Growth*, p. 53.
[11] William Gifford Palgrave, *A Personal Narrative of a Year's Journey through Central and Eastern Arabia, 1862–1863* (London: Macmillan & Co., 1868).

projects. The main stipulation of the agreement was that Kuwait could not cede territory to, nor have relations with, any nation until British consent had been received. Until full independence on June 19, 1961, with the abrogation of this treaty, Kuwait's foreign relations were handled through the British Foreign Office. The political relationship between Great Britain and Kuwait, lasting for over half a century, is reflected in such areas as trade, oil concessions, and the early direction of investment.

Kuwait was probably founded in the early part of the eighteenth century by two houses or families of the 'Anazah tribe of the Arabian peninsula. The Sabah and Khalifah settled near the harbor, where a fort, or "kut," stood. It is from the diminutive of this word that "Kuwait" is derived. By the second half of the 1700's, the Khalifah immigrated southward, eventually occupying Bahrain. The Sabah family has provided Kuwait's rulers since that time.[12]

The domestic political structure of Kuwait is headed by the Emir, a member of the Al-Sabah family, elected by the family; succession is not based upon primogeniture. Mention should be made of the stability and continuity of the Sabah rulers, which has been influenced by their longevity. In the 200 years from the beginning of the dynasty (Sabah I) in 1756 to 1956 (Abdullah III) only ten Emirs had ruled. Particularly beneficial was the continuity afforded under the extensive reign of Ahmad al-Jabir al-Sabah (1921-50), which spanned the initial leap from poverty to oil riches. The Emir and officials of the government have been and remain easily accessible to the Kuwaitis. This can be attributed to the small size of the indigenous population and the close-knit and personal Arab traditionalism. The absolute monarchy shifted toward a constitutional monarchical system with the election of a National Assembly in 1963.[13] The running of the government devolves upon 15 cabinet ministries headed by a prime minister.

Prior to independence, Kuwait participated in the Arab League

[12] For a brief but lucid history of Kuwait and its ruling house see Dr. George Rentz, "History of Kuwait and the Al-Sabah Dynasty," *Emergent Nations* (New York, Autumn, 1965), pp. 6-8.
[13] Elections are to be held at least every four years although the Emir has the power by decree to adjourn the Assembly for not more than one month or to dissolve it by an explanatory decree. The Assembly cannot be dissolved twice on the same basis. Following dissolution, new elections must be held within two months. *The Constitution of the State of Kuwait*, chap. 3, "Legislative Power" (Kuwait: Government Printing Press, 1962), pp. 17-26.

as a nonmember through support of economic and social agreements. Upon attaining full sovereignty, it immediately became a regular member of the League. Moving from the regional to the international sphere, Kuwait was accepted as the 111th member of the United Nations in May, 1963.

Two factors combined historically to turn Kuwaiti eyes seaward: first, the lack of land resources; and second, the geographical location, with the harbor providing accessibility. The sea provided Kuwait with its three predominant economic activities in pre-oil times—trade, fishing, and pearling. Trade was plied among the Arab states, Persia, and the Indian subcontinent. Pearling was a relatively large-scale industry. By 1912 a fleet of 812 ships employing 30,000 sailors and divers was engaged in this activity. During the summer months approximately one-third of the entire population would be at sea for the pearling season. By 1956 only five boats remained actively engaged in this industry as a result of the expansion of job opportunities at home through oil development; the gruelling nature of the work itself stimulated the movement to less demanding, more stable and lucrative jobs.[14] The growth of the cultured pearl industry, led by Japan, was also a factor in the decline of Kuwait's pearling activities. Shipbuilding has likewise suffered a drastic decline.

The characteristics which evolved from Kuwait's accessibility are not to be discounted lightly in the economic outlook or sociological makeup of the population. Kuwait is internationally minded, thriving on free trade; hence its economy is free. Trade, movement, and mercantile-entrepreneurial aptitude mark the Kuwaitis as distinct, for example, from their peninsula neighbors. This exposure to other lands and peoples, Arab and non-Arab alike, gave the Kuwaitis a relatively high degree of tolerance and a cosmopolitan attitude. Thus, when oil exploitation commenced and revenues began to accrue, the transition from poor to rich was smoothed by a background of contacts and knowledge of the world outside Kuwait. Such a mentality was evidenced by Abdullah al-Salem al-Sabah (1950–65), who as Emir was instrumental in constitutionalizing the government, attracting internationally respected financial experts as investment consultants, and initiating the Kuwaiti foreign aid programs.

[14] *Al-Kuwait Al-Youm Record,* January, 1956 (Kuwait: Government Printing Press), pp. 135–36.

Population and Labor

The unusual population explosion in Kuwait is traceable to immigration. With the possible exception of America at the turn of this century, no other country has witnessed such a mass movement of people, proportionately, as has Kuwait. Although the influx may have peaked, immigration still continues and turnover is high. Between 1957 and 1965 the total population of Kuwait rose from 206,473 to 467,339, an increase of 128 per cent in those eight years, with an annual average increment of 16 per cent.

The impact of the immigration is clearly seen from Table 3, which shows an annual 11.5 per cent average increase of Kuwaitis from 1957 to 1965, principally through naturalization. The non-Kuwaiti portion rose by some 20.5 per cent per annum for the same

TABLE 3

Population of Kuwait—Census of 1957, 1961, 1965[a]

	1957	1961	1965
Kuwaiti	113,622	161,909	220,059
Non-Kuwaiti	92,851	159,712	247,280
Total	206,473	321,621	467,339

Source: Central Statistical Office, The Planning Board, *Annual Abstract for 1966, Section Two,* "Population and Vital Statistics" (mimeographed, 1966), p. 19.

[a] The 1965 census covered the whole of Kuwait and its territorial waters but excluded the Neutral Zone.

period. The birth rate in the country was 4 per cent in 1961 and 4.7 per cent in 1965.[15] Such a rate of natural increment is very high by international standards.

The distribution of a population among different age groups has always been of importance to the social and economic development of any country. If a large portion of the population falls into the working-age group (15–64), it indicates that the nation's human resources are sufficient to cooperate with other economic factors for launching the process of development. On the other hand, should a large proportion of the populace be ranked as nonworkers (children under 15, aged persons 65 and over), then the country could face two problems. (1) Its human resources of productive

[15] This rate was obtained as the ratio between the number of live births during a year and the total population in the same year. Kuwait Chamber of Commerce and Industry, *Survey of Kuwait* (Kuwait, 1965), p. 1026 (in Arabic).

age might not be numerous enough to meet the demands for development. (2) This group needs special care in education, health, leisure programs, and retirement benefits, which represent heavy expenditures for social services.

From Table 4 it is clear that the working-age class among the Kuwaitis represented about 48 per cent of the indigenous population. In other words, 52 per cent of the total Kuwaiti population was either under 15 or over 64 years of age. This contrasts with the non-Kuwaiti portion, where 78 per cent of the males fell into the working-age category in 1965. Among the female non-Kuwaitis 71 per cent likewise were included in the 15–64 category, making the share of potential workers 74.5 per cent of total non-Kuwaitis, compared with 48 per cent for the Kuwaitis. The working-group mix, constituting 60 per cent of the total population, is marked by several features. The labor force is predominantly non-Kuwaiti. This grouping is one of new settlers in the prime age range, and there is a large turnover of the unskilled laborers, who generally are either unmarried or leave their families at home during their terms of employment in Kuwait. Among those immigrants who plan to settle in Kuwait the high level of social services is a drawing card.

Finally, the 15–64 guideline is being reduced from one direction and expanded in the other. With the emphasis on education, which is free throughout the university years, the youth will be spending a longer period in school and entering the labor market at a later age. At the other end of the spectrum, many persons over 64 either continue in private business or serve as consultants to government and industry. The older generation of Kuwaitis who have lived through the years of increasing affluence probably continue their pattern of work beyond the 64-year age limit used here to describe the working group.

Apart from grouping by age, the composition of the labor force shows that the ratio of employment to population is higher among non-Kuwaitis than among Kuwaitis. Non-Kuwaiti workers, numbering 138,994, form about 79 per cent of the non-Kuwaiti population in the 15–64 age range. The number of Kuwaiti workers was 40,140, or about 38 per cent of the working-age group. This disparity can be explained in part by the fact that the non-Kuwaitis come to the country specifically for work and are required to find employment in order to remain, while part of the indigenous

TABLE 4

Population by Age Group, Nationality, and Sex, 1965

Age Groups	Kuwaiti			Non-Kuwaiti			Total		
	Males	Females	Total	Males	Females	Total	Males	Females	Total
0-14	55,132	52,810	107,942	36,411	33,236	69,647	91,543	85,846	177,589
15-64	54,215	51,679	105,894	136,263	39,516	175,779	205,478	90,995	281,473
65 and over	3,222	3,001	6,223	1,069	785	1,854	4,391	3,986	8,277
Total	112,569	107,490	220,059	173,743	73,537	247,280	286,312	181,027	467,339

Source: Computed from *Annual Abstract for 1966, Section Two*, p. 22.

population is no longer in need of work as they have other sources of income. The broad categories of the labor force are indicated in Table 5.

TABLE 5

DISTRIBUTION OF THE LABOR FORCE, 1965

Employers	4,512
Self-employed	23,649
Wage earners	150,418
Employed in family business	504
Total employed	179,083
Unemployed	5,204
Total labor force	184,287

SOURCE: Computed from *Annual Statistical Abstract for 1966, Section Two*, p. 25.

As for the distribution of the population by economic sectors, one finds that services represent the largest single sector, with over 82,500 employed, largely by the government. The Kuwaitis are relatively well represented here (25,519), accounting for about 63 per cent of total Kuwaiti workers, as compared with 42 per cent of all non-Kuwaiti workers in this sector. Construction absorbs the second largest number of workers of any of the economic activities, reaching in 1965 almost 29,000. Construction is also distinguished by its near-saturation by non-Kuwaitis; only 1,264 Kuwaitis are involved in this area. Commerce, in which about one-quarter are Kuwaitis, ranks third, followed by manufacturing and transport. Agriculture ranks last as a sectoral provider of employment, as shown in Table 6.

The most striking fact shown in this table is that, although oil (included in mining) is the leading sector in contribution to the gross domestic product—61 per cent of the GDP—and is responsible not only for the bulk of governmental revenues but of export earnings, it is practically the least important sector in employment. Oil is a heavily capital-intensive industry, made more efficient through concentration and compactness in a small geographical area, thereby easing exploration, gathering, and movement of crude. Much of the labor needed is, moreover, unskilled.

Finally, we have perused the quantitative aspects of Kuwait's population, but of weight in the present prosperity and for future sustained development is the quality of the populace. Illiteracy in

Kuwait is just under 46 per cent of the total population, which is relatively low by the standards of neighboring Arab countries and, indeed, developing countries in general. A breakdown of literacy by Kuwaiti and non-Kuwaiti is somewhat misleading because of three elements. First, non-Kuwaiti as well as Kuwaiti students are receiving free education in Kuwait. Second, the spread of education has been fast and furious. Kuwait has over 400 students in U.S. colleges and universities alone, that is, one out of every 1,000 of the entire population.[16] Moreover, Cairo, Beirut, and European

TABLE 6

POPULATION[a] BY ECONOMIC ACTIVITY IN 1965 CENSUS

Sector	Kuwaitis	Non-Kuwaitis	Total
Agriculture, fishing	573	1,410	1,983
Mining, quarrying	1,349	5,643	6,992
Manufacturing	1,825	16,117	16,942
Construction	1,264	27,584	28,848
Power, water, sanitation	1,645	5,346	6,991
Commerce	5,129	17,916	23,045
Transport	2,613	7,412	10,025
Services	25,519	57,015	82,534
Others	249	675	924
Total	40,166	139,118	179,284

SOURCE: *Annual Statistical Abstract for 1966, Section Two*, p. 28.

[a] Does not include population less than 12 years of age and those of the status "unable to work".

universities, particularly those in England, have large numbers of Kuwaiti students enrolled. In addition the University of Kuwait was opened in the fall of 1966 and is projected to become a major center of higher education on the Gulf and in the region. Third, among the non-Kuwaitis, those skilled workers attracted are truly skilled, among the best the Arab world has to offer, while the unskilled are truly unskilled, largely from Iran and the peninsula states, some from Iraq. Because of the intense emphasis on education, the illiteracy rate should decline rapidly in the near future.

SECTORAL DEVELOPMENT

A cursory sectoral examination of the Kuwaiti economy shows that in terms of employment the dominant position is held by

[16] This probably is the highest ratio of foreign students to their respective country's population now in the United States.

services, which in its ability to absorb labor is the counterpart of agriculture in most developing countries. As for the distribution of the gross domestic product among the major sectors in 1965/66, mining and industry accounted for 69.9 per cent of which the lion's share, 60.7 per cent, was derived from oil while services represented but 29.7 per cent.[17] Agriculture and fishing contributed the unbelievably small portion of 0.4 per cent. The imbalance is apparent in the estimate that the contribution of manufacturing (other than oil-related industries) combined with agriculture accounted for only 2.2 per cent of the GDP, making this share one of the lowest for these sectors in the world.[18] By any standards, the oil industry is the leading sector except in its capacity to employ. Its growth rate has been high, in absolute and relative terms, in comparison with that of other sectors.

Historically, sectoral growth rates in most countries differed widely over any given span of time in the process of economic development. Overall growth, then, would appear to be touched off at various time junctures as the consequence, direct and indirect, of highly accelerated growth in one or more key sectors.[19] There are classical patterns of this condition, such as cotton textiles (from about 1780 to 1840) and later, steel, chemicals, and light-engineering products in England; the position of the railroads in the United States (*ca.* 1875–1900); wood products followed by steel in Sweden; and the growth of New Zealand's economy initiated by gold and continued thereafter through the development of wheat, wool, and dairy products.

For Kuwait the sectoral leadership of oil is more drastic and dominant than is the case of almost any other nation. This is primarily because there is no agricultural base. Yet there are three conditions ameliorating the entrenched sectoral imbalance.

[17] In computing these percentages, mining and industry were taken to include crude oil and natural gas and related industries, electricity and water, manufacturing and construction; services were taken to represent transport, storage, communications, wholesale and retail trade, banking, insurance, public administration, and defense.

[18] This percentage was figured from data in The Planning Board, *The First Five Year Plan for Economic and Social Development, 1966/67—1970/71* (Kuwait: Government Printing Press, December, 1965), p. 60 (in Arabic). Agriculture in Kuwait is limited to experimental farming, hydroponics, and some sparse grazing activities.

[19] The position of leading sectors in economic growth is dealt with by W. W. Rostow, *The Process of Economic Growth*, 2d ed. (New York: W. W. Norton & Co., Inc., 1962), pp. 161–62.

(1) Kuwait belongs to the "late-comers" which have at their disposal the great backlog of technological innovation evolved by the major advanced countries through their development. (2) Kuwait, through its capital surplus, could facilitate the application of these technological advances by procuring the equipment and services necessary. It could likewise become a leader, albeit on a modest scale, in eventually bringing about technical breakthroughs in problems peculiar to the region, such as the anti-desert attack, water resources, and natural gas and oil-based industrial research. (3) Kuwait's oil sector encompasses more than the "primary" element of supply which yields a growth rate that could be higher than that of other sectors through innovation and advances in technology; it includes "derived" growth elements closely related to the increase in demand which reflects the expansion of population, industrial production, and the increase in real income.[20]

In short, if a country is to have its economic growth advanced by a pronounced sectoral imbalance, then oil is one of the strategic sectors for leadership because additional units of investment will give the maximum increase in output. Theoretically, concentration on a leading sector may well drag along other sectors as increases in real income occur. This might lead to the ultimate development of the slower growing sectors. The Kuwaiti experience illustrates this trend.

A decade ago, as the boom in Kuwaiti oil was beginning to reach sizeable proportions, modern industry was virtually nonexistent apart from the oil industry itself. All developmental needs, even basic construction materials, were met through imports. Since the late 1950's the drive for diversification, aided by increases in oil income, has gradually gained momentum. The earliest industries to develop were connected with three major economic activities and were geared to serve mainly the needs of construction and oil industries and to provide a limited portion of consumer goods for local purposes. (1) In construction the cost of transportation was high, the demand for residential and public buildings was mounting swiftly, and some of the raw materials needed were available locally. (2) Industries related to water distillation (caustic soda, salt, hydrochloric acid) were soon established with Kuwait setting up some of the largest seawater treatment plants in the world. (3) The

[20] *Ibid.*, pp. 266–67.

final area of early industrial development was concerned with the Gulf fishing, specifically the processing of shrimp.

The underpinnings of the diversification program were the findings and recommendations of an industrial feasibility survey of Kuwait carried out by the Industrial and Process Engineering Consultants of London under the auspices of the Kuwaiti Ministry of Finance and Industry, the final report being submitted in 1963. Among the potential industrialization projects put forward was the manufacture of petrochemicals, with emphasis on fertilizers, refrigeration units, silicon-glass, tires, cement, plastics, aluminum smelting, and steel, the latter two through the utilization of natural gas.[21]

In 1961 the government embarked upon a policy of direct participation with private enterprise to initiate industrial ventures. The Kuwaiti government has subscribed to the original stock issues of 10 of some 14 industrial concerns organized by the beginning of 1965. Among the more ambitious enterprises are the Kuwait National Petroleum Company (KNPC) and the Petrochemicals Industries Company. In KNPC the government's share reached 60 per cent of the $21 million capital paid in by the beginning of 1965. In addition, the National Assembly approved a $70 million loan in the summer of 1965 to KNPC to finance the construction of a 95,000 barrel per day export refinery at Shuaiba, the site of the new industrial complex.[22] Government participation in the Petrochemicals Industries Company accounts for 80 per cent of the $44.8 million paid capital for the same year. The Kuwait Chemical Fertilizer Company's 2,000-ton-per-day petrochemical plant at Shuaiba has been completed and operations are under way. The Kuwaiti government's share in that firm is some 48 per cent of the capitalization, with Gulf Oil Company and British Petroleum each having 20 per cent interest in the concern.[23] By January, 1965,

[21] Ministry of Finance and Industry, *Industrial Survey 1963: By Industrial and Process Engineering Consultants, London,* vol. 2 (Kuwait, 1963) (mimeographed, in Arabic) lists the industries examined and evaluated.

[22] The loan reportedly carries terms of 10 years at 6 per cent. *Middle East Economic Survey,* July 9, 1965, p. 2. Negotiations were undertaken by KNPC with the U.S. Export-Import Bank and Chase Manhattan Bank. The terms of the loan from the former are some 8 years at 5.5 per cent on $50 million; the conditions for the credit of $7.5 million from the latter institution are not available. *Ibid.,* July 29, 1966, p. 2.

[23] The government's portion belongs to the Kuwait Petrochemicals Industries Company.

the total amount of capital paid in on the 14 industrial joint-stock companies, which excludes the banking, insurance, and transport companies and small industries, reached over $123 million.

Besides the direct participation in these companies, the government established the Savings and Credit Bank in 1965. Among its objectives is the extension of industrial loans although its activity in this sector has been modest compared with loans for other purposes. Its real impact has yet to be felt and assessed.[24]

Another step taken by the government was the establishment of the Shuaiba industrial complex south of the city of Kuwait. This center has been completed and stands as the largest such grouping of facilities on the Gulf and the most modern in the Middle East. Numbered among the infrastructure services provided are gas, power, water, cooling water, docking and handling facilities, and services to enable the various component industries to operate with minimum overhead charges. The priority in Shuaiba has been assigned to petrochemicals and is the site of the world's first all-hydrogen refinery under construction by the KNPC.

Finally, of overriding concern and possibly major implication is Law No. 6 of 1965, known as the National Industries Law. It provides for both regulation and encouragement of domestic industry by requiring government licenses for all processing and manufacturing activities and by proffering advantages through government aid including corporate income tax exemptions and indirect levies on imports of machinery, spare parts, and raw materials. The law also allows for the exemption from duties of exports of domestic products. Provision is made for tariff protection for a maximum period of 10 years under the condition of assurance that such action coincides with the interest of the local consumer vis-à-vis the quantity and quality of the commodities produced at home. Other advantages are given in site locations, low-interest loans, and government financial participation in pre-industry feasibility studies.[25]

In summing up the push for industrialization to improve sectoral balance and diversification, five principal obstacles have confronted

---

[24] *Law No. 30 of the Year 1965 Regarding the Establishing of the Savings and Credit Bank* (Kuwait: Government Printing Press, 1965). The capitalization of the Bank was $56 million, to be paid from the state reserves.

[25] Kuwait Chamber of Commerce and Industry, *Kuwait Chamber of Commerce and Industry Bulletin* (Kuwait, April, 1965), pp. 12–14 (in Arabic). (Hereafter cited as *Kuwait Chamber of Commerce and Industry Bulletin*.)

the drive: (1) shortages of primary materials other than oil, (2) the limited local market, (3) the lack of infrastructure and investment facilities, which led to (4) the reluctance of individuals to invest their capital in domestic industry, and (5) the shortage of skilled labor. Numbers one and two remain as definite problems, the third and fourth are being rapidly eased, and the fifth no longer stands as a real deterrent to industrialization because of the emphasis on education, through the immigration of trained persons and the utilization of international consultants. Owing to the tremendous spectrum of industrial possibilities inherent in oil and natural gas, the pressing shortages of primary materials has been mitigated somewhat, particularly when compared with the limitations of diversified industrial potential of primary products such as cocoa, cotton, copper, and coffee which form the major output of many developing nations. The rapidity with which industrialization has gone forward is not apparent in the GDP. So far the consuming task has been one of industrial infrastructure development, but the cutoff point between prerequisites for and actual operations of productive projects is drawing nearer.

TRADE AND THE INTERNATIONAL OUTLOOK

No better reflector of the Kuwaiti economy's degree of both growth and imbalance exists than the trends in and composition of foreign trade. The import growth rate has been consistently one of the highest among developed and developing countries alike. This growth of imports was stimulated by three factors: (1) the low tariff rate of 4 per cent ad valorem, full exemption of items imported by both the government and oil companies, foodstuffs, gold, silver, pearls, precious stones, and only a two per cent ad valorem duty on goods transshipped in Kuwait for reexport;[26] (2) the construction boom of the early years, especially in building and housing; and (3) the recent trend in industrialization.

From 1952 to 1965 imports increased eight and a half times while in the same period the population slightly more than tripled. (See Table 7.) Per capita imports have reached a world record level of $806 annually. This marks an increment of $516 per capita over the 1952 base of $290. The high growth rate of imports mirrors not

---

[26] A 100 per cent customs duty ad valorem is charged on liquid petroleum gas.

only the upward spiraling overall growth rate of the Kuwaiti economy but fluctuations as well, particularly the relative leveling-off in 1964. Such a condition was caused by business stagnation and excessive inventories, largely of consumption goods, built up in 1962–63. In 1965, however, the total value of imports rose once more because of developmental outlays by the public and private sectors. Even though the per capita level of imports in absolute terms is high, Kuwait's financial capacity is such that its imports absorb only about one-quarter of the exchange earnings, stemming mainly from oil and to a modest but increasing extent from returns on investments abroad. A similar proportion of the exchange earnings, approximately equal to that of imports, is going to foreign asset accumulation.

The percentage comparison of the value of non-oil exports to that of imports clearly delineates the dominance of petroleum in the Kuwaiti economy (Table 7). The situation is even more

TABLE 7

ANNUAL INCREMENT IN TRADE, PERCENTAGE OF EXPORTS TO IMPORTS, 1952–65
(IN MILLION DOLLARS)

Year	Value of Imports	Per Cent Change	Value of Exports[a]	Per Cent Change	Per Cent Exports to Imports	Population
1952	43.44	...	15.028	...	34.5	150,000[b]
1953	86.061	98	11.312	−25	13	...
1954	83.591	−3	11.928	5	14.2	...
1955	92.002	10	16.066	35	17.4	...
1956	115.013	25	14.753	−8	12.4	...
1957	155.716	36	13.798	−6.5	9	206,473
1958	210.42	35	15.478	12	7.25	...
1959	260.82	24	20.286	31	8	...
1960	241.92	−7	23.215	15	10	...
1961	249.2	3	25.659	11	10	321,621
1962	285.222	15	22.686	−12	8	...
1963	323.798	14	29.313	29	8	...
1964	322.221	−0.5	33.384	13.5	10.3	...
1965	377.154	17.5	39.589	19.3	10.5	467,339

SOURCE: *Survey of Kuwait*, p. 204; Central Office of Statistics, The Planning Board, *Yearly Summary of Foreign Trade Statistics 1965* (Kuwait: Government Printing Press, 1966), p. 5.

a Excluding oil.
b Estimate based on 1949 census.

unbalanced when it is realized that most non-oil exports are re-exports. From 1953 through 1965 the variation in the percentage of non-oil exports to imports was never higher than about 17.5 nor

lower than 8 per cent, averaging for those years some 11 per cent.[27]
We have excluded petroleum exports from the preceding discussion
in order to accentuate the critical position of the oil sector in the
economy, without which Kuwait would have a chronic balance-of-
trade deficit. But Kuwait is far from suffering under such a situation,
as we see in Table 8.

TABLE 8

THE SHARE OF OIL IN KUWAITI EXPORTS, 1958–65
(IN MILLION DOLLARS)

Year	Oil Exports	Other Exports	Total Exports	Oil as Per Cent of Total Exports	Value of Imports	Balance of Trade
1958	954.08	15.48	969.56	98	210.42	+759.14
1959	863.24	20.29	883.53	97	260.82	+622.71
1960	998.20	23.22	1,021.42	97.3	241.92	+779.50
1961	994.56	25.66	1,020.22	97.5	249.2	+771.02
1962	1,120.56	22.69	1,143.25	98	285.22	+858.03
1963	1,193.64	29.31	1,222.95	97.5	323.80	+899.15
1964	1,316.84	33.38	1,350.22	97.6	322.22	+1,028.00
1965	1,380.40[a]	39.59	1,419.99	97.2	377.15	+1,042.84

SOURCES: *Survey of Kuwait*, p. 227; *Kuwait—Economic Survey 1965/66*, p. 4.
[a] Estimated from fiscal year basis.

As for the composition of trade, Table 8 makes clear the paramount role of oil, which averages over 97 per cent of total export
revenues. Within the oil sector itself it is noteworthy that refined
products exports have expanded markedly, by about 65 per cent
from 1959 to 1965 with a 330,000 b/d capacity in the latter year.
The remainder of exports were reexports of vehicles and automotive
parts, sugar and tobacco products, oil equipment, and steel tubes.
The imports are far more diversified, ranging from foodstuffs to
autos and parts, air-conditioning equipment, tobacco products,
electronic equipment, and a wide variety of other consumption
goods, which account for two-thirds of the total value. In the last
year or so a new demand for capital goods has arisen to meet
industrial developmental needs, particularly in petrochemicals.
The Kuwait Oil Company reinjection plants and the Kuwait
National Petroleum Company refinery project have contributed to
and stimulated this trend in imports.

---

[27] *IBRD Report*, p. 83, indicates that the declared figures of exports are underestimated by almost 40 per cent of their value because of unrecorded movements
across the borders.

In trade, exports could be divided fairly distinctly between oil exports and non-oil exports (reexports). Kuwait Oil Company production represents over 90 per cent of the former category, which is directed primarily toward Italy (24.8 per cent of the total), Japan (17.9 per cent), the United Kingdom (14.6 per cent), France (8.4 per cent), Holland (5.7 per cent), and the United States (4 per cent), according to 1965 export figures.[28] Italy and Japan have recently become the major customers of Kuwaiti oil; both are energy-deficit, lacking indigenous resources of coal and oil, and both have heavy fuel oil requirements. The reexports, by comparison, are mostly regionally directed toward the peninsula states and other Arab countries, averaging about 60 per cent of total non-oil exports from 1960 to 1965.[29] As a source of imports, the United States has occupied a prominent position in Kuwaiti trade. This share has been increasing, and the U.S. stands as the greatest single exporter to Kuwait, fluctuating between 20 and 23 per cent in the first half of the 1960's. England, which for years has been the traditional supplier, ranked second in 1965, contributing around 16 per cent. The place of Europe in Kuwaiti imports has declined from 53.4 per cent in 1960 to 46.5 per cent some five years later, while that of Asia, specifically Japan, has risen from 18.4 to 23.5 per cent for the same span of time.

In short, there seem to have been no major structural changes in the composition of Kuwait's foreign trade although the drive toward diversification might bring eventual but certainly gradual modifications. Yet even with industrialization, Kuwait will likely remain trade-oriented, as most of the commodities produced will need export markets. Moreover, the mercantile mentality is a clear facet of the economic characteristic of the Kuwaitis and has helped to forge Kuwait's international outlook. The close ties between the Kuwaiti and world economies could be summed up along the following lines. (1) A major part of Kuwait's economy stems from the oil sector, and demand for oil is contingent upon external factors such as world consumption, distribution of investment in oil production, and oil companies' policies. (2) The Kuwaiti economy relies heavily on imports for consumption and capital purposes. While the amount of imports depends upon the local

[28] Kuwait Oil Company, Limited, *Annual Review of Operations 1965* (Kuwait: Mogahwi Press, 1966), p. 33.
[29] See Table 4, chapter 5.

forces of supply, still the prices of Kuwaiti needs are largely reflec-
tions of the world demand. (3) The amount invested abroad by
both public and private sectors constitutes a major portion of total
Kuwaiti savings. Returns on such investments are dependent upon
the world economic situation, and hence a spread of distribution
might be helpful. (4) A liberal trade policy and liberalism in general
in economic ties are followed by Kuwait. This is quite suitable for
Kuwait because of its favorable balance-of-payments situation.
(5) Kuwait's policy of investing in the efforts of the developing
countries through the evolution of its aid programs is yet another
facet of the Kuwaiti international economic outlook.[30]

In the following chapters some questions will be raised not only
referring to Kuwait's economic growth but also to its relationship
with its African and Middle Eastern neighbors. Why does Kuwait
offer a vivid example of an export economy, and what elements
contribute to its vulnerability? Any answer involves the intricacies
of the oil industry in its domestic and international operations. An
attempt will be made to focus the position of Kuwait vis-à-vis
consumers and other producers within the world market. Issues
such as price stabilization, production programming, and multilateralism (including the Organization of the Petroleum Exporting
Countries) hold deep ramifications for Kuwait's economic future.

Given the background of Kuwaiti prosperity due to oil, an
examination of the characteristics of the economy raises questions
concerning the government's role in financing development and
the place of entrepreneurial ability. In a capital-surplus economy
need the government play the same part as in a capital-deficit
country? What is the efficacy of macroplanning in Kuwait, with
its abundance of capital? Would the goal of balanced growth be
relevant to a nation the size of Kuwait? There exists in the country
today a real drive toward a more balanced economy, whether
justified or not. Perhaps the most critical factor in sustaining
development lies in the utilization of human resources and the
relationship between effort and economic reward. How much longer
can the government serve as the major employment base in the
nation and what impact can this policy have on incentive?

Shifting then to the broader scope of regionalism, to what degree
does size affect economic cooperation in the Middle East and

[30] Report of the Minister of Finance and Oil on the 1966/67 budget in *Kuwait
Chamber of Commerce and Industry Bulletin*, March, 1966, p. 6.

Africa? With the apparent advantages of economies of scale and the applicability of sectoral and factoral balance within a larger geographical area, why and how does the implementation of collective measures lag so far behind the numerous plans put forward for the Arab world? It is necessary to assess Kuwait's place in the context of regionalism and trade and within the newly formed Arab Common Market.

In the first half of the 1960's the idea was conceived and then realized of instituting a foreign aid program involving the movement of considerable capital funds. It stands as an experiment in intra-help among the developing nations where a surplus factor, in this instance capital, is extended. In addition to any altruistic and political motivations for an assistance program, does a drive for investment enter the Kuwaiti picture? What measures are taken to dissociate the economic from the political rationale, with the objective of raising the level of efficiency in this factoral movement? To accurately evaluate the power exerted by this small country counting less than half a million inhabitants, within the realms of finance and development, Kuwait's aid-investment activities should be studied in the regional as well as the international perspective.

The Economics of Oil 2

To the uninitiated, the economics of the oil industry appears a labyrinth. Its worldwide scope and the attendant pressures, economic and political, make its study intriguing but complex. The economics of oil may be viewed from the standpoint of the producing countries, the operating companies, and the consumers. It is affected by trade restrictions, competitive energy sources, political conditions both national and international, and the level of development and prosperity throughout the world. Producing countries are concerned with the terms of trade, the best utilization of a wasting asset, and revenue requirements for stability and developmental purposes. Operating companies are subject to demand fluctuations, supply priorities, the host country's needs, often to the governments in which the parent company is located, and to competitive and market problems. Consumers want sufficient security of supply and reasonable prices and must deal with the political, social, and economic problems when a domestic energy supply is in competition with imported oil. Any attempts at price stabilization and production programming must function within this milieu of sometimes divergent, sometimes complementary, and sometimes identical interests of the various components of the industry.

Bilateral arrangements, such as company-producer and company-consumer, continue but with less prominence as more sophisticated multilateral groupings have arisen in recent years. The oil companies have, for some time, experienced some elements of multilateralism because of the degree of vertical integration, the joint operation of concessions, and the complicated contracts of crude supply and marketing arrangements. Now consumers and producing countries are participating in groups to protect and extend their interests.

The common energy policy of the European Economic Community is of vast importance to the oil industry, as Western Europe is the largest importer of oil. Producing countries in the Middle East have been meeting to share knowledge and coordinate policies through the Arab Petroleum Congress, and more recently an international group of producers joined in the establishment of the Organization of Petroleum Exporting Countries (OPEC).

Just ten years ago the world oil industry still lay largely unexamined by scholars. In the last half decade, however, a number of outstanding books and articles have been published on the practical and academic aspects of this vital industry.[1] Today the student of petroleum affairs is fortunate indeed in having a substantial, sound, and growing volume of data and studies.

Kuwait is the world's second largest exporter of crude oil, the holder of the greatest reserves, and the largest producer in the Middle East; it suffers from a nearly total dependence on oil for revenue. Therefore, fluctuations and trends within the oil industry as a whole have widespread implications for Kuwait. The oil industry in Kuwait cannot be discussed in a vacuum. The principal

[1] M. A. Adelman, *The Supply and Price of Natural Gas* (Oxford: Blackwell, 1962); Helmut J. Frank, *Crude Oil Prices in the Middle East* (New York: Frederick A. Praeger, 1966); J. E. Hartshorn, *Oil Companies and Governments* (London: Faber & Faber, 1962); David Hirst, *Oil and Public Opinion in the Middle East* (London: Faber & Faber, 1966); Charles Issawi and Mohammed Yeganeh, *The Economics of Middle Eastern Oil* (New York: Frederick A. Praeger, 1962); Wayne A. Leeman, *The Price of Middle East Oil* (Ithaca, N.Y.: Cornell University Press, 1962); S. H. Longrigg, *Oil in the Middle East, Its Discovery and Development*, 2d ed. (London, 1961); George Lenczowski, *Oil and State in the Middle East* (Ithaca, N.Y.: Cornell University Press, 1960); Ashraf Lutfi, *Arab Oil* (Beirut: Middle East Research and Publishing Center, 1960); Zuhayr Mikdashi, *A Financial Analysis of Middle Eastern Oil Concessions: 1901–1965* (New York: Frederick A. Praeger, 1966); articles include: M. Adelman, "The World Oil Outlook," in *Natural Resources and International Development*, ed. Marion Clawson (Baltimore: Johns Hopkins Press for Resources for the Future, Inc., 1964); M. Adelman, "Efficiency of Resource Use in Crude Petroleum," *Southern Economic Journal*, October, 1964; M. Adelman, "Oil Prices in the Long Run," *Journal of Business*, April, 1964; Edith T. Penrose, "Middle East Oil; The International Distribution of Profits and Income Taxes," *Economica (London)*, August, 1960; E. T. Penrose, "Profit Sharing Between Producing Countries and Oil Companies in the Middle East," *Economic Journal (London)*, June, 1959; E. T. Penrose, "Vertical Integration with Joint Control of Raw-Material Production: Crude Oil in the Middle East," *Journal of Development Studies (London)*, April, 1965; trade publications include *The Oil and Gas Journal* and *The Middle East Economic Survey* among several; proceedings of the Arab Petroleum Congress; publications of the Organization of the Petroleum Exporting Countries; publications of the First National City Bank of New York and the Chase Manhattan Bank.

areas of study include production costs, reserves, concessions and oil agreements, stabilization of prices, production programming, and oil-producer groupings.

PRODUCTION AND RESERVES

In no other country has oil been discovered and produced more advantageously to both the producing nation and concessionaire than in Kuwait. A combination of factors coalesced to bring about this favorable situation. The backbone of Kuwaiti output has been the Greater Burgan—the largest single deposit of crude yet discovered. Two major economic criteria for gauging the rate at which development and exploitation take place and the profitability of operations are the reserves and the accessibility. The Burgan and smaller fields in Kuwait account for 19.5 per cent of the world's proven reserves, concentrated in an area of only 6,000 square miles.[2] Thus, any oil field in Kuwait is not far from the coast because of the country's small size, and the Burgan has the added advantage of being only 15 miles from a highly suitable deep-water loading area. The ease with which Kuwaiti oil can be extracted and moved to the shipping point might be singled out as one of the most important aspects, if not the most influential element, in the high profitability of Kuwaiti production.[3]

It might be beneficial to offer a simplified comparison of Kuwait's profitable and efficient production with that of its neighbor, Saudi Arabia, another large-volume and relatively low-cost producer. The oil-producing sands of the Kuwaiti fields are more than 1,000 feet thick, while in Saudi Arabia the sands are mostly 200 feet. Moreover, the porosity and permeability of the Kuwaiti sands are the highest of the Middle East. Whereas a natural-water drive most often lifts oil in Kuwait, the principal drive in lifting Saudi Arabian oil is natural gas. Finally, Saudi Arabian oil fields are far inland, while in Kuwait crude from the fields is pumped a short

---

[2] Samir Shamma, *The Oil of Kuwait* (Beirut: Middle East Research and Publishing Center, 1959), p. 20. See also Table 3 in this chapter. Figures on reserves must not be accepted as definitive as they are subject to change and vary according to the publishing source.

[3] Leeman, *Middle East Oil*, p. 74. Because the Kuwait Oil Company produces 92 per cent of total Kuwaiti crude output (1965), unless otherwise specified the figures given on the oil industry in Kuwait refer to this company and its operations.

distance to Ahmadi Ridge (390-foot elevation) and from there flows by gravity to the waiting tankers in the port of Ahmadi.[4]

Such factors have contributed to its level of production costs, the lowest in the world. Recent figures show the Kuwait Oil Company's cost (the single largest producer in Kuwait and also in the world) at 6.26 cents per barrel. Of this total, 4.1 cents account for the cost of producing and gathering the oil, 0.66 cent the cost of transport to the export point, and 1.5 cents the cost of amortizing the capital employed.[5] The total cost of production (excluding royalties) compares favorably with production costs of 20 cents per barrel in the Middle East as a whole, 51 cents in Venezuela, 82 cents in Indonesia, and $1.75 in the United States.[6] Table 1 ranks oil

TABLE 1

MAJOR PRODUCERS AND THEIR SHARE OF TOTAL OIL RESERVES AND PRODUCTION
IN 1965
(IN PER CENT)

	Share of Reserves of World Total	Share of Production of World Total
Kuwait	19.4	7.2
Saudi Arabia	18.7	7.04
Iran	11.3	6.3
United States	10.0	25.4
U.S.S.R.	9.1	16.15
Iraq	7.1	7.1
Venezuela	4.8	12.1
Libya	2.8	4.7

SOURCE: *Kuwait Chamber of Commerce and Industry Bulletin*, 7, no. 58 (June, 1966): 36 (Kuwait; in Arabic); *Oil and Gas Journal*, Worldwide Issue, December 27, 1965; British Petroleum Company, Ltd., *Statistical Review of the World Oil Industry 1965* (London, 1966), p. 5.

producers by their position vis-à-vis reserves. "Proven reserves," while used widely as a yardstick within the industry, remain open to question because companies are understandably hesitant to publish precise figures on their reserves. Moreover, new discoveries make for a wide margin of fluctuation in estimated proven reserves.

[4] Leeman, *Middle East Oil*, pp. 74–76. Although water drive is common to most Kuwaiti fields, gas does contribute to some lifting.

[5] *Middle East Economic Survey*, Supplement, May 20, 1966, p. 3. This is the first time such detailed figures have been given.

[6] In 1946, the first year of commercial production, Kuwaiti production costs were estimated at about 27 cents per barrel based upon known reserves and output. By 1956, costs were down to 10 cents p/b based upon larger reserves (10 times that of 1946, that is, 4 milliard barrels) and throughput of over 1 million b/d. Mikdashi, *Financial Analysis*, p. 123. *Middle East Economic Survey*, Supplement, December 23, 1966, p. 2, gives the U.S. figure.

The combined factors of vast reserves and lower unit costs enhanced the rapid expansion of oil production in Kuwait and at a rate much higher than that experienced by other Middle Eastern producers. Although oil was discovered in 1938, the Second World War caused a suspension in petroleum activities. Actual production began in 1946, and the succeeding years saw a sharp upsurge, until the mid-1950's. From 1956 on the rate continued to rise, but more sporadically and at a slower pace, as seen in Table 2.

TABLE 2

CRUDE OIL PRODUCTION IN KUWAIT AND THE NEUTRAL ZONE
(IN MILLION U.S. BARRELS)

Year	Kuwait Oil Company	Aminoil	Arabian Oil Co. (Japan)	Total Kuwait Share[a]	Actual Increase in Kuwait Share (Per Cent)
1946	5.9	...	...	5.9	...
1947	16.2	...	...	16.2	174.0
1948	46.5	...	...	46.5	187.0
1949	89.9	...	...	89.9	93.0
1950	125.7	...	...	125.7	39.0
1951	204.9	...	...	204.9	63.0
1952	273.4	...	...	273.4	33.0
1953	314.6	...	...	314.6	15.0
1954	347.3	2.4	...	349.8	11.0
1955	398.4	4.3	...	402.8	15.0
1956	399.9	5.6	...	405.5	0.6
1957	416.0	8.8	...	424.8	4.7
1958	509.4	13.0	...	522.4	23.0
1959	504.9	21.0	...	525.9	0.6
1960	594.3	24.8	...	619.2	17.7
1961	600.2	29.3	7.5	633.3	2.2
1962	669.3	34.3	21.9	714.6	12.8
1963	705.4	35.6	48.3	765.2	7.0
1964	774.8	35.5	63.6	842.2	10.0
1965	791.8	36.5	33.1	861.4	2.28
1966	830.7	29.6	47.1	907.4	5.3

SOURCE: Kuwait Currency Board, *Fifth Annual Report for the Year Ended 31st March 1966* (Kuwait: Government Printing Press), p. 21.

[a] Kuwait's share is the total production of Kuwait Oil Company, Aminoil in the Neutral Zone and half the production of Arabian Oil Company which operates in the off-shore area in the Neutral Zone between Kuwait and Saudi Arabia.

While the rate of exploitation of Kuwaiti oil has been unsurpassed by a similar rate of development of any natural resource elsewhere in the world, it could be noted as well that because of the exceptional size of the reserves, such rapidity of exploitation has not been out of balance. On the contrary, it might be argued that such vast reserves would justify an even higher rate of exploitation. With a high reserve-production ratio, as seen in Table 3, arguments for an increased rate of output center upon three major considerations. First, whether there is a steady rise or possibility of a future rise in oil prices; second, whether the per unit purchasing power of oil revenues remains the same or increases; and third, whether the producing country has no need for an increment in revenue. In Kuwait's case international and regional financial commitments have become an important segment of total revenue requirements and are therefore to be included in the last consideration above.

TABLE 3

OIL PRODUCTION AS PER CENT OF RESERVES OF MAJOR PRODUCERS, 1965

	Production Estimates (1,000 bbl.)	Proven Reserves (1,000 bbl.)	Production as Per Cent of Reserves
Iran	678,498	40,000,000	1.7
Iraq	466,433	25,000,000	1.9
Indonesia	128,400	9,500,000	1.3
Kuwait	861,400	68,700,000	1.25
Libya	452,272	10,000,000	4.5[a]
Qatar	78,730	3,000,000	2.6
Saudi Arabia	728,613	60,000,000	1.21
United States	2,848,825	35,400,000	8.05
U.S.S.R.	2,912,000	32,000,000	9.1
Venezuela	1,262,498	17,250,000	7.3

SOURCES: *Oil and Gas Journal*, December, 1965, pp. 82–83; *Kuwait Chamber of Commerce and Industry Bulletin*, June, 1966, pp. 36–37.

[a] Because exploration is still being pursued intensively, additional discoveries will probably increase reserves and bring down this relatively high percentage.

The ramifications of these commitments, and their impact on the Kuwaiti economy, and of all the three elements will be discussed in succeeding chapters. It suffices to point out here, however, that in the first condition, concerning oil prices, no increase has occurred in the last six years since the two reductions of 1959 and 1960. In fact, the more realistic attitude is one based on stability at the present price levels rather than on projections of an increase. The second element is again not likely to materialize as the trade terms of oil exporters (as with other raw-material-producing countries) have not improved but have as often as not deteriorated.

On the other hand, a slower rate of exploitation of Kuwaiti oil need not be totally negative. If the cost to the economy in the future is less than at present, there will be a higher recovery and wider utilization of the natural gas associated with crude oil production. It appears, however, that it is in the general interest of both the companies and the government to accelerate output.

Ordinarily slower production rates might be in line with a con-
servationist policy aimed at lengthening the period of exploitation,
and hence revenue, as with the Venezuelan policy toward oil
resources. Yet where the reserves are so vast and considered practically a near-economic "free good," and with conservation measures
for natural gas proceeding as quickly as possible, such a policy
would not reap greater benefits.[7] Kuwaiti production is one of the
lowest as a percentage of reserves (1.25 per cent in the 1965
estimate), as compared with the U.S. at the other end of the
spectrum, which showed its output as 8.05 per cent of reserves.[8]

Such a variation cannot be explained solely by business risk in
operations.[9] Other factors, political and economic, which would
have a retarding effect on the rate of exploitation include trade and
exchange restrictions and protective energy policies in the consuming
countries, all of which will be examined later.

UTILIZATION OF NATURAL GAS

Natural gas production in Kuwait can be examined from three
viewpoints. The first and most traditional aspect is the abundance
of this resource and the great possibility of its waste. Second is the
present drive to make natural gas a more important foreign exchange
earner through export of such products as LPG. The final area of
investigation is the industrialization base natural gas offers for the
domestic economic development of the country through its utilization as a chemical raw material, fuel, and reducing agent in
metallurgical operations.[10] As Kuwaiti crude oil production is
accompanied by mass production of gas, the quantity of the latter
is wholly dependent on the output level of the former. Rough
estimates of present output are in the order of 1,000 million cubic
feet per day, of which just over 20 per cent is being economically

---

[7] Leeman, *Middle East Oil*, p. 24, considers Kuwaiti oil a "free good."

[8] Computed from Kuwait Currency Board, *Fifth Annual Report* (Kuwait: Government Printing Press, 1966), p. 21; and *Kuwait Chamber of Commerce and Industry
Bulletin*, June, 1966, p. 37.

[9] United Nations, Economic Commission for Europe, *The Price of Oil in Western
Europe* (Geneva, March, 1955), p. 13, contends "even the most generous allowance
for the greater risks of production in the Middle East could only reduce slightly
the difference between the profit margins there and in the U.S." See Mikdashi,
Financial Analysis, p. 93, for discussion of this facet.

[10] A good description is found in *IBRD Report*, pp. 114–18.

used.[11] As of early 1965, gas reserves were estimated to exceed 30 trillion standard cubic feet.[12] By far the largest share of natural gas in Kuwait consists of the two true gases, methane (75 per cent) and ethane (12 per cent), with some propane (4.5 per cent) and smaller amounts of butane and pentane.[13]

The economic potential of this resource is of almost unlimited magnitude.[14] With such vast production of gas, waste is an extremely sensitive issue to both the operating companies and the host country. Because of the limited domestic demand and the technical obstacles to gas injection in earlier years of production, flaring off large quantities was unavoidable. Rapid innovation and technological change are responsible for advances in liquification processes, transport facilities, and reinjection. Although the venting and flaring of gas in the past may be described as wasteful in terms of burning energy without concurrent benefits, it could be viewed as not wasteful in that there was no alternative use. The difficulties in transport of LPG have been rapidly overcome. For example, in 1963 the quantity of LPG exports rose by 75 per cent over that of 1962.[15] Such developments outdate earlier writings which were severely critical of gas waste.[16]

From 1960 to 1964 the increase in gas utilization was greater than the increase in its production. Utilization doubled while output increased only by 33 per cent in that period.[17] Accordingly, the share of used gas of total production is the highest in the Middle

[11] "The Mineral Industry of Kuwait," by James A. West, reprint from U.S. Department of the Interior, *Bureau of Mines Minerals Yearbook 1964*, p. 2.

[12] *Ibid.*, p. 5.

[13] The true gases, methane and ethane, must be substantially cooled before liquification by pressure can take place. Vapors such as propane and butane may be liquified by compression alone while the liquid gases, including pentane, are already in liquid form except for some small amount in the vapor state due to the volatibility of the gas.

[14] Recently it has been estimated generously that the amount of natural gas being flared off in the production of the Gulf, and to which Kuwait is the major contributor, is alone sufficient to supply two-thirds of the world's nitrogen consumption and could be processed into 20 million tons of nitrogen compound annually. *New York Times*, May 2, 1966.

[15] E. L. Klinger, "The Mineral Industry of Kuwait," reprint from U.S. Department of the Interior, *Bureau of Mines Mineral Yearbook 1963*, p. 7209.

[16] As, for example, Shamma, *Oil of Kuwait*.

[17] General Oil Affairs Department, Ministry of Finance and Industry, *The Oil of Kuwait, Facts and Figures*, 1965 edition (Kuwait: Government Printing Press, 1965), p. 27. (Hereafter cited as *The Oil of Kuwait [1965]*.) This is for KOC production, which accounts for 92 per cent of total oil output.

East. In 1965 Kuwait Oil Company's (KOC) liquified petroleum
gas facilities doubled.[18]

Since natural gas in its various forms is usually more difficult to
transport than oil, this petroleum product is primarily used for
domestic development. Specialists in Kuwait have been giving
serious study to the question how best to institute its utilization,
economically and rapidly, thereby reducing the waste. As crude oil
remains the most important petroleum product, planning natural
gas development must be done without adverse interference with oil
output. For this reason, gas injection into the fields to maintain
pressure is given first priority. To date, two injection plants are in
operation, one of 90 million c.f.d. and the other of 50 million c.f.d.
in the Burgan and Raudhatain (North Kuwait) fields respectively.
A third is under construction at Minagish. The second most
important area in which gas consumption can be expanded is the
production of energy. Gas is scheduled as the energy base of the
Shuaiba complex, with consumption expected to be about 300
million c.f.d. Electric power from this source is used in Kuwait's
distillation plant, the world's largest, which produces over 6 million
gallons daily. With concurrent plans for industrial and agricultural
development, greater demand for water may well necessitate
expanded gas use for distillation. Equally significant for Kuwait's
economic future is natural gas as the raw material for petrochemicals
and fertilizers, as mentioned earlier.

Because of the vast price differential between crude oil and natural
gas, the latter is likely to remain a by-product of the former's
production.[19] Thus, industrial planning, which projects natural gas
as its energy base, must take this factor into account; that is, in the
event of a crude production cutback, it would prove too expensive
to produce the oil simply to derive the natural gas.[20] Consequently
some calculated waste of gas, a margin to absorb oil production
fluctuation, must be allowed to cover any such eventuality.[21]

[18] The British Petroleum Company, Ltd., *Annual Reports and Accounts 1965*
(London, 1966), p. 23. (Hereafter British Petroleum Company, Ltd. will be
abbreviated as BP.)

[19] In Kuwait, oil and natural gas occur together, whereas in some areas separate
natural gas deposits have been found.

[20] In periods of bad weather which restrict the loading of tankers, oil output
can be reduced, although tank storage can be used to give an element of control
to this possibility.

[21] This view is given by Faisal Mazidi, *Natural Gas in Kuwait and Its Utilization*
(Kuwait: Government Printing Office, 1963), p. 5 (originally presented as a
paper to the Fourth Arab Petroleum Congress, Beirut, November, 1963).

REFINING

Among the oil producing countries which are largely dependent upon oil for government revenue and the growth of national production, there has been rising concern about and increased pressure for the establishment of a domestic refining industry and an expansion of the units in existence. Two motivations for such a condition in Kuwait were (1) the drive for economic diversification within the oil sector itself, since limited opportunities existed elsewhere, and (2) the vast earnings derived from the petroleum industry. Kuwaiti attempts at diversification within the industry have been concentrated on refining and transport, the former being the most strongly supported as a national policy requiring the local refining of the largest amount possible. What was begun in 1949 by KOC to process crude to meet local demand (capacity 25,000 b/d) on a limited product mix line of kerosine and gas oil has repeatedly been expanded to a total refining capacity of 250,000 barrels of crude per day with a widespread base to include light and heavy gas oil as well as kerosine, bitumen, and other materials.[22] By blending, still other products are derived, including gasoline, light distillates, aviation turbine kerosine, and diesel and fuel oil. Today the product mix varies to accommodate not only local requirements but also foreign demand. Over 10 million tons of refined products (or one-tenth of all KOC exports, including crude) were exported in 1964–65.[23]

A program for naphtha has been initiated which involves reinjection into the original source wells rather than flaring this product off with natural gas. This distillate is a light, volatile liquid with solvent

---

[22] *The Oil of Kuwait (1965)*, p. 36, gives the breakdown of the four categories as 42.5 per cent of the first four products and 57.5 per cent bitumen and other materials.

KOC—Crude Oil Processed at Mina Al Ahmadi Refinery 1950–1965
(Average in 1,000 Barrels per Calendar Day)

1950— 21.4	1951— 23.4	1952— 25.0	1953— 29.0	1954— 29.0
1955— 29.4	1956— 28.8	1957— 27.3	1958—119.9	1959—143.0
1960—177.0	1961—171.0	1962—191.7	1963—202.9	1964—217.7
1965—220.0				

Source: Kuwait Oil Company, *Annual Review of Operations 1965* (Kuwait: Mogahwi Press, 1966) p. 29. (Hereafter Kuwait Oil Company will be abbreviated as KOC.)

[23] *The Oil of Kuwait (1965)*, p. 34. In 1965 production did not vary greatly.

characteristics which, by reinjection, tends to dissolve some of the heavier constituent elements in the crude oil and thereby increases the total amount of crude likely to be lifted. During the last 15 years a total of 31 million barrels of light petroleum products has been reinjected together with 2.6 million barrels of natural gasoline. Such a program was dual-purposed. In addition to the naphtha effect on the heavy oil components of the unlifted crude, it served as a conservation measure, a form of storage until demand for local consumption and export would warrant its reextraction and re-refining. It is apparent that current demand for naphtha and other light products for the petrochemical industry, feedstock, and urban gas usage is such that reinjection has been sharply reduced.[24]

The second major refinery, with a capacity of 110,000 b/d of refined products, is operated by Aminoil in the Neutral Zone. The two principal products are naphtha and fuel oil. The original refining plant was established to separate the sulfur compound (H_2S) from the crude prior to shipment. The Arabian Oil Company's Khafji refinery in the Neutral Zone is capable of refining some 30,000 barrels daily of crude. The main products include bunker oils for use by tankers arriving at Khafji ports, some unfinished naphtha, and diesel oil needed for local operations. Finally, Kuwait National Petroleum Company, begun in 1960 with the overriding objective of increasing the participation of Kuwaiti nationals in petroleum development, has been mainly involved in the distribution of KOC refined products in the domestic market. In 1967 KNPC commenced large-scale refining in its all-hydrogen plant completed that year in Shuaiba.[25] It will be recalled that Kuwait's low-gravity crude, with its sulfur content, is about 40 to 50 per cent classified as heavy fuel oil and is used mainly for industry and as a maritime fuel. Hydrogen processing is designed to upgrade most of the heavy oil into more profitable light products such as kerosine and diesel. The growth rate of refining in Kuwait has been greater than that in the Middle East as a whole.[26]

---

[24] The average quantity of naphtha reinjected for 1965 was 5,783 b/d, as compared with an average of 6,251.9 b/d for 1950 to 1965 of light products of which naphtha is by far the largest portion. *Middle East Economic Survey*, Supplement, May 20, 1966, pp. 2–3.

[25] See *Middle East Economic Survey*, Supplement, March 11, 1966, for details on the Shuaiba refinery.

[26] BP, *Statistical Review of the World Oil Industry 1965* (London, 1966), p. 13.

STRUCTURE OF THE KUWAIT CONCESSIONS AND ROYALTY EXPENSING

Five oil companies, one of which is a national firm, operate in Kuwait today. The largest and oldest producer, responsible for 92 per cent of the total output of crude, is the Kuwait Oil Company Limited (KOC). The parent companies, British Petroleum Company Limited and Gulf Oil Corporation, share equally in KOC's concession for Kuwait proper and the extension to the six-mile limit of territorial waters.[27] The original term of the concession was 75 years from December 23, 1934. In 1951 the concession was amended with an extension of 17 years, fixing the expiration date for 2026. Again in 1962 the concession was amended, this time resulting in KOC's agreement to relinquish 3,961 square miles, over half the original concession area.[28] The first well of producing capacity was found in 1938, and until 1942 drilling continued only to be halted because of World War II. By 1946, however, the first commercial shipment was exported. The rate of KOC's output has been phenomenal. In almost two decades (1946–65), the company was responsible for the production of over 1,000 million tons of crude oil.[29]

Because British Petroleum and Gulf are among the least vertically integrated of the international major oil companies, both have made

[27] Gulf is an American firm while British Petroleum Limited (BP) is a British firm in which the British Government owns the controlling interest. The original concession was granted to Gulf and the Anglo-Persian Oil Company (APOC), the latter firm becoming the Anglo-Iranian Oil Company (AIOC) and finally British Petroleum Limited. It has been argued that Kuwait's political ties with Great Britain were a dominant factor in the manner in which the concession was given and in the makeup of the terms. Mikdashi maintains, "It may be concluded that owing to the dependent political status of Kuwait (1) it took six years to have the British Government sanction a concession agreement, (2) a British company, viz. APOC, had to be invited to participate although its geologists were throughout pessimistic and unfavorable to such concession, and (3) the financial terms obtained by Kuwait were certainly less favorable than those obtained by neighboring Iraq, Saudi Arabia, or Persia."—Mikdashi, *Financial Analysis*, p. 83. The terms of all Kuwaiti concessions and the operations of the various concessionaires may be found in Mikdashi, pp. 312–14; Leeman, *Middle East Oil*, pp. 23–29; Issawi and Yeganeh, *Economics of Middle Eastern Oil*, pp. 178–79; *The Oil of Kuwait (1965)*, pp. 15–55; Penrose, "Crude Oil in the Middle East," pp. 251–68.

[28] Organization of Petroleum Exporting Countries, "From Concessions to Contracts," Vth Arab Petroleum Congress, vol. 1: *Economics*, 19(A–Z) (Cairo, March 16–23, 1965), p. 11, notes that relinquishing of the area is to be completed prior to May 8, 1967, with the final 386 square miles of offshore concession to the six-mile limit.

[29] KOC, *Annual Review of Operations 1965*, p. 18.

long-term contracts to supply crude to other large firms which in turn affect Kuwaiti production.[30] In 1947 Gulf entered into an agreement to sell Royal Dutch/Shell a good portion of its share of Kuwaiti crude output.[31] The contract was to run until 1956, but two extensions now schedule deliveries to be made until 2026. Instead of a fixed pricing formula by which Shell would buy from Gulf, the two firms agreed that Shell and Gulf would share equally the profits on the production, transport, refining, and final marketing of the crude involved in the transaction. In this manner, Shell became, for all practical purposes but without legal title, a partner in the operation of the KOC concession.

British Petroleum likewise has entered into crude sale contracts which could affect the level of Kuwaiti output. In 1947 and 1948, BP, then Anglo-Iranian Oil Company, arranged to supply quantities of crude oil to Standard Oil Company (New Jersey) and Socony-Vacuum Oil Company (now Socony-Mobil) for twenty-five years.[32] The important element vis-à-vis Kuwait in these contracts was the right of crude delivery to Jersey and Socony from BP's output of either Kuwait or Iran. The control over the level of production in Kuwait is further strengthened by the provision between British Petroleum and Gulf in their original agreement whereby the former company reserves the right to supply the latter's crude oil needs from other BP holdings (i.e., Iran and Iraq).[33]

Revenue to the Kuwaiti government was based, until 1951, upon tonnage royalty. Two major advantages of this method as compared with the profit sharing system include (1) administrative ease for both government and company in assessing the quantities of oil produced and exported, as opposed to the difficulties in computing profits, and (2) greater net profits to the companies involved in

[30] See Penrose, "Crude Oil in the Middle East," n. 8, p. 265.

[31] As a measure of the share involved in this transaction, it is helpful to note that in 1958 Gulf sales to Shell averaged 413,000 b/d, that is, 58 per cent of its Kuwaiti output and 9.7 per cent of the average daily production of the Middle East as a whole. Leeman, *Middle East Oil*, p. 161.

[32] Details in Leeman, pp. 161–68. A third contract between Sinclair and BP is of less importance, involving several marketing arrangements for entry into the Americas. Shamma, *Oil of Kuwait*, p. 28; also, Leeman, pp. 27–28.

[33] Mikdashi, *Financial Analysis*, p. 82, "Thus, when pressed for economic or political reasons to increase its Persian oil production, APOC could, in principle, always reduce Kuwait's production, and still satisfy the requirements of its partner, viz. Gulf. Such a measure might reduce its liability to find outlets for Kuwait's oil at a time when it was under pressure to raise production in Persia or Iraq."

the event of a rise in profits.[34] The 1934 agreement granted a 13-cent equivalent per barrel royalty payment which, it is interesting to note, falls far below the approximate 22-cent per barrel payment to Iran, Iraq, and Saudi Arabia.[35] In 1951 a new agreement between KOC and the government of Kuwait made provision for an income tax payment over and above the 1934 agreement. The tax due is computed in such a way that, together with other payments (royalties, rent), it would provide an income equal to 50 per cent of KOC's realized profits on oil exports.[36] (Included as cost items for the computation of the tax were the costs of production, exploration, drilling, development, depreciation, and other capital extinguishment costs.)

Four years later a supplemental agreement was concluded with the parent companies of Kuwait Oil Company whereby the royalty payment was to be 12.5 per cent of the posted price of crude oil rather than the 13 cents per barrel (the basis known as royalty tonnage). Moreover, the royalty payment was accepted as an advance on account of the income tax due Kuwait by KOC. In the same year, British Petroleum (Kuwait) Ltd. and Gulf Kuwait Company guaranteed that the aggregate income from exports of crude and refined products would not fall below a minimum level which, in the case of crude oil, would be the value of the crude calculated at posted prices.[37] Computation on the basis of posted rather than actual prices is more advantageous to the host governments, as the posted level has seldom been realized (except for the sales to affiliates) in recent years. It has been pointed out that posted prices may be viewed as a reflection of long-run conditions of supply and demand while actual prices may include a discount for quantity or for long-term buying commitments. Other devices by which the price is actually lowered are particularly favorable tanker rates and/or credit terms or special refinery processing

[34] *Ibid.*

[35] *Ibid.*, p. 83; for full details of fiscal arrangements, pp. 312–13. See also Longrigg, *Oil in Middle East*, p. 111.

[36] Mikdashi, *Financial Analysis*, p. 313.

[37] The agreement further guaranteed that the aggregate income from exports of refined products would not be less than posted price of crude equivalent plus refinery costs plus a refining fee of 5 shillings (about 28 cents) per ton. *The Oil of Kuwait (1965)*, p. 58. BP (Kuwait) Ltd. and Gulf (Kuwait) Company were also allowed in this 1955 agreement to deduct volume discount and a 2 per cent selling charge. The volume discount has since been abolished and the selling charge reduced to 1 per cent.

agreements.[38] It has been estimated that "Arabian crude . . . [on the average] today is posted at $1.80 and realizes something around $1.40, and sometimes less."[39]

Royalty Expensing

As KOC is by far the largest producer and since this discussion has centered on the terms of the concession to and subsequent agreements with this company, a short study of the implications of the royalty expensing issue would be useful at this point. In the 1951 KOC-Kuwaiti government agreement, royalty payments were not considered a production cost. In recent years there has been a general concern among Middle Eastern producers that royalties should be expensed as a cost rather than treated as a credit against income tax liabilities, particularly as it is so treated in the oil company accounts. It has, moreover, been accepted practice in the U.S., the world's largest oil producer. The essence of the Kuwaiti argument, and that of other oil exporters, is that petroleum is a wasting asset and accordingly a compensation must be proffered for the intrinsic value of this raw material apart from the standard tax on company income. The Organization of Petroleum Exporting Countries, to which Kuwait belongs, has made uniformity of royalty expensing a major objective since members such as Venezuela already have reached agreement on this issue.[40]

The negotiations involved the OPEC members' consent to an allowance of 8.5 per cent off posted prices in exchange for royalty expensing at 12.5 per cent. A subsequent decision called for a gradual reduction of the 8.5 per cent allowance by one per cent a year in 1964 and 1965. Thereafter the applicable rate of discount was subject to further negotiations. The monetary impact of such a change in royalty expensing is estimated to reach an average net gain of about 11 cents per barrel in the oil revenues of the member

[38] For a good, general yet brief discussion of the meaning of posted prices, see Leeman, *Middle East Oil*, pp. 3–4.

[39] Adelman, "Crude Petroleum," p. 109. This is an average figure for Arabian and Gulf crude. Kuwaiti crude posted price is lower because, as pointed out earlier, the lower gravity ("heavy crude") contains less of the high-priced distillates.

[40] OPEC, *Resolutions Adopted at the Conferences of the Organization of the Petroleum Exporting Countries*, Resolution IV. 33, p. 47. See also the paper by Khader Ibrahim Herzallah, "Expensing of Royalty: Its Necessity and the Various Stages through which It Passed in the Middle East," Vth Arab Petroleum Congress, vol. 1: *Economics*, ser. 5 (A-4).

countries.[41] With reference to the Kuwaiti position, agreement was reached between the government and the Kuwait Oil Company in January, 1965. However, ratification by the National Assembly was delayed pending agreement on arbitration clauses and quit claims. Objection to the latter condition, that the agreement would be in full and final settlement for all outstanding claims on the companies prior to January 1, 1964, was based upon the seeming contradiction to the OPEC demand for a return to the pre-August, 1960 price levels. Meanwhile, the lack of immediate ratification led to the stoppage of payment of an estimated $28 million per year for 1964 and subsequent nonpayments until ratification.[42]

A revised agreement between KOC and its parent companies, British Petroleum and Gulf Oil, and the government, however, was ratified by the National Assembly in May, 1967. Back payments to the government as a result of the application of the OPEC royalty expensing formula are in the neighborhood of $92.4 million. The major benefits of the final accord are four. (1) Kuwait may take in cash or kind up to 12.5 per cent of production. (2) While a discount allowance for tax purposes was set up for the years 1964 through 1966, the government has retained the right to cancel these discounts after 1966 if it so desires. (3) Although the government has settled on the question of posted prices for previous years in this agreement, it holds the right to inspect the production and operating costs for all past years. Moreover, Kuwait may challenge the posted price level after 1966. (4) Finally, KOC agreed to submit any dispute involving Kuwaiti income tax legislation to the jurisdiction of the Kuwaiti national courts, whereas the earlier draft agreement specified arbitration.[43]

Aminoil

The concession for the Neutral Zone, shared by Kuwait and Saudi Arabia, was granted in 1948 to the American Independent Oil Company (Aminoil), now jointly owned by eight U.S. firms, the largest holders being Phillips Petroleum Company and Signal

[41] OPEC, "OPEC and the Principle of Negotiation," Vth Arab Petroleum Congress, vol. 1: *Economics*, ser. 20 (A-2), p. 9.

[42] *Middle East Economic Survey*, December 31, 1965, p. 2; February 18, 1966, p. 1.

[43] *Middle East Economic Survey*, May 5, 1967, pp. 1–3. The discount allowances, in accordance with the OPEC formula, were 8.5 per cent in 1964, 7.5 per cent the following year, and for 1966, 6.5 per cent.

Oil and Gas Company.[44] The duration is for 60 years to explore for and produce Kuwait's undivided half-interest in the onshore area. Export began in 1954. The following year, another 60-year concession was granted to Aminoil for exploration and production of crude in the territorial waters to a six-mile limit, including the islands of Kuber, Qaru, and Umm Al-Maradim. The terms of the payment were the highest at that time in the Middle East; a royalty of $2.50 per ton and 15 per cent of the shares of the operating company.[45]

In 1961 an amended agreement was concluded between Aminoil and the government in which the company agreed to pay the greater of either 57 per cent of profits based on realizations or 50 per cent of profit based on posted prices, to be discharged by a payment of a royalty at 12.5 per cent of the posted price of oil "won and saved," the Kuwaiti income tax with the royalty credited against this tax, and a make-up payment if needed.[46]

The Arabian Oil Company

The offshore Neutral Zone concession, for $44\frac{1}{2}$ years, was granted in 1958 to the Arabian Oil Company, Limited (AOC), which is the operating subsidiary of the Japan Trading Company, a grouping of some 60 Japanese firms.[47] First exports to Japan took place in 1961.

---

[44] The exact breakdown of Aminoil ownership is:
(1) Phillips Petroleum Company—37.30%
(2) Signal Oil and Gas Company—33.54%
(3) Ashland Oil and Refining Company—14.13%
(4) James S. Abercrombie—7.06%
(5) Sunray Mid-Continent Oil Company—2.95%
(6) Lario Oil and Gas Company—1.77%
(7) Globe Oil and Refining Company—1.77%
(8) Pauley Petroleum—1.48%
The identical Saudi share of the Neutral Zone onshore was granted in a concession to the Pacific Western Oil Company, now Getty Oil Company.

[45] Also included was a bonus of $7.5 million, rental of $625,000 until the discovery of oil in commercial quantities and a tax exemption fee (one-eighth of gross sales proceeds from gas less cost of handling and transport to final buyers and $7\frac{1}{2}$ cents per ton in lieu of present and future taxes). See Issawi and Yeganeh, *Economics of Middle Eastern Oil*, pp. 37–38; Mikdashi, *Financial Analysis*, p. 313; *The Oil of Kuwait (1965)*, p. 59.

[46] See *The Oil of Kuwait (1965)*, p. 59, and Issawi and Yeganeh, p. 38.

[47] AOC also received the offshore concession from Saudi Arabia for that country's share of the Neutral Zone, thereby gaining exploration and production rights over the entire offshore Neutral Zone, with the exception of the 6-mile limit on territorial waters and the islands of Qaru and Umm Al-Maradin and their surrounding

AOC agreed to pay the greater of either (1) 57 per cent of profits based on posted prices (including royalty as a payment on account), or (2) royalty at 20 per cent of posted prices plus 40 per cent of profit based on posted price after charging royalty as an expense.[48] Moreover, the Kuwaiti government is to receive 57 per cent of the profits of refining and marketing, with such operations kept separate from production, that is, any losses in refining and marketing cannot be set off against the production profits. Finally, upon the discovery of oil in commercial quantities, the government exercised its right to purchase at the original issue 10 per cent of the share capital of AOC, thereby receiving 10 per cent of the dividend of the company in addition to the royalty and tax payments.[49]

KSPDC

In 1961 the fourth concessionaire, Kuwait Shell Petroleum Development Company Limited, concluded an agreement with the government of Kuwait with rights to explore for, drill, and produce crude for 45 years. The concession area included offshore seabed pertaining to Kuwait in the Gulf outside the territorial water limit of six nautical miles from shore.[50] Exploration activities were carried out in 1962 and 1963 but were discontinued the following year pending settlement of the border dispute among Kuwait, Iraq, and Iran. The revenue aspects of the agreement are the company's payment to the government of 50 per cent of its profits based on posted prices, to be discharged through a royalty at 12.5 per cent of the posted price of oil won and saved; the income tax (royalty being a credit against the tax); and a make-up payment when necessary. As with the AOC agreement, the Kuwaiti government, upon discovery of crude in commercial quantities, has an option to

---

waters to 3 nautical miles. It should be noted that oil from the Khafji field, the only producing AOC field to date, has 27–28° A.P.I. gravity and a sulfur content of 2.75 per cent. Daily producing capacity is 210,000 bbls. Some 36 million c.f.d. of natural gas is now mostly flared off. See *The Oil of Kuwait* (*1965*), pp. 48–49.

[48] The amount due to be discharged by a payment of (1) royalty at 20 per cent of posted price of oil won and saved, (2) Kuwait's income tax, royalty being a credit against income tax, (3) a make-up payment if needed. *The Oil of Kuwait* (*1965*), p. 60. An annual deed rent of $1.5 million was included. Issawi and Yeganeh, *Economics of Middle Eastern Oil*, p. 38.

[49] *The Oil of Kuwait* (*1965*), p. 60.

[50] Covering about 1,500 square nautical miles, the islands of Warbah, Bubiyan, Failakah, Mashjan, and Auha. *The Oil of Kuwait* (*1965*), p. 53.

take up to 20 per cent interest in KSPDC.[51] Morevoer, the government may take part or all of its 12.5 per cent royalty in kind and is entitled to all natural gas without cost which the company cannot utilize or sell.

Kuwait National Petroleum Company

The single local company holding a concession is the Kuwait National Petroleum Company (KNPC), founded in 1960 with the Kuwaiti government subscribing to 60 per cent of original shares. KNPC was involved only with the local marketing of KOC refinery products until KOC relinquished about 9,262 square kilometers of its concession area. KNPC petitioned the government for a concession, and the government has announced its intention of granting the concession upon the conclusion of negotiations over terms. KNPC is involved in refining with its plant at Shuaiba as well as in other oil activities.

ELASTICITY AND PROJECTION OF DEMAND FOR CRUDE OIL

Oil is subject to substitution by various energy sources (with a few exceptions where the uses of energy are not interchangeable, as in gasoline for automotive use and kerosine for jet propulsion). With the development of technology and research, coal, gas, and nuclear power are progressively nearing the substitution level for oil in industrial usage. The choice among these various energy sources is, however, still determined not only by relative prices but also by the cost of investment, the convenience of use, and last but not least, the security of supply.[52]

Before discussing the degree of response to demand for change in

---

[51] The option can be taken by the government itself or by a company it nominates and in which it has a controlling interest. The 20 per cent interest in the venture is against a cash payment in proportion to the total expenditures (excluding rents, bonus payments, and other accruals to the government) incurred by the company up to the discovery date in respect of its operations; it then shares in all further assets and liabilities. *The Oil of Kuwait (1965)*, pp. 60–61. Another clause is the section which stipulates relinquishment to the government of 20 per cent of the unexploited area, beginning three years after the discovery of commercial quantities of oil and at five-year intervals thereafter. Issawi and Yeganeh, *Economics of Middle Eastern Oil*, p. 36.

[52] Bela Balassa, *Trade Prospects for Developing Countries* (Homewood, Ill.: Richard D. Irwin, Inc., 1964), p. 268.

the price of oil, it may be helpful to recall that oil is not a homo-geneous commodity; quality and location of crude might also have a decided effect on the elasticity of demand. Generally speaking, the recent experience of alterations in demand for oil resulting from changes in price shows a high degree of inelasticity. By comparing the percentage growth in demand following the 1959 and 1960 price cuts, we can estimate the relationship between the price of oil and the total demand. When prices declined in the two instances above, the rate of increase did not diverge greatly from the average level of 7 per cent annually for the decade 1952–63. The actual rate of increase in demand was 7.7 per cent in 1960 and 6.5 per cent in 1961.[53] While these figures leave the impression of demand inelasti-city, they are not conclusive evidence. Other factors such as excess capacity and the reentry of Soviet oil into the world market contributed to the market condition.

A further examination of price elasticity requires, first, an analysis of the impact of a change in the price of crude on the ultimate price of refined products, and second, a study of the relative elasticity of demand for the refined products. In examining the effect of a change in the price of crude oil at the source (in this instance, the Middle East) on the price of refined products paid by the individual consumers in Western Europe, the slight importance of the cost component of the crude relative to the total price charged to the ultimate consumer is evident: about 16 per cent of the final average price ($11 per barrel) is accounted for by the share of crude ($1.75 average Middle Eastern price).[54] An estimated increase of 10 per cent in the price at the source, if completely passed on to the ultimate consumer, would cause only an additional 1.54 per cent hike to the final price of the refined product. Such an increase would cause a slight change in consumption, if any.[55]

---

[53] OPEC, *Elasticity of Demand for Crude Oil; Its Implications for Exporting Countries* (1964), EC/64/II, p. 15.

[54] Of this $11 per barrel of finished oil products, in Western Europe, about $3.50 accounts for "downstream operations" costs (that is, transport and refining); an average of $5.75 is direct and indirect taxes imposed by the consumer govern-ment; and $1.75 represents the costs, taxes, and royalties paid at the production stage of the crude oil as well as company profits. *Ibid.*, p. 8.

[55] If an assumption is made that the elasticity of demand for finished products is as high as unity, then consumption is figured to drop, in this case, by an equal proportion, 1.54 per cent, giving a numerical measurement of elasticity of crude oil of 0.15, indicative of high price inelasticity. See also Leeman, *Middle East Oil*, p. 177, on excise and protectionist practices.

For Kuwaiti oil, the cost component of crude is only $1.59 per barrel, and thus the burden to the ultimate consumer of a similar 10 per cent increase in price at the source would be still lighter, amounting to about a 1.47 per cent rise. The low cost of Kuwaiti crude in comparison with the average Middle Eastern figure is largely a reflection of the low cost of exploitation, considered the lowest in the world, and of the heavy grade (low gravity) of oil in the Kuwaiti fields.

The price elasticity of demand for refined petroleum products varies widely in response to the availability of substitutes. Demand for these refined products is mainly derived from and is dependent upon the demand for other goods or services and accordingly could be considered relatively inelastic, mainly because a change in price usually has little effect on the final price ("derived demand"). Any examination of the refined products, however, would reflect a wide range of elasticities. If these products are classified according to their demand elasticities, gasoline would be considered the most price inelastic, followed by kerosine, gas, diesel oil, and fuel oil, with the latter being relatively more elastic.[56]

The tax policies of the consuming countries in Western Europe may also mirror the degree of elasticity of demand for these specific petroleum products. It has been suggested that these fiscal measures are largely revenue-raising in purpose and therefore would tend to maintain the highest possible intake.[57] Such an assessment is valid as one of the considerations in consumer-nation tax policies. These fiscal measures may likewise be protectionist, with regard to indigenous energy sources, and could be designed to either encourage or discourage substitution for oil in the consumer's national interest. On the whole, however, there has been a clear correlation between the tax level and price elasticity—the more inelastic the demand for a petroleum product, the higher the tax. Gasoline, the most heavily taxed (about $15.50 average tax included in the average per barrel cost of $23), is considered the most price inelastic. Correspondingly, the tax component declines to $5.50 per barrel on kerosine (total price $13.50), to $4.50 per barrel on gas and diesel

[56] The demand for residual fuel oil is more elastic than that of distillate fuel oil because of the greater availability of substitute products for the residual type, through the use of change-over equipment. Issawi and Yeganeh, *Economics of Middle Eastern Oil*, p. 64.

[57] Cf. *Elasticity of Demand for Crude Oil; Its Implications for Exporting Countries* pp. 13–14.

($11 total price) and averages 60 cents on fuel oil (average total Western European price of $4.60 per barrel).[58] The demand elasticity for the latter product has been conditioned by competition resulting from greater efficiency in the use of coal and natural gas, and from the potential of nuclear power.

Demand Projection for Oil

Traditionally, changes in the demand requirements in energy in industrial countries have been predominantly responsible for the expansion of the oil industry in the petroleum exporting countries and their foreign exchange earnings. Reliance on energy has been a symptom and a cause of economic development interwoven in almost all stages of economic activity in industrialized nations. Such a relationship could best be illustrated by comparing measurements of changes in energy consumption with those of the GNP of the major consumer countries. At the end of the 1950's a glance at data of the per capita GNP in the U.S. (the world's largest energy consumer) and those of per capita energy consumption shows that with about $2,400 per capita income, the energy consumption per person was equal to 8 tons of coal equivalent as compared to $1,500 per capita income and 5 tons in the United Kingdom, and $1,300 with 2.4 tons in France. A closer examination indicates that during the 1950's in the United States, a one per cent increase in the GNP was accompanied by a 0.84 per cent rise in energy consumption.[59] However, increased efficiency in this originally high-base energy economy, combined with continued shifts toward services, is causing an expected slight reduction of energy requirements in relation to continued increases in the GNP.[60] Accordingly, recent projections forecast an increase between 0.73 per cent and 0.80 per cent in energy consumption associated with each 1 per cent in GNP rise.[61]

[58] *Ibid.*, p. 30.

[59] Balassa, *Trade Prospects*, pp. 270–71.

[60] These projections are tentative, as technological developments have always played, and will continue to play a major role in shaping energy markets. For example, the development of air-conditioning on a national rather than a regional scale in the U.S. will cause a large energy consumption. Monthly review of the Petroleum Department of the Chase Manhattan Bank, *The Petroleum Situation*, March, 1966.

[61] The 0.73 per cent estimate given for 1960–70 is in Hans H. Landsberg *et al.*, *Resources in America's Future* (Baltimore: Johns Hopkins Press, 1963), p. 292. The 0.8 per cent for 1955–75 is given by S. M. Schurr, Bruce C. Netschert *et al.*, *Energy in the American Economy, 1870–1975* (Baltimore: Johns Hopkins Press, 1960).

In his recent study, Balassa projects a 0.75 per cent increase, or a total income elasticity demand for energy estimated at 0.75. Based on this percentage, energy is projected to increase from 1.45 billion tons of coal equivalent in 1960 to 2.20–2.27 billion tons of coal equivalent in 1975.[62]

Energy consumption in Western Europe, although lagging substantially behind that in the United States, has witnessed a lower income elasticity of demand during the 1950's.[63] This may be largely attributed to the intensified drive toward the substitution of oil, with its greater efficiency, for coal, which in the 1960's began to level off. Nevertheless, projections indicate that total energy consumption associated with increases in the GNP for Western Europe is likely to grow as illustrated in Table 4.

Turning to an examination specifically of oil consumption we find that while there is a rapidly upward spiral of petroleum demand, the rate has decreased from the earlier, phenomenal upsurge and has become more steady. A recent study by the Petroleum Department of the First National City Bank of New York has revealed that during the first five years of the present decade, the demand for petroleum increased at a rate of 7.8 per cent, compared with 4.3 per cent for energy emanating from all sources.[64] The characteristics of efficiency, and the price level, have contributed to the advantageous position achieved by oil in the energy market. The leveling-off of the rate of increase in petroleum demand may be attributed to a recent comparative increase in efficiency in the coal industry in the U.S. and to the reaching of the minimum limit to which Western European governments could reduce coal production. These conditions in the coal industry and the prospects of other energy sources will be discussed later in this chapter.

Nonetheless, the rate of rise in demand, though less than during the postwar "oil boom," will remain large. In the span 1965–70,

[62] Balassa, *Trade Prospects*, p. 271.

[63] The share of liquid fuels increased nearly threefold in the Common Market and the United Kingdom between 1950 and 1960 as compared to one-fifth that rise in the United States. *Ibid.*, p. 272.

[64] Edward Symonds, *Energy Memo* (New York, First National City Bank, April, 1966), p. 1. Cf. same study, p. 4, for the statistics given below:

World Oil Demand (in thousands of barrels per day)

	1959	1964	1969
World (excluding Soviet-Communist areas)	19,770	28,720	39,370
U.S.S.R. and other Communist consumers	2,640	4,170	6,370

TABLE 4

ENERGY CONSUMPTION IN DEVELOPED COUNTRIES
(IN MILLION TONS OF COAL EQUIVALENT)

	1960		1970[a]		1975[a]	
	Million Tons	Per Cent	Million Tons	Per Cent	Million Tons	Per Cent
United States						
Solid fuels	357	25	458	23	505	22
Liquid fuels	590	41	796	41	925	40
Natural gas	482	33	662	33	740	33
Hydroelectricity	19	1	29	2	39	2
Atomic power	...	...	...	...	...	...
Total Energy	1,448	100	1,965	100	2,267	100
European Common Market						
Solid fuels	285	65	260	40	250	31
Liquid fuels	129	29	324	49	436	55
Natural gas	14	3	48	7	75	9
Hydroelectricity	13	3	17	3	19	2
Atomic power	...	...	8	1	20	3
Total Energy	441	100	657	100	800	100
United Kingdom						
Solid fuels	197	76	188	58	184	50
Liquid fuels	61	24	116	36	150	41
Natural gas	0	0	4	1	6	2
Hydroelectricity	0	0	...	...	...	...
Atomic power	...	...	18	5	24	7
Total Energy	258	100	326	100	364	100
Japan						
Solid fuels	62	57	80	37	90	31
Liquid fuels	38	35	120	56	187	63
Natural gas	1	1	3	1	3	1
Hydroelectricity	7	7	12	6	16	5
Atomic power	...	...	...	...	...	...
Total Energy	108	100	215	100	296	100

SOURCE: Bela Balassa, *Trade Prospects for Developing Countries*, pp. 276–77.

a Using Balassa's maximum projection figures.

the yearly increase is estimated to be 2.1 million barrels per day.[65]
The level of investment already attained by the present producers
is such that output in many areas can be greatly expanded with
little additional investment. This is particularly true in the Kuwaiti
case.

[65] *Ibid.*, p. 1. Thus, although the percentage of increase (1965–70) is less than
for the 1960–65 period, the actual barrels per day increase is greater than the
1.8 million b/d of the first half of the decade.

Within this overall picture of total energy demand and the portion held by oil (which is leveling off but will retain a healthy percentage increment annually), there are regional and product-market conditions which will have a more definite impact on Kuwaiti output and its export position. In Western Europe, because of the protection of domestic coal interests and a slowdown of the economic growth to a more normal level of activity (mentioned earlier), an average annual increment of 8.6 per cent is estimated for the 1964–69 period, compared with an average yearly rise of 15 per cent the previous five years. Likewise Japan's demand is projected to fall from the extraordinarily high 27.1 per cent average annual increase (1959–64) to 12.5 per cent (1964–69), but it will still prove the most actively growing market.[66] During the same periods, the annual average increase for the Western hemisphere showed 3.4 per cent and 3.6 per cent for the second period.[67] It is the latter two areas, Western Europe and Japan, that furnish major markets for Kuwaiti output. In fact, the Japanese consumption share of Kuwait's production has been growing steadily in recent years.

Another factor affecting the Kuwaiti trade prospects is the change in the product mix which, in long-range market planning, may prove more important. It should be recalled that Kuwait's heavy crude is a major source of residual oil. In mature economies, particularly those with indigenous, efficient coal production, the share of residual oil is either a declining or static proportion of total oil demand. In the United States residual oil has declined to about 14 per cent of all petroleum product consumption while in Western Europe residual oil demand has leveled off at 37 per cent of the total, as compared with the gasoline share of 42.6 per cent in the U.S. and 16.5 per cent in Western Europe. In Japan, which lacks efficient, good-quality coal, residual oil still accounts for over 50 per cent of the petroleum market. In the developing countries as a whole, the residual oil share remains high, about 37 per cent. The future market trend is likely to include a further relative contraction of demand for residual oil in industrialized nations. It appears, however, that the potential expansion of oil in general and its

[66] Balassa, *Trade Prospects*, p. 281; largely due to the abandonment, in 1962, of the "coal before oil" policy in Japan. However, the coal resources of this nation are of relatively poor quality.
[67] E. Symonds, *Energy Memo*, April, 1966, p. 2.

heavy types in particular will be in those developing countries undergoing industrialization, where oil consumption presently accounts for 14 per cent of the total world demand and where the per capita consumption is about one-twentieth of that of the United States.[68]

Yet the ultimate amount of imports to consuming countries, theoretically or without political and fiscal obstacles, will depend on production cost advantages and changes in the cost of transport. Kuwait already enjoys, and is likely to continue to enjoy, the lowest production costs in the world, and although North African and Nigerian oil benefits from lower transport cost, the difference between freight costs of African and Gulf crude is being lessened through larger tankers and pipeline schemes. If cost were the only criterion, then Kuwaiti crude could compete in North American markets.

PRICE STABILIZATION

Two major issues continue to confront oil exporters in general and Kuwait in particular. One is the price structure; the second is maintaining the rate of production growth. Oil, as a primary commodity, has suffered from the general decline in the price of raw materials that has caused a deterioration in the terms of trade of the producing countries.[69] It is even more serious for petroleum producers because the commodity is a wasting asset. A price cut cannot be offset by a value-equivalent increase in production as greater output would further act as a price depressant and would hasten depletion of the resource. In the 1964 United Nations Conference on Trade and Development, this problem was recognized through suggestions that action be taken to improve the revenues accruing to the developing countries which produce and export minerals and fuels, to insure maximum utilization of such resources

[68] *Ibid.*, p. 9; per capita consumption of one barrel in the developing countries as compared to some 20 barrels in North America. Also, see E. Symonds, *Financing Oil Expansion in the Development Decade* (New York: First National City Bank, 1963), p. 1.

[69] Posted crude prices reached their peak in 1958 but have since declined by 13 per cent from that level. The terms of trade dropped after 1955 but recovered in 1958 and declined again from the 100 base in 1958 to 84 in 1962. F. Parra, *Exporting Countries and International Oil* (OPEC, 1964) EC/64/I, p. 29.

in their own industrial development on the basis of coordination and cooperation.[70]

A widespread weakening of the price structure took place in 1959 and again in 1960 when the companies, without consultation with the producing countries, lowered posted prices on crude oil.[71] This action brought about an immediate reaction among the exporting nations which led to the creation of a grouping, the Organization of Petroleum Exporting Countries, of which Kuwait was a founding member. Yet underlying the cuts in posted prices has been the continued deterioration in actual prices. This decline, while having more significance to the producing countries where taxes are based on actual sales prices, is also important to others, including Kuwait, where the terms of supplemental agreements on the expensing of royalties add obstacles in the elimination of the presently permitted allowances and are contingent upon improvement of the market situation. Kuwait has been more sensitive to

[70] United Nations, Conference on Trade and Development, *Final Act* (E/CONF.46/L.28, June, 1964), Annex A, p. 57.

[71] The following table gives an idea of the price fluctuation which affected the major oil exporters and original members of the OPEC.

Posted Crude Prices 1955–65
(In U.S. Dollars)

Country Gravity Port	1955	1956	1957	1958	1959	1960	1961	1962	1963	1964	1965
Iran 34/34.9° f.o.b. Abadan	1.86	1.86	1.99	1.81	1.73	1.73	1.73	1.73	1.73	1.73	1.73
Iraq 36/36.9° f.o.b. Tripoli	2.39	2.46	2.69	2.49	2.31	2.21	2.21	2.21	2.21	2.21	2.21
Kuwait 31/31.9° f.o.b. Ahmadi	1.72	1.72	1.85	1.85	1.67	1.59	1.59	1.59	1.59	1.59	1.59
Qatar 40/40.9° f.o.b. Umm Said	2.08	2.08	2.21	2.21	2.03	1.93	1.93	1.93	1.93	1.93	1.93
Saudi Arabia 34/34.9° f.o.b. Ras Tanura	1.97	1.93	2.08	2.08	1.90	1.80	1.80	1.80	1.80	1.80	1.80
Venezuela Oficina 35/35.9° f.o.b. Puerto la Cruz	2.88	2.80	3.05	3.05	2.80	2.80	2.80	2.80	2.80	2.80	2.80

SOURCES: OPEC, *Note on Resolution IX, 61* (1965), p. 5; 1965 figures from calculations of Petroleum Department, First National City Bank, New York.

pricing of crude than other principal exporters, as the Kuwaiti governmental revenue per unit has been consistently lower, mainly because of the lower gravity of its crude and the sulfur content, which lower its price on the market.

Some countries such as Libya and Iran are eager to expand the rate of production. The former is a newcomer to the industry and the latter is seeking to reestablish its pre-nationalization share of the market. In their efforts to expand production, they have been giving secondary consideration to raising the posted price of crude and accepting flexible company realizations.[72] The Organization of Petroleum Exporting Countries has put forward a plan of linking the prices of crude oil to an index of prices of essential imports. This scheme, which was designed to offset the decline in the terms of trade of the oil exporting countries, thus far has not been realized because of the technical difficulties in drawing up the indices. There are as well the basic obstacles to the present oil market conditions characterized by an excess capacity. First, newcomers in the export of oil, including Nigeria, Algeria, and the Arabian Gulf states, and the reentry of Soviet oil into the world market, have compounded the recent weakness in prices. Second, the trade restrictions and fiscal measures imposed by certain advanced consuming countries such as the United States, Great Britain, France, and Germany act as a depressant on attempts to raise the price of crude. Third, and of growing importance, is the competition, existing and potential, of other energy and fuel forms, particularly nuclear power.

With reference to the first factor, increasing competition in production and marketing of petroleum, it suffices to point out that in two countries, Algeria and Nigeria, the annual average increase from 1959 to 1964 was some 84.5 per cent and 60.5 per cent respectively as compared to an average of 9 per cent for Kuwaiti production for the same period.[73] Admittedly the production base of

---

[72] Frank, *Crude Oil Prices*, p. 176. On the other hand, some members of the Organization of Petroleum Exporting Countries are willing to reduce their expansion rate to avoid the sale of their oil at discount prices. Recently the system of posted prices was applied to Libya in conformity with OPEC resolutions concerning this matter.

[73] BP, *1964 Statistical Review of the World Oil Industry* (London: British Petroleum Company, Ltd., 1965), p. 7. Another example is the 22 per cent estimated production increase from 1965 to 1966 of Abu Dhabi, which reportedly hesitated to join OPEC because such a connection might lead to production restrictions.

these African examples, particularly Nigeria, was comparatively low; yet the increase is, by any standards, remarkable. The Soviet Union's drive to increase the marketability of Russian oil has been intensified in recent years. Petroleum is the Soviet Union's prime commodity export, and in the 1950's its production quadrupled while the world output doubled. Moreover, domestic demand has not been rising proportionately and has allowed for a fourfold increase in exports during the 1955–60 period.[74]

The second element hampering efforts to improve the price position is the trade restrictions and fiscal measures, referred to earlier, which are imposed by the advanced importing nations. The United States restricts the international producers and protects its domestic market through import controls, prorationing, and depletion allowances, adversely affecting the oversupply situation in the rest of the world.[75] For example, before the 1958 mandatory controls on oil imports to the U.S., Gulf Oil Corporation imported 14 per cent of its Kuwaiti oil production for its own system and sold up to 8 per cent to other American importers.[76] As a result of the restraints on trade, Gulf Corporation and other American firms have had to seek other markets. Conversely, if the United States allows freedom of entry of foreign oil, such oil would be available at over $1 less per barrel than the domestic price and its entry would tend to minimize the inefficiency in U.S. crude production.[77] Additional restraints on imports into the United States have been advocated recently because of the deficit in the balance of payments. Considering that the gross value of oil imports accounted for 10 per

[74] D. L. Spenser, "The Role of Oil in Soviet Foreign Economic Policy," *American Journal of Economics and Sociology*, January, 1966, p. 98. It is interesting to note that the 1965 plan envisaged slightly less than 30 per cent of total oil production for export (*ibid.*). Soviet oil production growth rate has been about 9.5 per cent in recent years but is projected to drop to about 8.7 per cent for the 1965–70 period. Symonds, *Energy Memo*, April, 1966, p. 2. An example of Soviet marketing in the West is the 1965 long-term agreement between the Raffineries du Rhone for its refinery in Switzerland. The price of the oil is significantly below the level at which major international companies can sell crude. Argentina, Brazil, Italy, and Japan also buy Soviet oil. *New York Times*, August 23, 1965.

[75] See Marwan Iskandar, "World Oil Surplus in Relation to United States Imports, Depletion and Prorationing Policies," Vth Arab Petroleum Congress, vol. 1: *Economics*, ser. 4 (A-4), pp. 1–25.

[76] U.S. Congress, *Energy Oil Lift Program and Related Oil Problems, Hearings*, 4 vols. (Washington, D.C., 1957), p. 1333.

[77] M. Adelman, "Crude Petroleum," p. 105. He estimates that over $4 billion annually could be saved by allowing freedom of oil into the United States.

cent of the total value of U.S. imports in 1964, petroleum appears a rational target for cuts. Approximately 45 per cent of oil imports to the United States are derived from Eastern hemisphere sources, and reductions in American foreign oil requirements would adversely affect the marketability of Eastern supplies as well as the Venezuelan supply, which alone accounts for some 50 per cent of U.S. oil imports.[78]

While attention has largely been fixed on American restrictions, protectionist and restrictive fiscal policies have been followed by other industrialized countries and accordingly influence the price of crude and impede the substitution effect which tends to allow for greater use of oil. France's attitude toward Saharan oil, which is still looked upon mainly as a French "national" source, is reflected in the preferential market allowed for oil from this source that inhibits imports from other producers. Protective measures for indigenous energy resources remain a potent element in pricing and importation of petroleum and its products. The EEC countries, with the exception of Italy and England, have imposed either quotas or relatively high taxes to protect domestic energy sources, particularly coal.[79] While the traditional and overriding protectionist concern is for the European coal industry, the fairly new discoveries of natural gas have contributed to an alteration of the balance between total energy requirements and European energy output. Recent estimates anticipate the eventual production of EEC natural gas to equal the amount of energy presently derived from all its coal mines. If the well-head cost of this natural gas is as low as it

---

[78] E. Symonds, *Oil in the National Balance* (New York: First National City Bank, 1965), p. 2. It should be noted, however, that U.S. foreign earnings from direct investment in total overseas oil exceed the investment outflow of capital by approximately $1 billion annually.

[79] The following table gives some idea of the part played by the tax component in the consumer countries in the cost of oil products to the individual consumers.

Recent Prices (January 1964) for Regular-Grade European Petrol
(in U.S. cents per gallon)

Country	Pump Price	Tax	Excluding Tax Price
France	72.6	55.3	17.3
Germany	53.9	32.4	21.5
United Kingdom	50.9	32.3	18.6

SOURCE: OPEC *Cheap Energy, Diversification of Sources and Security of Supply* (OPEC, 1966), p. 13.

is now estimated to be, 0.4 cent per cubic meter, then energy imports must be able to compete.[80]

The exceptional case is Italy, which because of the scarcity there of indigenous energy sources does not impose any serious restrictions. In recent years over 20 per cent of oil imports to that country were of Soviet petroleum, which competes with Kuwaiti and other Middle Eastern and African petroleum for the Italian market.[81] Italy became the main market for Kuwait Oil Company crude in 1965, taking 24.8 per cent of KOC total exports.[82] In Germany, a tax of DM 25 per ton on heavy fuel oil and DM 10 per ton on light oil illustrates the scale of the coal protectionist policy in that country.[83] Since Kuwaiti crude is heavy and contains a greater potential of fuel oil products, such a taxation policy does have a direct bearing on the asking price for Kuwaiti crude and its ability to compete with other fuel energy sources such as coal.

Along with its high taxes on fuel oils, Germany has actively sought to impede refinery expansion. France uses a quota system and administrative pressure to control the growth of fuel oil consumption. In 1960 Belgium put a "special" tax on oil, and a year later England imposed an excise tax on fuel oil.[84] Such restrictions have a very real impact on Middle Eastern and North African producers as Western Europe obtains about 73 per cent of its oil imports from these areas. Moreover, because of the Iranian nationalization incident and the Suez crisis, some economic considerations in procurement of petroleum have been subordinated to the drive for greater supply security.[85] A call for lower prices has been heard

[80] Lucio Corradini, "Communauté Européenne et Transformation du Marche de l'Energie," paper presented at the International Conference on "Energy, An Essential Element for Cooperation Among Countries of the Mediterranean Area," Rome, March, 1965 (Doc. No. 2136/65f, Communauté Européenne du Charbon et de l'Acier, Autres Sources d'Energie), p. 13.

[81] Spenser, "Role of Oil in Soviet Foreign Policy," p. 100.

[82] *Middle East Economic Survey*, July 1, 1966, p. 3.

[83] Frank, *Crude Oil Prices*, p. 203.

[84] *Ibid.*, p. 165.

[85] F. R. Parra, Chief of OPEC Economics Department, OPEC Statement at the International Conference on "Energy, An Essential Element for Cooperation Among Countries of the Mediterranean Area," Rome, March 1965; résumé in *Middle East Economic Survey*, May 7, 1965, p. 5. This Conference is considered important as the first attempt at "consumer-producer dialogue." It is scheduled to meet annually. At the first conference, representatives attended from OPEC, ENI (the Italian Government's oil company), the government of Italy, the Arab League, and the European Coal and Steel Community.

persistently from the developing nations which suffer from chronic foreign exchange shortage. A specific case which had repercussions in the 1960 cuts of posted crude prices in the Middle East was the Indian government's stand on lower c.i.f. prices.[86] Such conditions, particularly in the advanced countries, are a potential threat to the low-cost oil producers through the development of other sources of energy, such as shale oil, tar sands, and nuclear power. Although the present production cost of these three sources is still too high to make them widely commercially competitive, they remain alternative energy possibilities.[87]

It is in this realm of competitive energy sources that the oil exporters face the third element involved in the pricing of petroleum. In the long-run, nuclear power offers the greatest threat to the marketability of oil. The application of atomic energy is limited at present to electrical generation and motive power for large vessels. However, the possibility of utilizing atomic power for light transport is distant. Still, Kuwait, as a major exporter and producer of heavy crude, is likely to be more concerned with the development of nuclear fuel than the producers of the lighter grades. With the emphasis of nuclear fuel in the generation of electricity and for industrial purposes, keener competition with heavier, residual oil should evolve. In turn, the anticipated reduction in the cost of nuclear power will make demand more elastic for heavy crude.

---

[86] Some developing oil importers in Latin America, particularly Argentina and Brazil, secure lowest rates through their government agencies which accept competitive international bids. The lower prices of independent suppliers, including the USSR, bring pressures to lower the actual prices charged by the major international companies.

[87] The estimated cost has been given of oil from U.S. oil shale at $2.75 per barrel laid down Los Angeles and $3 per barrel in Chicago; Canada's Athabasca tar sands would cost $3 per barrel at eastern seaboard as compared to Kuwaiti crude at 31° APL sold at full posted price f.o.b. the Persian Gulf which could land in Los Angeles at a price of only $2.45 per barrel. Private experimental investigation is being continued in the oil shale deposits in Colorado by the Oil Shale Corporation, which gives tentative estimates at the retort to be $1.15 to $1.30 per barrel at a level of 50,000 b/d production. These costs are competitive with domestic petroleum. A main attraction of shale oil is that it can be produced without the burden of exploration costs to replace reserves. On the other hand, the initial capital investments required ($1,500–$2,000 per daily barrel) prior to receiving any income are much higher for shale than for petroleum. Charles Prien, "The Miracle of Shale Oil," *University of Denver Magazine*, March, 1965, p. 27. There is, as well, the question of the immense waste disposal from the oil shale processing which poses a large-scale economic and technical problem.

Already nuclear energy has moved from the experimental to the production stage and from military to civilian use. Recent cost estimates of a commercially operated and privately owned nuclear plant in the United States is a weighted average of just over 26 cents per million BTU, which is equivalent to $1.59 per barrel of fuel oil or $6.80 per short ton of coal.[88] One negative feature of nuclear fuel, however, is the problem of waste disposal and potential nuclear pollution. With the growing sensitivity to pollution of the environment in developed countries, this aspect is not a minor factor, realistically or psychologically. On the whole, the threat of losing markets to nuclear energy has performed a key role in the revitalization of measures to increase efficiency in the American coal industry. The reduction of production costs and prices is enabling the United States to assume the position of the major coal exporter to Europe. In this decade trans-Atlantic freight rates for American coal have been cut almost in half to the present figure of $3.50 per ton. Greater transport efficiency with larger, special vessels is expected to lower this rate still further by over one-third in the 1970's.[89]

Thus Middle Eastern and North African oil has to compete progressively not only with nuclear energy but also with American coal within both the U.S. and Europe. It is therefore the middle and heavy grades of oil rather than the lighter types which will be facing stiffer competition and accordingly must adjust to conditions of elastic demand. The cost of nuclear energy will finally set the maximum prices at which fossil fuels may be sold. Just how soon this ceiling will be established will largely depend upon the pricing

[88] This estimate is derived from the Jersey Central Power and Light nuclear plant, Adelman, "Crude Petroleum," pp. 112–13. The U.S. Atomic Energy Commission has published its findings on the competitiveness of nuclear power with both coal and oil as follows:

Nuclear Plant			Competitive with Fossil Fuels Costing:		
Size (MW)	Year Start	Year Operate	cents/million BTU	dollars/barrel (fuel oil)	dollars per short ton (coal)
500	1967	1972	36.2–43.2	2.21–2.64	9.50–11.15
500	1972	1977	27.2–35.1	1.66–2.14	7.10–9.20
1,000	1980	1985	21.1–26.1	1.29–1.59	5.53–6.81

Source: M. Adelman, "Efficiency of Resource Use in Crude Petroleum," p. 122. (National Power Commission, National Power Survey, Advisory Committee Reports No. 15.)

[89] Corradini, "Communauté Européenne," p. 16.

of fossil fuels in the immediate future. A tentative guideline may be the competitive level of oil and coal, which would be equivalent to the conservative cost estimate of 28 cents per million BTU of nuclear fuel.[90]

Finally there is the question of nuclear energy in underdeveloped countries. The disposal of oil in developing areas has been increasing at a rapid rate although its level falls far below that of the advanced consuming regions. The traditional Kuwaiti markets in Europe have been strong, but the increased competition from North African petroleum and other sources of energy has led to a fall in the European share of total Kuwaiti crude exports from 64.8 per cent in 1960 to 59.6 per cent in 1964.[91] The slack is being taken up by exports to Japan in the Eastern hemisphere and to the developing countries.[92] The vulnerability to price fluctuations of oil exports to developing nations is likely to be greater than to advanced consumers. First, there are the foreign exchange shortage and severe balance-of-payments difficulties; second, although the percentage increase in consumption is high, the base is low. If petroleum prices become prohibitive, the developing nations, with limited industrial facilities committed to oil as a fuel and as a generator of power, can exploit domestic hydroelectric potential or leap directly to nuclear energy. Presently no developing country of any magnitude or size has failed to include at least one nuclear reactor in its economic development plan, whether for prestige or economy.

The combined impact of the entry of newcomers, policy changes by the importing countries in trade and fiscal spheres, and the development of non-oil sources has made the attainment of stable crude prices a difficult objective. Such developments have been reflected in the inability to market crude at posted prices; on the whole, posted prices have been maintained at the reduced level of 1960. The primary goal of the exporting countries—to restore the original price—has been made more difficult to realize by the persistent declines in actual prices.

[90] Adelman placed the 28-cent nuclear price as equivalent to $7.35 per short ton of coal and $1.74 per barrel for heavy fuel oil, which is about the present going price for this crude. Adelman, "Crude Petroleum," p. 113.

[91] *Kuwait Chamber of Commerce and Industry Bulletin*, March, 1966, p. 7, gives the statement of the Minister of Finance and Oil.

[92] However, lower European actual prices for crude have seeped into the Eastern markets with a weakening of prices there as well. *Middle East Economic Survey*, October 29, 1965, p. 1.

PRODUCTION PROGRAMMING

Within this context the most logical instrument left in the hands of Kuwait and other major exporting countries would be a design for production allowances or controls. Proposals along these lines have been given but secondary importance, and this only recently, by most of the Middle Eastern exporting nations. The lack of immediate concern can be traced to two factors. The first is attributable to the relatively high rates of output growth, particularly for the post-Iranian nationalization crisis period. With the obvious exception of Iran,[93] other oil producers have witnessed continued growth. Kuwait recorded an annual average increase from 1954 to 1964 of 8.5 per cent; Iraq, 7 per cent; Qatar and Saudi Arabia, 6.5 per cent.[94] (See Table 5 for production bases.) The second factor lies in the lowest cost of production, that of the Middle East. Thus the incentive to expand its output is inherent in the situation itself.

Kuwait manifests the reaction perhaps to a greater degree than its fellow producer-exporters in both instances. Comparatively, Kuwait's production was given a larger boost, almost quadrupling from 1949 to 1954 as a result of the Iranian oil crisis and kept gaining momentum, clearly illustrated in Table 5 where Kuwaiti production is shown in perspective with other Middle Eastern producers. Second, the cost of production of Kuwaiti crude is the lowest among all exporters. With other producers faring well in output, the exporters' pressure was directed toward an improvement in price rather than an increase in the relative shares of the producing countries. Undoubtedly the lack of emphasis on production was also motivated by the fear of aggravating an increase in the total producing capacity which might, in turn, cause a further deterioration in prices. But with the recent development of oil exploration and production in such areas as Algeria and Nigeria, and the fairly new natural gas discoveries in Europe (mainly in Holland and the North Sea by those companies involved in Middle East production), more attention has been directed toward the total supply of the

---

[93] See Issawi and Yeganeh, *Economics of Middle Eastern Oil*, pp. 9–11. Oil production declined from 242 million barrels in 1950 to 8 million in 1952. However, after the settlement of the nationalization problem, production resumed, reaching its previous records in 1960.

[94] BP, *1964 Statistical Review of the World Oil Industry*, p. 18.

TABLE 5

Production of Crude Petroleum in the Middle East by Countries, 1913–65
(In Thousands of Barrels)

Period	Bahrain	Iran	Iraq	Kuwait	Neutral Zone	Qatar	Saudi Arabia	Total
1913–33	34	536,768	5,411	...	...	...	...	542,210
1934	285	57,851	7,689	...	...	...	...	65,825
1936	4,645	62,718	30,406	...	...	...	20	97,589
1938	8,298	78,372	32,643	...	...	...	495	119,808
1940	7,074	66,317	24,225	...	...	...	5,075	102,691
1942	6,241	72,256	19,726	...	...	...	4,630	102,735
1944	6,714	102,045	30,943	...	...	...	7,794	147,496
1946	8,010	146,819	35,665	5,931	...	...	59,944	265,369
1948	10,915	190,384	26,115	46,500	...	...	142,853	416,767
1950	11,016	242,475	49,726	125,722	...	12,268	199,547	640,752
1952	11,004	7,800	141,100	273,433	...	25,255	301,861	860,453
1954	10,992	21,500	228,432	347,319	5,995	36,450	347,845	998,623
1956	11,015	197,148	232,307	399,874	11,684	45,300	360,923	1,258,231
1958	14,873	301,526	266,102	509,382	29,310	63,910	370,486	1,555,589
1960	16,500	390,755	354,592	594,278	49,830	63,908	456,453	1,726,306
1962	16,362	496,630	366,825	600,226	81,760	61,346	555,056	2,178,205
1964	18,000	618,616	456,814	772,698	132,196	77,589	628,095	2,704,008
1965	20,788	688,214	480,032	791,902	131,717	84,335	739,078	2,935,066

Sources: Issawi and Yeganeh, *Economics of Middle Eastern Oil*, p. 183; computed from figures in KOC Ltd., *Annual Review of Operations 1965*, p. 19; for 1964, 1965 figures, *World Oil*, August 15, 1966, p. 89; for 1962, *World Petroleum*, February, 1964, p. 33.

exporters and the defining of proportions of the offtake from individual countries as well as finding an equitable basis for doing so.[95] The Organization of Petroleum Exporting Countries is attempting a production program.

Kuwait and other members of OPEC have indicated interest in the fact that while the average percentage increase for the entire grouping did not vary greatly from one year to another (a change of from 9.6 per cent to 9.8 per cent annually from 1961 to 1964), the individual production rates have fluctuated more sharply. Kuwait's annual rate of output increase has varied from 6.5 per cent to about 13 per cent; Iraq has witnessed a range from 0.7 per cent to 15.2 per cent, and Saudi Arabia from 6.3 per cent to 11.1 per cent.[96]

The principle of production programming was adopted by OPEC for the first time in 1965 and was advanced as a "transitory measure" mainly to define the allowable growth rates among its members with 1964 production as a base. These growth rates, as shown in Table 6, were considered the maximum ceiling levels to combat excessive supply and halt the downward trend in actual prices. While this schedule was adopted by the group, some reservations were voiced by certain members, such as Libya, because of opposition to production programming per se, or because of objections to the rate assigned them (Saudi Arabia). In terms of implementation, realized rates often differed widely from those allotted. For Libya, the actual output was running almost double its programmed share while Kuwaiti production was lagging over 50 per cent behind its OPEC growth rate. Saudi Arabian production has surpassed its OPEC quota as well. Objections generally centered on the inability to balance actual output with quotas.

---

[95] At the Ninth Conference of the Organization of Petroleum Exporting Countries held in Tripoli, Libya, July, 1965, a clearly stated resolution was drawn up giving the position of the oil producers. "The Conference . . . with a view to counteracting the continuing erosion of crude and production prices; considering that one of the contributing factors to the deterioration of crude and product prices is the unrestricted competitive use of the excess producing capacity; recognizing the need for a steady flow of oil to international markets on the basis of equitable and stable prices; considering that there is an immediate need to formulate a programme to achieve the objectives set out in the Resolutions of the Organization, resolves (1) to adopt as a transitory measure a production plan calling for rational increases in production from the OPEC area to meet increases in world demand; and (2) to submit a production programme to the Governments of Member Countries for approval." *Resolutions Adopted at the Conferences of the Organization of the Petroleum Exporting Countries*, Resolution IX.61, p. 103.

[96] *Middle East Economic Survey*, August 27, 1965, p. 26.

More important, while the production program was designed mainly with the goal of price stabilization in mind, it did not guarantee the total revenue growth rate for the producing countries. An optimal and more equitable allocation may have to include fixed increases (while allowing for revisions arising from alterations in commercially usable reserves) according to the ratio of oil income to the budgetary revenue of the producing country as well as to the historical output growth of individual members. In addition to an attempt at price stabilization through prorationing, and thus control of total output, an effort should be made to adjust quotas to output capabilities and requirements of economic development of each producer. In the former effort, OPEC production programming

TABLE 6

OPEC OIL OUTPUT GROWTH RATES
(IN PER CENT)

	Change 1964 over 1963	Change Annual Average (1959–64)	OPEC Growth Rates (1965/66)[a]
Indonesia	6	4.5	10.0
Iran	15	13.0	17.5
Iraq	9	8.0	10.0
Kuwait	10	9.0	6.5
Libya	87	300+	20.0
Qatar	−2	2.5	32.0
Saudi Arabia	7	10.0	12.0
Venezuela	5	4.0	3.3

SOURCE: *Middle East Economic Survey*, August 27, 1965, p. 5; June 18, 1965, p. 7.

[a] For a 12-month period ending June 30, 1966.

is handicapped by the alternative suppliers outside its scope (Nigeria and Algeria) plus the fact that total OPEC production is only about 43 per cent of the world output even though its share of the world reserves is 69.9 per cent.[97]

Using the major guidelines for production programming, i.e., the reserves and the developmental revenue requirements, we find the case of Kuwait exceptional. In the section dealing with production and reserves in this chapter, it was shown that Kuwaiti production has not been commensurate with its proven reserves (Table 3). If compared to the situation in the United States, we

---

[97] Low quota allocations or inability to realize projected allotted targets could lead to enhancement of investment in non-OPEC countries and a loss of market position which might prove difficult to reclaim by OPEC members.

note that while Kuwaiti proven reserves are roughly double those of the United States (excluding shale oil and tar sands), the annual output of Kuwait is about one-fourth that of American production. [98] Production programming need not be visualized as a means of creating an artificial scarcity solely for the purpose of raising prices. The alternative sources of energy and the inability to control all oil production for export make such a course inadvisable. The basic reasoning behind the OPEC programming appears, however, to aim at meeting the rising consumption requirements while providing strengthened *stability* to prices through coordination of the individual and control of the total output of its members.

Kuwait's position in production programming is likely to continue to be conditioned by the relative abundance of reserves. This, coupled with world marketing projections for the immediate future, necessitates adoption of and adherence to the highest possible production quota. Kuwait would defeat its own economic purposes by pursuing a policy of excessive caution in drawing on its reserves. Time preference, in terms of present exploitation, is a potent consideration which can only be offset by a rise in oil prices or an improvement in the terms of trade (that is, the per unit purchasing power of oil income), both of which appear unlikely. [99]

Aside from reserves the second influence in production programming decisions is the developmental revenue requirements of the producer. In this aspect, Kuwait is preponderately dependent on oil income, and its budget is a direct reflection of oil exploitation, concomitant with all the advantages and drawbacks of such a single-commodity reliance. On the whole oil revenue has been well utilized for the welfare of the average individual. The size and population of the country have facilitated the establishment of an unprecedented level of social services, yet without government control of the factors of production. Revenue requirements are channeled into three major areas: domestic economic development, a relatively extensive foreign aid program, and diversified investment to offset depletion of its primary commodity. Through the initiation

[98] In 1964 the U.S. output was 7.4 per cent of its proven reserves while Kuwait exploited only 1.1 per cent of its reserves. More importantly, while the American crude production is basically for domestic consumption, Kuwaiti output is almost totally earmarked for export. An additional factor to be kept in mind is that Kuwait enjoys the lowest production cost per unit in the world.

[99] *Middle East Economic Survey*, December 10, 1965, p. 8. These ideas were expressed by Ashraf Lutfi, Secretary General of OPEC.

of an economic aid program, the only one of its type—development lending and grants extended by a developing nation—Kuwait has assumed something of a "pioneer stance" among oil exporters as well as among the developing countries. As Kuwaiti assistance is carried out largely on a regional basis, it serves to de-emphasize the disparity between the oil "haves" and "have nots" which has long characterized the area.

Within this context, Kuwait can ill afford any sizeable cut in its production rate. A decrease in or stagnation of governmental revenues would be felt not only domestically in the development and diversification programs but also internationally in those areas which are recipients of Kuwaiti assistance and/or investment. In the first nine months of the OPEC program, the organization's production increase lagged behind the 10 per cent target by some 2.2 points. Libya and Saudi Arabia have averaged more than their allotted quotas while production in Venezuela and more specifically in Kuwait has given a poor showing.[100]

In the latter country, output was actually lower than for the same nine-month period of the previous year.[101] As a key producer and holder of the single largest proven reserves, Kuwait is quite naturally one of the principal supporters of the OPEC production programming. Because of its regional position as a lender and

[100] The Saudi Arabian government has been pushing for a rapid increment in output because of its revenue needs arising from noneconomic commitments abroad.

[101] *Middle East Economic Survey*, April 29, 1966, p. 6. Kuwait's estimated output for the first nine months of the OPEC program was, in thousands of barrels per day:

July 1965– March 1966 (OPEC program)	July 1964– March 1965	Actual % Change	% Increase Allowed for Program Period
3,327	3,350	−1.0	6.5

The following table shows the actual production growth of major Middle East producers.

	Annual Average Production			
	1960/65	1966	1965	% Increase
Kuwait (KOC)	6.0	2,223.2	2,181.4	1.9
Saudi Arabia (Aramco)	10.0	2,378.0	1,994.3	19.2
Iran (Consortium)	12.5	1,997.0	1,776.2	12.4
Iraq (IPC Group)	6.5	1,363.2	1,268.9	7.4

SOURCE: *The Middle East Economic Survey*, November 4, 1966, p. 3.

investor, pressure to meet continuing and increasing revenue requirements is greater than what an individual country, small in size and population, might otherwise feel. It is of more than passing importance that a relatively stable condition in the Middle East, and hence security of supply, has been aided through the regional and international financial activities of Kuwait.

Initial reaction to the production programming resolution of the Tripoli Conference of OPEC included the opinion that it was a direct challenge to "what many people would consider their [the international oil companies] most essential day-to-day management decisions."[102] An assured minimum level of planning is valid for both the companies and the producers. The "offtake" programs of the companies are the counterpart of OPEC's projected system of production programming. The oil companies are not only vertically integrated but geographically diversified in holdings as well. In this manner they maintain a constant cushion of surplus capacity over and above the amount necessary to take care of seasonal fluctuations in demand, and thereby increase security of supply and hold a stronger position in unilateral negotiations with any single host government.

Nearly all the production in Venezuela, Indonesia, Africa, and the Middle East is handled by seven major internationals—Standard Oil (New Jersey), the Royal Dutch/Shell Group, British Petroleum, Socony-Mobil, Gulf Oil, Standard Oil of California, and Texaco—and the French firm, Compagnie Francaise des Petroles.[103] Company interests are intertwined as they operate in varying degrees of conjunction with each other in the producing countries. A glance at the international majors' activities shows that all of them participate in the Iranian Consortium, about 70 per cent of Iraqi oil is produced by four of them, and four are responsible for 100 per cent of Saudi Arabian production, excluding the Neutral Zone. In partnership, two majors control 90 per cent of Kuwaiti output although in this instance, as mentioned earlier, the operating company KOC has long-term supply contracts with other major companies.

Perhaps more realistic and equally important for the entire question of keeping supply in hand and prices stable is to arrange a system whereby minimum rates of production increase would be

[102] "OPEC Gets to Essentials," *The Economist (London)*, August 28, 1965, p. 800.
[103] Details of ownership of the operating companies in the producing countries may be found in Leeman, *Middle East Oil*, pp. 10–15.

ensured. The realization of such an objective would give the needed revenue base for economic development. Planning is relatively new to most of the oil exporting countries. The final draft of Kuwait's First Five Year Plan was completed in 1967. Iran, Iraq, Saudi Arabia, and other nations have likewise initiated planning for development. Establishing a system of minimum production increases would simultaneously provide for some latitude in offtake for the companies and at the same time enhance orderly economic development and political stability through a guaranteed level of income to the producing countries. Moreover, greater economic and political stability in individual countries assists regional stabilization and development, making more secure the functioning of foreign investment and foreign enterprises in the area. This specific element of stability and security of supply in the Middle East is often cited as the reason for the decision of oil companies to invest in exploration and production in other regions, even when the production costs are higher than for greater output from Arab sources. It should be noted, however, that the Arab world has no monopoly on instability, and in fact has been relatively stable, particularly the oil producing countries. No civil strife rages, as in Nigeria, nor has nationalization been undertaken, as by Iran. Security of supply is a valid motive for diversification of sources. It would be advantageous to final consumers, importers, and companies as well as the producer to make some production programming arrangement so that output could be based more solidly on economic factors such as reserves and cost.

MULTILATERALISM IN OIL

Kuwait's interest in a multilateral approach for the stabilization of oil prices and in maintaining the rate of growth in production is influenced by three factors. First, the Kuwaiti economy is almost totally dependent on oil, as manifested in the exceptionally high portion of governmental revenues attributable directly to oil, the heavy dependence of the economy on imports, and, subsequently, the interest in the terms of trade. Second, the high reserve-production ratio, possibly the highest in the world, accentuates the concern over adequate exploitation. Underlying this situation is the feeling that the longer the period over which oil is not fully exploited and exported, the more severe will be the negative impact on the Kuwaiti economy of declines in the value of its principal export owing to competition from other sources of energy and from old and new petroleum producers. Third, Kuwait, being a small country in size and population and only recently independent, feels that its ability to safeguard its interests and to apply pressure will be enhanced through a multilateral approach.

There are two multilateral groupings in which Kuwait participates. The first, the Arab Petroleum Congresses, is basically regional with all members of the League of Arab States included, oil and non-oil producers alike. Invited as delegates or observers to the annual meetings which began in 1959 have been representatives of the oil companies operating in both the Arab and non-Arab countries. The essence of the resolutions adopted by the Congresses is to increase the participation of Middle Eastern countries in the oil industry and to protect the rights of the region in the exploitation of its wasting asset. Repeatedly the Arab Petroleum Congress has emphasized the need for assimilating basic knowledge of petroleum in its various stages—oil economics, engineering, and legislation—on a wide spectrum by acquainting the population as a whole and specialists in particular through training and the creation of a petroleum institute.[104] Other resolutions have dealt with the strategic and sensitive question of gas conservation, employment of Arab technicians and workers, and forging a network of regional pipelines and refineries. The Congresses have provided a forum for the exchange of oil facts and ideas current in the Arab world. The resolutions have most often been statements of purpose rather than definite programs, which could not be implemented directly through the Congress as it lacks the institutional authority.

Individual countries have varied in the intensity and degree of realization of the Congress resolutions. In Kuwait implementation has been comparatively thorough. Examples are Kuwait's consistent

---

[104] The lack of general knowledge concerning the oil industry has been cited as a major problem in Middle Eastern development and as contributing to friction through misunderstanding between governmental policy formulation and the operating companies as well as the transit nations. "It is indeed strange that very few of the inhabitants of the Middle East have actually seen crude oil," Ashraf Lutfi, *Arab Oil*, p. 3. The idea of a petroleum institute was originally advanced in 1959 at the First Congress and has gradually moved from a mere idea into the final planning stage (Fourth Resolution of the Vth Arab Petroleum Congress, 1965).

push for priority for Arab workers in the oil industry, its striving to coordinate its policies regarding petrochemicals, and the intensification of its natural gas utilization and conservation. Perhaps more important, Kuwait has taken positive steps through its aid programs to actualize the sharing of its oil revenues on a regional scale, thereby reducing the gap between the oil "haves" and "have nots" in the Middle East.[105] The Arab Petroleum Congress was instituted before the establishment of the second multilateral organization of which Kuwait is a member. The second grouping is international although Arab representation is strong, actually the majority; credentials for membership include status as a substantial oil exporter.[106] The goals and objectives of both organizations are, for the greatest part, complementary and supportive rather than competitive.

The weakening of the price structure by the companies in 1959 and again in 1960 without consultation with the producing countries triggered a response from the major exporting nations.[107] Shortly after the second price cut, Kuwait joined with Iran, Iraq, Saudi Arabia, and Venezuela in the formation of the Organization of the Petroleum Exporting Countries, with the first meeting held in September, 1960. These five countries were then responsible for some 80 per cent of the world trade in oil.[108] The OPEC was formed to enable "regular consultation amongst its members with a view to coordinating and unifying the policies of its members."[109] Specific areas of coordination for OPEC activities included resolutions that the companies keep prices steady and free from

[105] There is a strong impression that "Arab oil" is something of a regional asset to be utilized for the benefit of the entire area. An example is the resolutions of the IVth Congress which stressed "the importance of Arab oil as a national resource which has a vital bearing on the development of the Arab economy and the raising of the standard of living in the Arab homeland" and the "heavy responsibility of the Arab States in this regard." IVth Arab Petroleum Congress, Beirut, November 5–12, 1963, vol. 1: *Economics*, "Resolutions," p. 1 (in Arabic).

[106] The smallest member of OPEC, Qatar, currently exports an average of 200,000 b/d, which gives a guideline on the necessary level considered adequate for membership.

[107] Posted prices were cut by major companies by 18 cents per barrel in February, 1959 and by an additional 10 cents per barrel in August, 1960. Mikdashi, *Financial Analysis*, p. 172.

[108] J. E. Hartshorn, *Oil Companies and Governments*, p. 18. Since the founding of OPEC, additional members have been admitted—Indonesia, Libya, and Qatar.

[109] OPEC, *Resolutions Adopted at the Conferences of the Organization of the Petroleum Exporting Countries*, Resolution I.2, p. 3.

unnecessary fluctuations, a call to return to pre-August 1960 levels, uniformity in royalty expensing, and finally, stabilization of prices through the regulation of production, among other possible means.

OPEC represents a new force in the oil industry, but because it was so recently organized it is still in the process of developing its functions and spheres of interest. Coordination of member countries' production and marketing in petrochemicals and fertilizers is a pressing matter for OPEC consideration, particularly since these products are export oriented. Not only would such coordination control wasteful competition and duplication among the members, it would also allow for a more concerted effort to break into the world petrochemical and fertilizer markets where producers of longstanding are firmly established. Kuwait has been able to move from the planning to the production stage in fertilizers, putting it somewhat ahead of its Arab neighbors and other OPEC members, and accordingly its stake in such coordination is pronounced. The Arab Petroleum Congresses and Arab League are pushing for a regional planning scheme in this specific area as well.[110]

In its attempts to stabilize prices of crude oil and to facilitate the export of semifinished and finished petroleum products, specifically petrochemicals, to the advanced countries, OPEC could utilize the facilities of the recently founded United Nations Trade and Development Board. The objectives of this U.N. agency include the improvement of the terms of trade and the removal of trade barriers by the industrialized countries to both the raw materials and industrial commodities of the developing nations. OPEC has been recognized by the 75 developing countries participating in the 1964 U.N. Conference on Trade and Development. The effectiveness of channeling endeavors of the OPEC members through UNTAD is likely to be contingent upon the development and acceptance of the tasks of this U.N. agency as well as upon a reconciliation of the interests of both consumers and producers to provide a meeting of interests on some middle ground.

Finally, multilateralism, whether through OPEC alone or in combination with other regional or international agencies, such as the Arab Petroleum Congress or UNTAD, offers a potentially orderly way in which to balance and reconcile the numerous

[110] In May, 1966, a special section was established in the Kuwaiti Ministry of Finance and Oil which will act in a liaison capacity between the government and OPEC and other similar international and Arab organizations.

interests interwoven in the entire business of producing and exporting oil. The companies may view OPEC as a contender for control of production and exports. While this may be true in certain instances, the Organization itself must deal with three forms of competition: (1) intra-OPEC, among the members themselves, particularly in the rates of output growth; (2) between OPEC and nonmember producers; and (3) between petroleum and other energy sources. The consumer interest involves dependable supply, freedom of choice of area of production and variety of fuel, and stability of price. Companies seek profitable operations, security of investment, and freedom to balance the output from their scattered holdings. To all concerned parties, oil is of no value unless it is efficiently produced and marketed. A very real mutuality of interest exists in (1) production and (2) orderly economic development of the producer economies, giving greater stability, which in turn increases security of supply (consumers' interest) and security of investment (companies' interest). Some substratum giving minimum functioning levels for both producing countries and the companies is needed.

Financing
Domestic Development

3

THE CAPITAL-SURPLUS ECONOMY

We have seen in the preceding chapter the rapid and relatively steady development of oil in Kuwait. Kuwait has been forced to make radical adjustments to the pace of this petroleum exploitation. The increase in government revenue bears witness to the rising oil output. In 1950 government revenue from oil was estimated at $11.48 million. It jumped to $281.4 million in 1955 and reached $719.6 million in fiscal 1964/65. Besides direct payments to the government, the oil companies are responsible for sizeable purchases in the domestic market, which have approximately doubled since 1958, as indicated in Table 1. Considering the scope of the Kuwaiti local economy, the companies' spending is not a negligible portion.[1]

The oil boom and labor needs brought a swift rise in the population, largely through immigration, which was discussed earlier. Yet this 127 per cent increase from 1957 to 1965, while widening the local market and fulfilling unskilled and skilled labor requirements, nonetheless placed added responsibilities upon the government in terms of social services and resettlement. Not only has the influx in expatriates left the Kuwaitis a numerical minority (although the largest single group), there has been a shift in the economic outlook, away from the sea and toward the riverless, arid, and nonagricultural land.

While the initial reaction to the process of oil and natural gas exploitation was one of greater activity in contracting, construction,

---

[1] Newly created local industries now supply the oil companies with such items as steel pipe, asbestos pipe, bricks, industrial gases, and flour. Caustic soda, refined salt, and hydrochloric acid are also purchased by the companies.

and transport, oil and oil revenue largely confined themselves to an economic enclave pattern. Thus the question posed was how to diffuse the governmental wealth and encourage redistributional development. The post-World War II pattern of agricultural land reform programs as a method of redistributing income was not applicable in the Kuwaiti case, as the agricultural land base was nonexistent. The only land which had any value, or potential value, was the area in and surrounding the city of Kuwait. In the absence of a progressive personal income tax (and in the early years most Kuwaiti incomes were so limited that their ability to pay was restricted and practically nil), the government undertook a program

TABLE 1

OIL REVENUES AND COMPANIES' CURRENCY PURCHASES 1958—1964/65
(IN MILLION DOLLARS)

Year	Oil Production[a] (In millions of Long Tons)	Payments to the Government	Local Currency Purchases by the Oil Industry
1958	71.2	359.8[a]	n.a.
1959	71.5	447.44[b]	34.72
1960/61[c]	84.2	444.08	28.0
1961/62	86.1	467.32	40.32
1962/63	97.2	484.4	43.12
1963/64	104.2	533.68	50.96
1964/65	114.6	719.6[d]	53.76

SOURCE: Ministry of Finance and Industry, Kuwait.

a These figures are for the calendar year.

b For 15 months of production, ending March 31, 1960.

c Beginning in 1960, the fiscal year was begun on April 1 for 1960/61.

d Includes the KOC tax payment for 16 months' production.

of overwhelmingly urban land purchase and resale as the principal instrument for distribution of oil revenues among the general population. This program was envisaged primarily as a method of dispersion of wealth, so much so that for quite some time urban planning and the concept of land economics were neglected.[2] The land purchase program has been criticized as a naive and crude means of distributing income. While there were unevenness of distribution and relative ineffectiveness in activating the domestic

[2] Urban planning and land usage in Kuwait have been discussed capably by Saba George Shiber, *The Kuwait Urbanization* (Kuwait: Government Printing Press, 1965). The distinctions between control of land and government ownership of land have been clearly traced by R. J. Burroughs, "Should Urban Land Be Publicly Owned?" *Land Economics*, February, 1966, pp. 11–17.

economy through productive investment, on the other hand (in the milieu of Kuwait then, at the beginning of the program) there were no other easily implemented alternatives short of donations and "handouts." In any case, a rather large outflow to foreign investment would probably have occurred. The Kuwaiti population already suffers from a dimming of the relationship between effort and reward; the latter alternative might have led to a further weakening of this relationship.

A portion of the purchased land has been utilized in expanding the network of roads within the city and its sprawling suburbs, and some has been used for public construction. The major parts, however, were resold to the private sector at nominal prices. There has been a heavy reliance on land purchases for dispersion, which accounted for 50 per cent more in the expenditures from 1958 to 1964 than that expended on an alternative method of capital projects for the same period. The total amount spent on the program has reached over $1 billion since 1957. In recent years this activity has been condemned as a subsidy system for landowners, particularly the wealthy, since urban land, largely worthless fifteen years ago, has skyrocketed in value and now ranks among the most high-priced in the world. The situation has been aggravated by the lack of a capital gains tax to curb land speculation. It has been reported that land prices in the center of the city of Kuwait can reach as high as $160 per square foot.[3] Although the land purchase program will be studied further in the analysis of the budgets, it should be pointed out here that allocations for this purpose have been reduced in absolute and relative terms of governmental expenditures.

Capital surplus is evidenced in three areas: (1) in the gap between government revenues and its expenditures, (2) in a comparison between the total savings and the total amount invested in Kuwait, and (3) in the balance of payments. In the first comparison in Table 2 the revenue side of the general budget is divided into the external and domestic sources, with oil revenue and investment income grouped in the former and with custom duties, public utilities, and the proceeds of land resales contributing to the latter. Revenue in general has been growing rapidly, particularly in the oil sector, which has averaged an annual rise of over 8 per cent in recent years, although the returns on investment abroad have given

[3] *IBRD Report*, p. 89, wherein the cost of land for parking a car in the city of Kuwait is placed at $19,600.

a steadily rising performance. The estimate of oil revenues for fiscal 1964/65, excluding the accelerated tax payment of $145.6 million as the first of three annual installments from the Kuwait Oil Company, was about $574 million.[4] The projected contribution from oil to the budgetary revenues was scheduled to reach $609.28 million in 1965/66 and $651.28 million the following fiscal year. Yield from foreign investment has increased by almost 30 per cent between 1961/62 and the 1965/66 level. The domestic revenue producers, although minor in their share, have continued to grow annually, making up a nearly constant 7 per cent of the total, as seen in Table 2.

TABLE 2

GOVERNMENT BUDGET AND SURPLUS, 1961/62—1963/64
(IN MILLION DOLLARS)

	1961/62	1962/63	1963/64
Total revenue	542.08	575.12	622.72
Oil	467.32	484.40	533.68
External investment income	36.68	43.68	42.00
Public utilities	8.68	11.48	12.60
Resale of land	9.52	13.16	9.24
Other[a]	19.88	22.40	25.20
Total expenditures	449.96	462.00	493.64
Current expenditures[b]	211.40	256.76	301.00
Capital expenditures	73.64	75.04	103.04
Land purchases	164.92	130.30	89.60
Budget surplus	92.12	113.12	129.08

SOURCE: Ministry of Finance and Industry, Kuwait.

a Includes customs and port dues.

b Includes security, health and education, operating costs and current expenditures for public works and public utilities, and all other expenditures.

Mention should be made of the tax system prevailing in Kuwait. There are no income taxes except one of 50 per cent on income from non-Kuwaiti participation in Kuwaiti business when the net income exceeds $1.05 million. This levy is actually directed toward the oil companies operating in the country. It has not as yet become a major factor in joint foreign-Kuwaiti undertakings, but it could have a negative impact as the tax is imposed on equity income

[4] Until an agreement was reached between the government and KOC in April, 1964, the company had paid taxes based on the production of the previous calendar year; that is, taxes for 1963/64 were computed on the 1962 production figure. Thus the 1964/65 KOC payment covers the 1964 production and one-third of the 1963 production taxes.

rather than on loan interest. If large-scale foreign financing and/or participation is needed for industrial enterprises, such a condition might involve an imbalance between the debt and equity relationship. Other taxes include import and export duties, with the former set at 4 per cent ad valorem on most commodities and the latter, applying to goods transshipped in Kuwait for reexport, amounting to 2 per cent ad valorem. Although the duties are comparatively low in both instances, the expansion of dutiable imports and reexports is steady, if modest, and supplements the oil and foreign-investment revenues of Kuwait.

Yet although government expenditures have been on the rise, it has been at a markedly slower rate than that of revenues. The surplus cannot be traced to a lag in government measures in development needs nor in the allocations for social services. For example, in 1961/62 Kuwait paid out $240 per person for such services, as compared with $210 in Great Britain. Health and education are the recipients of a sizeable percentage of total expenditures. From fiscal 1963/64 through the 1966/67 budget estimate, education, health, and other social services accounted for an average of 25.5 per cent per annum of total expenditures.[5] It is small wonder, then, that Kuwait has been dubbed the "welfare state."

The current outlays are substantially increased by the government's position as an employer—almost one of every six persons in the country is on the government payroll. As has been pointed out, the oil industry is capital-intensive and offers employment to only 7,000 or so, of whom approximately 5,000 are manual and unskilled laborers. Without an agricultural sector to absorb labor and with industry in its formative stages only, Kuwait has been forced to expand governmental jobs, which has in turn raised the

---

[5] *Kuwait Chamber of Commerce and Industry Bulletin*, May, 1966, pp. 6–8. Misconceptions about and lack of awareness of developments in the Middle East are evident in many scholarly writings. Although a high level of social services has been attained in Kuwait, one still finds statements like the following: "... per capita income can be a misleading index of the state of development or the economic welfare of the country. A striking illustration of this is the case of Kuwait, which has an exceedingly high level of per capita income but which, by no stretch of the imagination, can be considered a developed country. Because of extensive royalties from oil, its aggregate income is very high relative to its small population; nevertheless, almost the entire population lives in poverty because the bulk of royalties accrue to the country's ruler." Bernard Okun and Richard W. Richardson, *Studies in Economic Development* (New York: Holt, Rinehart & Winston, 1961), p. 233.

question of overstaffing. The government employed 73,779 persons, ten times the number employed in the oil industry. In the 1965/66 budget 62.6 per cent of current expenditures, or 39.6 per cent of total outlays ($247.52 million), was earmarked for salaries and wages. In that same year additional employees were estimated to push the number in government employ over 80,500. Since the total population of Kuwait is less than half a million, the impact of the government as an employer cannot be overemphasized.[6]

Current expenditures rose by about two-thirds again from the 1961/62 level in the five years following that base. But more important as an indicator of the economic development taking place in Kuwait is the simultaneous decline in land purchase allocations and the rise in capital expenditures, tripling in the five years from 1961/62 to 1966/67.[7] The development outlays are premised upon a low base in comparison with the capital capabilities of the country. The level and allocation of these outlays are determined by the Planning Board. Most infrastructure requirements in port facilities, highways, and government buildings have been met; the level of school, hospital, and clinic construction is in for normalization in the near future. In the three-year period ending March, 1963, the capital expenditure breakdown showed about 18 per cent geared toward education and health facilities, 24 per cent in housing and government buildings, and 58 per cent invested in infrastructure and public utilities. Among the remaining large projects are the completion of a modern, outstandingly equipped airport, low-income housing units, and the development of the industrial estate at Shuaiba.[8] Thus, capital expenditures will necessarily level off although the demands of industrialization, which are now stimulating the increase in these outlays, will continue for some time.

[6] *Report of the Minister of Finance and Industry on the General Budget of the State of Kuwait, 1965/66* (Kuwait: Government Printing Press, 1965), pp. 14–15 (in Arabic). (Hereafter cited as *General Budget for 1965/66*.)

[7] *Kuwait Chamber of Commerce and Industry Bulletin*, May, 1966, p. 6.

[8] Even to affluent Americans, the requirements for obtaining a "low-income" designation are most liberal. Keeping in mind that there is no personal income tax, an individual whose monthly income does not exceed KD. 150 ($420) is eligible to participate in low-income housing programs. The dwellings are purchased over a 25-year period, interest free. Under certain conditions, such as poverty, death, or disability of the head of the household, payments may be waived. Transferring the home to a non-family person is not allowed, thereby keeping the housing in the hands of lower-income Kuwaitis. *IBRD Report*, p. 103. From 1957 through 1963 some 2,182 low-income homes had been built by the government.

The third major item in government expenditures other than current and capital expenditures is the land purchase program. Even though allocations were on the decrease from the earlier phenomenal highs, land purchases accounted for 28 per cent of the oil revenues from 1956 through 1965/66.[9] The two Missions of the International Bank for Reconstruction and Development to Kuwait in 1961 and 1963 recommended a reduction in this allocation, which at that time was consuming about one-quarter of the oil revenues, and a partial replacement of that expenditure in the economy by government investment in private or quasi-private industry and increased capital spending on public works, although the latter has definite limits of absorptive capacity. The Mission concluded that outlays of about $112 million per year could be usefully expended on capital projects from 1963/64—1965/66.[10] The Kuwaiti government has, for the most part, followed this pattern in recent years, as seen in Table 3. The method does retain some

TABLE 3

THE SHARE OF CURRENT AND DEVELOPMENT EXPENDITURES IN TOTAL BUDGETARY OUTLAYS, 1961/62—1966/67
(PER CENT OF TOTAL EXPENDITURES)

	1961/62	1962/63	1963/64	1964/65	1965/66	1966/67
Current	41.5	49.1[a]	50.6	52.8	55.0	55.2
Development	22.1	21.6	26.5	22.3	25.8	33.8
Transfers	...	0.8	1.7	2.6	6.1	6.9
Land purchase	36.4	28.5	21.6	22.3	13.1	4.1

SOURCES: *IBRD Report*, p. 172; *Kuwait Chamber of Commerce and Industry Bulletin*, May, 1966, p. 6.
a Includes an allocation of $13.58 million to "emergency fund."

allure as an immediate way of pumping capital into the economy: for example, the sharp rise in 1964/65 in an attempt to stimulate activity. The government has recognized, however, that this system has outlived its original purposes and that it has tended to weaken entrepreneurial ability because of the growth of dependence on the government as a source of income.[11] Thus, although the program continues, the reductions in allocations have been drastic and a directional shift has been implemented, away from the wealthy owners benefiting largely from earlier purchases, toward medium- and low-income landholders who are likely to have a

[9] *Kuwait Chamber of Commerce and Industry Bulletin*, May, 1966, pp. 6–8.
[10] *IBRD Report*, p. 87.
[11] *General Budget for 1965/66*, p. 10.

lower marginal propensity to save. It would seem that a program directed in this manner would offer a greater possibility of invigorating the domestic economy, by a high consumption level, than the previous direction, which led to a high outflow of capital.

From the above discussion certain economic characteristics emerge. Although there has been a rising rate in current expenditures, this has been accompanied by stability in capital outlays and a decline in allocations for land purchases. Correspondingly, revenues have been on the increase and the surplus condition continues and is expanding. In comparing the budgetary estimates with actuals, a tendency can be discerned of underestimating revenue and overestimating expenditures in drawing up the budget. Hence, the surplus is usually greater than is apparent by the budget figures. Because of the limitations of the Kuwaiti economy, the government budget acts as a major indicator and gives ample control of the level of economic activities within the country.[12] The surpluses are, for the most part, added to the government's foreign assets, while a minor portion is maintained with domestic banks. By the beginning of 1965, public accumulated foreign assets totaled about $1.4 billion, and rough estimates place private sector accumulations abroad at some $1.3 billion.

In the realm of savings and investment, the level of per capita income in Kuwait has allowed the attainment of an extremely high savings rate, 44 per cent of the GNP. Thus far, however, the country is capable of absorbing only 41 per cent of total savings in investment at home. It is becoming more apparent that this limited effect on domestic capital formation is a measurement of the need for flexibility and "capacity to transform" in the economy. The capital growth capabilities are inhibited by the lack of natural resources other than oil. Such obstacles as high transport costs of raw materials, high wage rates estimated to be at least double the level of neighboring countries, narrowness of the domestic market, and the lack of agriculture (and hence, agricultural fibers and products required for industrialization) have hindered the development of these industrial opportunities open to the economy. The

[12] The "Western welfare states" are so classified by the importance of the public sector's share in the national production, ranging from 30 to 40 per cent. Ursula K. Hicks, *Development Financing* (New York: Oxford University Press, 1965), p. 20. Kuwait, therefore, can be grouped accordingly as the public sector's portion of the national production is nearing the 40 per cent level. *General Budget for 1965/66,* p. 11.

meager water resources are not only a restrictor of agricultural development, they are also an impediment to industrial growth. Finally, the existence of a high propensity to import serves to dampen the multiplier effect of domestic expenditures.

Another limiting factor in channeling savings was the low interest rate prevailing in Kuwait, which until 1964 was about 2.5 per cent for savings accounts and only slightly higher for time deposits. Even with the current hikes, the 1965 rates remained below the six plus per cent in Great Britain and the seven per cent offered in Switzerland. Moreover, as Kuwait has not yet instituted a central banking system, although one is planned, the interest increases are of an *ad hoc* nature with wide divergence among various monetary institutions.

The third area in which a capital-surplus condition is reflected is the balance of payments. The surplus here has been progressively increasing, estimated at about $168 million in 1964/65 alone. With no official figures on balance of payments, Table 4 gives a rough

TABLE 4

SUMMARY OF BALANCE OF PAYMENTS ESTIMATES, 1965/66
(IN MILLION DOLLARS)

1. *Transactions of the Oil Sector*		840.0
Estimated receipts from exports of oil and oil products	1,380.4	
Factor income transfers by oil companies	−686.0	
Extra payment by the Kuwait Oil Company due to the change in the accounting year	145.6	
2. *Other Current Transactions*		−296.8
Exports and reexports, f.o.b.	36.4	———
Imports, c.i.f.	−378.0	
Balance of trade[a]	−241.6	
Income on government foreign assets	47.6	
Income on private foreign assets (including commercial banks' assets)	84.0	
Other invisibles	−86.8	
3. *Balance of* (1) *and* (2)		543.2
4. Net assets of commercial banks (increase)		−56.0
5. Official foreign assets		−224.0
6. Miscellaneous capital movements (including net errors and omissions)		−252.0

SOURCE: The Planning Board, *Kuwait—Economic Survey 1965/66*, p. 9.

[a] Data are for the calendar year 1965.

and tentative estimate for 1965/66. The most significant source of foreign receipts comprises the oil companies' taxes, rents, and royalty payments. It should be recalled that the expenditures of these companies in the domestic market in terms of contracts, salaries, and wages contribute to the favorable balance (see Table 1 for amounts). The returns on capital invested abroad also are included. Non-oil exports, particularly reexports, are increasing annually but can contribute as yet only a minor positive share to the financial situation. These exports have increased over threefold, from $11.2 million in 1957 to $36.4 million in 1965/66. The regional direction of these reexports based upon Kuwait's geographical location, liberal trade policies, and mercantile-oriented population is discussed at some length in chapter 5.

Capital movements, on the other hand, specifically through government investments, are recorded as reaching an average of one-quarter of the proceeds of oil production annually since 1950. Private capital outflow, excluding the transfers of funds by non-Kuwaiti residents, is rather elusive when it comes to exact figures; a rough estimate is about $90 million for 1962/63.[13] Also contributing to the negative factors in the balance of payments is the high level of imports, unparalleled elsewhere in both developed and developing nations. In recent years a relatively slow decline in construction activities and a more rapid reduction in the allocations for land purchases have figured in the stabilization, since 1963, of the total value of imports at about $322 million per year and in a reduction in the non-oil trade deficit. Thus, given the present situation and future prospects based upon the uninterrupted rate of oil production, and with the growth of industrialization and expanded exports, the outlook is for continued improvement in the balance of payments and for sustained growth in surpluses.

Independent Budgets

Apart from the main state budget, there are six independent budgets. These are for (1) the Kuwait Fund for Arab Economic Development, (2) the Shuaiba Board, (3) higher education, (4) the Kuwait Currency Board, (5) Kuwait Airways, and (6) the Credit and Savings Bank. In 1966/67 half are expected to show a surplus.

[13] Because of the lack of a central banking system, an exact figure for private outflow must be approximate at best. The estimate here is based upon interviews with government and banking officials in Kuwait.

The successful operation of the KFAED is projected to have a $9.5 million surplus over its expenditures of $700,000 which will be added to the Fund reserves. A sound financial position and efficiency of management are of paramount importance if the Fund's capital is to be revolving and thus insure a continued level of development lending. Likewise, the estimated surplus of $2.2 million of the Kuwait Currency Board will be channeled to that agency's general reserves over the $270,000 outlays for the year. The Credit and Savings Bank's budget expects expenditures to reach $870,000 and revenues $1.8 million, leaving a surplus of about $900,000 for the Bank's general reserves. This institution, created in 1965, took over the functions of the former Credit Bank.

An independent budget for higher education was established in 1966/67 for the first time, having previously been included in the general budgets. The $3.5 million expenditure is to be financed from the state reserves. The $23.8 million outlay for the Shuaiba Board is to be covered by loans extended through the Ministry of Finance and Oil. As Shuaiba is not yet in full operation, no revenues have been estimated. (In 1965/66, the Board's budget similarly projected no revenues and an expenditure of $30.8 million.) The only independent budget with estimates for a deficit in 1966/67 is that of Kuwait Airways. Expenditures should reach $17.9 million, revenue some $14 million, leaving a loss of almost $4 million to be financed through the state reserves.

GOVERNMENT PARTICIPATION IN JOINT-STOCK VENTURES

The private sector in Kuwait is favored by the absence of any major taxes, and it receives the services of public utilities at non-commercial rates. Business also benefits from government participation—equity and loan. There are certain background elements which have led to public participation in mixed enterprises. (1) The first is the cohesiveness between the merchant-businessman and the government; this class traditionally provided the basic support to the administration. Therefore, the Kuwaiti businessman tends to regard government participation as a boon rather than as a case of "creeping socialism." (2) The government is the largest single consumer for Kuwaiti products and services, a specific example being the construction materials industries. (3) Governmental overstaffing and bureaucratic inefficiency led the government to relinquish management of all industrial plants, excepting an asphalt installation. The Ministry of Public Works' brick and cement products factories have been turned into a share company, the National Industries Company, with a 51–49 per cent government-private division of ownership. (4) Conversely, an enlarged industrial sector would ease the problem of underemployment and provide job opportunities to the young educated Kuwaitis entering the labor market. (5) The government policy has been designed to break the economic enclave pattern of the oil industry and bring the private sector into closer contact with the predominant source of wealth. (6) Certain undertakings in which the government has participated directly through equity or indirectly through loans are of a public service nature such as the transport system.

Finally, in addition to the benefits of expanded productive employment opportunities and diversification, government partici-pation has been visualized as a means to fill the gap caused by the leveling-off of the construction boom and the reduction in govern-ment allocations for land purchases. Participation in quasi-private ventures offers a more sophisticated, equitable, and productive means of diffusing the wealth and, at the same time, gives a better chance of success in invigorating the economy. This was, it will be recalled, a consideration of no small importance in the land purchase scheme. Government presence in industry proffers the stability and assurance which might be the key to luring expanded domestic investment of savings and possibly even a return of capital from foreign banks and real estate. The mere presence of government participation, however, does not remove the possibility of mis-investment or overextension. There are indications that the private shareholders may have expected too much from public subscription's role in the various endeavors. Mixed enterprises should, nevertheless, encourage a sense of belonging to the development process of the country among the population. While this is in itself a positive factor, it could become detrimental should overdependence evolve.

Government participation has been concentrated in investment companies, amounting to 51.5 per cent of total commitments; followed by oil and petrochemicals, 38.1 per cent; transport, only 5.5 per cent; industry, 3.9 per cent; and services, just 1 per cent or so. These percentages indicate the level of commitment to non-oil industry. They are also indicative of a capital-surplus condition because of the predominant share of public partnership in monetary investment. There are nine companies in which the government has participated directly in the fields just mentioned. In 1966 the public share in these areas of economic activities amounted to $127.02 million of total capitalizations of $169.4 million, or 75 per cent. By 1966 the government had paid in $61.6 million, or about 48.5 per cent of its commitment. Besides the government participation in those joint-stock companies cited in Table 5, equity commitments totaling $13.89 million for subscriptions to capitalization in four additional enterprises have been carried out through

TABLE 5

GOVERNMENT PARTICIPATION IN JOINT-STOCK COMPANIES AS OF JANUARY 1, 1966
(IN MILLION DOLLARS)

	Total Capitalization	Government Share	Government Share (Per Cent of Total)
Oil and Petrochemicals			
Kuwait National Petroleum Company	21.0	12.6	60
Petrochemicals Industries Company	44.8	35.84	80
Investment			
Kuwait Investment Company	21.0	10.53	50.1
Kuwait Foreign Trade, Contracts and Investment Company	56.0	54.99	98.2
Transport			
Kuwait Transport Company	5.6	2.8	50
Kuwait Navigation Company	5.6	4.2	75
Industries			
The National Industries Company	4.2	2.14	51
Kuwait Flour Mills Company	5.6	2.8	50
Services			
Kuwait Hotels Company	5.6	1.4	25

SOURCE: *Kuwait Chamber of Commerce and Industry Bulletin*, May, 1966, p. 10.

intermediary companies. For example, the 48 per cent share ($11.2 million) of the government in the Kuwait Chemical Fertilizer Company belongs to the Kuwait Petrochemicals Industries Company. A 38 per cent portion of the Kuwait Asbestos Industries is held by the Kuwait National Industries Company, which also participates by holding the 50 per cent government share (with the Kuwait Investment Company) of the Kuwait Prefabricated Building Company. Finally, the Kuwait National Petroleum Company (KNPC) owns 51 per cent of the Kuwait Aviation Fueling Company.

The two investment joint-stock companies receiving the lion's share of government participation are the Kuwait Investment Company and the Kuwait Foreign Trade, Contracts and Investment Company (KFTCI). (The Investment Company has been relatively successful in its real estate investments both domestically and in advanced countries.) Their projects include low-income housing construction in Kuwait and involvement with the Prefabricated Building Company there. Numbered among their international schemes are the establishment of a real estate company in England, participation in a Kuwaiti bank in London, and the construction of two hotels, one in Paris and the other in Lebanon. The KFTCI has a greater capitalization and larger share of government participation. While it is early to view its financial activities, since it was established only in 1965, its most sweeping project is connected with the Kuwait-United Arab Republic loan agreement of February, 1966, wherein it is expected to take part in specific schemes in the U.A.R., notably the establishment of a phosphates complex, construction of a shipyard, and implementation of a land reclamation program.

Turning to the oil sector, note should be taken of the rapid growth of the Kuwait National Petroleum Company (KNPC). Beginning with distribution for local markets originally handled by the Kuwait Oil Company, it has expanded its range of activities to encompass refining and eventually plans its own exploration and extraction operations upon securing the concession for the relinquished KOC area, almost half the size of the original concession. The Petrochemicals Industries Company has been associated with the entire scope of petrochemical development. It owns 60 per cent of the Kuwait Chemical Fertilizers Company (with the remaining 40 per cent of ownership divided equally between British Petroleum and Gulf Oil Corporation), which began operations at its $33-million Shuaiba fertilizer complex in the summer of 1966. In August the company made its first export to Iraq. The direction of its first year's exports appears to be regional, toward Africa and the Middle East. Thus a step has been taken to bring oil closer to the private sector by widening the possibilities for participation in the various aspects of the industry through the enterprises described above.

With the initial preoccupation with oil accompanying the swift rise in petroleum production, two of the three traditional occupations suffered from a decline of interest—pearling, which had already been hit by a fall in prices around 1930, and shipbuilding—although the third, trade, continued to flourish and expand. The Kuwait Navigation Company should help to revitalize interest in the sea as it pursues operations in buying and selling ships and dealing with other areas of water transport. The company, which was formed in May, 1965, has two cargo ships in service and has ordered an additional three vessels. The Kuwait Transport Company operates the local bus system, and its sphere of activities is to include public transport on a regional basis between Arab countries.

In the industrial sector, the most important joint-stock enterprise is that of the National Industries Company, which was created with the purpose of purchasing and establishing all types of industries. Among its activities can be listed its participation in the Kuwait Asbestos Industries and its part holdings, with the Kuwait Investment Company, of the 50 per cent government share in the Prefabricated Building concern.

Another means of government support for the quasi-private sector has been through the extension of loans. This trend appears to be gaining wider application. Among the more recent credits was $70 million loaned to KNPC to partly finance the all-hydrogen refinery at Shuaiba. The Kuwait Oil Tanker Company, with 100 per cent private capital subscription, also received a loan of $8.4 million from the government for the purpose of assisting in capitalization. Two vessels of the supertanker category (160,000 tons dead weight) are on order.

The venture by a government into mixed enterprise explores a new avenue in that it seeks to encourage rather than control or inhibit the private sector. Such an investment technique could have a great impact on a small-size private investment market like Kuwait's, where ownership is restricted to citizens. Perhaps its most significant contribution in Kuwait is that it is providing additional public income but without the application of additional taxation. The system has met with some reverses traceable, for the most part, to the ease with which stock can be bought. The Company

Law (Article 102) allowed for installment buying over a five-year period, which led to speculative overextension. The inability to meet the payments combined with recent business fluctuations to increase government caution and selectivity in joint-stock company participation.[14]

In June, 1966, Law No. 49 was enacted to regulate government lending to joint-stock ventures. It gave the Minister of Finance and Oil authority, with approval of the Cabinet, to extend loans to such corporations with a total maximum limit of funds available for this purpose of $140 million to be granted from the state reserves. Five contingencies for advancement of credit are (1) subscription of the company must be open to the public; (2) the government or one of its agencies must have already subscribed original capital; (3) one-half of the capitalization must have been paid in; (4) the total of government loans or guarantees must not be higher than the paid-up capital; (5) banking and investment companies must be excluded as potential recipients. The rate of interest charged is not to exceed three per cent. Thus it would appear that the government loans to industrial corporations, including those in oil and petrochemicals, could be facilitated, and that support with developing lending terms would be available for those already aided through government partnership, a possible move toward depth rather than a wide spread in the public sector's role in mixed enterprise.

BANKING AND CAPITAL MARKET

In reviewing the role of the banking system in financing development a summary of the makeup and activities of Kuwaiti banks will help to define their spheres of interest and functions.

Four commercial banks operate in Kuwait, three Kuwaiti owned (the National Bank, the Gulf Bank, and the Commercial Bank of Kuwait), the fourth a foreign institution (the British Bank of the Middle East) established in 1942. The first joint-stock company set up in Kuwait was The National Bank, which today has the largest balance sheet, over $230 million. Despite the business slump of the mid-1960's, the institutions have shown consistent profits. At the end of fiscal 1965/66 the combined balance sheets of the

[14] See Fakhri Shehab, "Public Sector Plays Unique Economic Role," *Emergent Nations*, Autumn, 1965, pp. 58–59.

banks reached $943.88 million, a substantial sum within the perspective of the national income of the country and the size of the population. Government deposits in 1965/66 with these concerns were up 19 per cent over the previous fiscal year, reaching about $131 million. The backbone of the banking system is the private accounts. Although this is a relatively recent trend it seems strong, with a 23 per cent increase from 1964/65 to 1965/66, reaching almost $389.5 million in time and savings deposits. This increment in private time and savings deposits was primarily the reason for a rise in the banks' foreign assets.[15] The 1965 interest rate adjustment and that of the following year undoubtedly helped to lure some savings home from foreign institutions. Demand deposits declined for the same period by $18.2 million to $142 million, perhaps attributable to the attraction of the time and savings deposits. The orderly transition from the financial stagnation of the 1963–65 period reinstated a measure of confidence in the economy.

Bank advances as of the 1966 fiscal year amounted to just under $220 million. Such advances are once more being geared toward the movement of goods rather than a high level of financing for consumer credit, which marked the years of slack business activity. The interest rates charged in Kuwait are generally lower than those prevailing in neighboring countries. The major business of the commerical banks is in the financing of imported goods. Bank participation assisted in the formation of numerous local import companies which have been capable of attracting stockholders without difficulty. The long-standing Kuwaiti interest in trade and the scale of imports make investment in such enterprises natural and offer a good return. The commercial banks have not only been involved in the establishment of import contracting firms, but actually buy up the imported goods from the foreign exporter. The importer then repays the bank on time. Previously the interest on such loans has run at about 5 per cent if repaid within fifteen days of the arrival of the shipment in Kuwait and 7 per cent per year if it is paid after that time. As most of these credits are short-term, the money available for such loans can be used as much as three or four times a year. Kuwaiti banks have neither a service charge for current accounts nor do they pay interest on the account.

[15] Kuwait Currency Board, *Fifth Annual Report for the Year Ended 31st March, 1966* (Kuwait: Government Printing Press, 1966), p. 11.

They also have a high proportion of unsecured loans paid out on the good name of the borrower.[16] The Commercial Law of January, 1961, fixed the maximum rate at 7 per cent although the prime borrowers get loans at around five per cent.[17] Actually, it should come as no surprise that money is comparatively cheap in Kuwait due to the capital-surplus condition of the economy.

While borrowing from these banks has been on the rise, the dominant monetary role is still played by the government in lending and transfers. Most of the credits extended by the banks are geared toward foreign trade; in a few cases, toward support of private concerns involved with government contracts. Another major interest of the banking system in Kuwait is handling the sale of original issues of joint-stock companies, an area of operations which has not come up to expectations because of severe fluctuations. The extent of the slight recession, which has had wide implications for the government and business policy, is seen in Table 6 with the changes in the value of securities traded on the Kuwaiti Stock Market.[18]

TABLE 6

ANNUAL PER CENT OF CHANGE IN MARKET FLUCTUATIONS
(1961 BASE YEAR = 100)

Year		Per Cent Change over Previous Year
1961	100.0	...
1962	143.5	+43.5
1963	127.0	−11.5
1964	102.0	−19.8
1965	94.5	−7.4

SOURCE: *Kuwait—Economic Survey 1965/66*, p. 9.

The place of the banks in developmental financing has been limited. Besides being primarily commerce-oriented in its lending, its major effect was felt in increasing the supply of money through lending to the private sector, reaching at times as high as half the

[16] Because of the small number of Kuwaiti borrowers out of a small entire population, such practices are not so dubious as they would appear. The investing and business group is limited and closely knit.

[17] Ministry of Commerce, *Law No. 2 of 1961* (Kuwait: Government Printing Press, 1961), Article 483, p. 123.

[18] By the end of 1965 some 28 joint-stock companies had been established with a total nominal capital of $226.8 million.

increment in the money supply in the economy. Such conditions have led to a greater reliance on the banking by the private sector to finance current transactions and immediate requirements. This in turn has freed private funds, which generally were directed toward foreign investment.

Through coordination with the banks, the Kuwait Currency Board controls the availability of currency notes. The Kuwaiti dinar (1 KD. = $2.80) is issued through the Board in exchange for sterling and other convertible currencies.[19] By law the backing of currency is fixed at a minimum of 50 per cent in gold with the remainder in convertible currencies or financial obligations payable in these currencies. The backing consists now of gold and British and U.S. government securities. As the statistical correspondent for the International Monetary Fund, the Board has been active in gathering financial, monetary, and economic data. The envisaged Central Bank would carry out similar operations and in time produce official balance-of-payments statements and compile national accounts. However, the Central Bank in Kuwait would not be called upon to function as many such institutions in developing countries often do; specifically, as there is no balance-of-payments difficulty and freedom of trade and mobility of capital are the hallmarks of the Kuwaiti economy, the Bank need not act as a restrictor of operations in these economic activities.

The government became a banker with the creation of the Credit Bank in 1961. The functions of this institution were taken over by 1965 by the Savings and Credit Bank. The underlying *raison d'être* for the establishment of the Credit Bank was to institutionalize the channeling of investment into domestic projects with an eye toward diversification. Loans made by the Bank are low-interest and long-term, paid out in installments with some form of security required. Some control exists in the manner in which the borrowed money is spent. Loans for house construction, for example, are intended only for the borrower's domicile, to curtail speculation with low-interest government money. The low-interest credits likewise give a financing source to low-income Kuwaitis other than

---

[19] From 1959 to 1961 the currency of Kuwait had been the "Gulf" rupee, convertible into sterling through the Reserve Bank of India. Prior to 1959 the Indian rupee served as currency throughout the Gulf states. It is through the 1961 currency exchange that India incurred an obligation to Kuwait to be settled by 1972.

money-lenders or well-to-do individuals whose rates are uncontrolled and usually higher.

The government's desire to encourage industry was not being fulfilled sufficiently by the commercial banks. Government participation in joint-stock companies through equity and loans became increasingly burdensome and fragmented, specifically with the smaller companies. Therefore, the Credit Bank seemed to offer a method of coping with the situation and to create an atmosphere conducive to local industrialization and diversification; it had a broader objective than the traditional commercial banks' fields of interest, which had centered upon trade. Applications for loans for small industrial projects are given a review by bank technicians to assure the soundness of the investment. Either the factory, equipment, or personal assets can form security for the credit. If the borrowers should put up the factory as security, the Bank will loan up to 50 per cent of the total cost of the venture, otherwise up to 60 per cent of the total cost can be extended on property or other assets. The interest on these industrial loans is 3 per cent, repayable in 5 years, although this limit is extendable should the money be plowed back into the business. Such a loan application can be for an enterprise in a field sufficiently covered, but it will most often be refused, although credits can be extended to those plants already existing. Such measures decrease the chances of business failure, thereby increasing the chances of repayment of the loans. The government leases industrial land on fifty-year leases at a nominal rate to enhance the growth of small industries. In addition to borrowing for actual plant construction and equipment purchases, small industries may receive a credit at the industrial rate in order to build housing for employees.

The capitalization of the Credit Bank was set at $21 million. With Law No. 30 of 1965, however, the Savings and Credit Bank's capital was placed at $56 million, to be paid from the state reserves, with all sums paid into the 1960 institution shifted as part of the new bank's paid-up capital. The Savings and Credit Bank has an independent budget, as discussed earlier in this chapter. Three purposes are decisive in making the operations comprehensive. The first is to facilitate industrial, real estate, and agricultural credit for agencies and individual Kuwaitis. Investment in real estate and construction is by far the most ingrained and common activity into which funds have been channeled. Although support of industry is no innovation, the attention directed toward agriculture is noteworthy as in this sector Kuwait's backlog of experience is minimal.[20]

Second, the Bank is designed to extend loans to individual Kuwaitis on a "personal" rather than "project" lending basis. Third, it is empowered "to accumulate and *invest* savings and to pay the returns of such investment to the savers."[21] All savings and returns are under governmental guarantee. The significance of the third area of operations lies in the relative inability of Kuwait to move even half of its enormous savings into investment; such an institution is a step toward closing the gap. To carry out one of its secondary functions there is a department to advise would-be entrepreneurs in medium- and small-scale ventures, to prepare pre-industry studies, and to assess potential business enterprises.

According to its charter the Savings and Credit Bank has considerable potential. It may issue bonds and borrow, from the government or under its guarantee, up to the limit of its paid-up capital. Thus, if the institution implemented but the borrowing provision, it could theoretically have a working capital of $112 million. For those appraising the Bank's functions to date who are interested in balanced development via diversification, its operations have been somewhat disappointing as it has fallen into the traditional Kuwaiti form of fund utilization—real estate. In 1965 the Bank's decisions on applications showed 1,265 credits to real estate, with a total value of about $17 million; 17 loans to agricultural projects, totaling approximately $173,000; 7 loans to industrial schemes, representing $380,000; and 188 personal loans, totaling $308,000, almost equal to the amount lent to industry. Of the total value of decided credits 95.3 per cent went to real estate; 2.1 per cent to industry (a distant second); 1.7 per cent to personal loans; and only 0.97 per cent of the total to agriculture. This offers a picture of how private investment is channeled in Kuwait at present. Its accuracy can be questioned on the ground that the loans were of small size and that any sweeping and serious industrial development will be of a larger scale.

[20] Agricultural loans may be repaid when the farmer has marketed his crop. Moreover, the Bank's agronomists are available for advisory purposes.

[21] *Law No. 30 of the Year 1965 Regarding the Establishment of the Savings and Credit Bank* (Kuwait: Government Printing Press, 1965), Article 4. The emphasis is mine.

A summing-up would be advantageous at this point. We have seen the benefits and disadvantages attending oildom in Kuwait. The reserves are vast, the production costs low, and given a reasonably steady growth in output and stability of crude prices at the present level, Kuwait is assured a source of income and a raw material base for almost a century. This gives an element of certainty, but at the same time, because of the overdependence there are uncertainties, largely the uneasiness which attends having all one's eggs in a single basket. At least Kuwait has some eggs; the problem is to manufacture additional baskets. In comparison some developing nations in Asia and the Middle East suffering from overpopulation have but little idea how adequate their resources will be to meet their needs in just two decades. Owing to the peculiarities of the Kuwaiti economy and its size, both in monetary assets and physical dimensions, developmental financing becomes critical.

Domestic possibilities for investment appear to have limitations. Demand in certain activities has reached the near-saturation point; the low marginal propensity to consume has become a constricting and chronic element in the economy. To contain inflation and to market its industrial output, Kuwait must maintain its trade-orientation. Mixed financing in diversification will probably be continued because of the benefits of involving the small-sized Kuwaiti population in the developmental efforts. If liberality of trade and competitiveness of products are to characterize the industrialization process, then the stress in government participation will likely remain a form of partnership for the encouragement rather than the control of the private sector.

In the following chapters the discussion will turn to the issues in balanced growth, the efforts and efficiency of planning, and finally, the economic ramifications of Kuwait's place within a region capital-deficit yet having great potential in marketing and productive investment opportunities, some of which are unavailable in Kuwait and may be complementary to Kuwaiti domestic diversification efforts.

Balanced Growth and Planning 4

PLANNING IN A CAPITAL-SURPLUS ECONOMY

In the field of economic growth, planning for developing countries has been studied within the context of shortage of capital, lagging natural resources, and a generally slow rate of growth in the per capita income. Under conditions of strictly limited resources priorities must be established and allocations cannot be left to accident. Because the majority of developing countries fall into this category, planning literature has failed to make allowances for exceptional instances where a nation, through indigenous or external developments, has accumulated abundant capital.[1] Indeed, the attitude has been one of writing off such cases as merely exceptions to the rule. Capital is overestimated where and when it is needed and tends to be underestimated when it is available. In the latter case, economic planning is required to minimize waste which could accompany a capital-surplus condition, especially when the surplus accumulation takes place rapidly and is unmatched by similar increases in other factors of production.[2]

In situations where a natural resource has been discovered and speedily exploited on a massive scale, as with petroleum, or where a large-scale transfer of funds has been carried out through foreign assistance, an examination of the problems of rapid growth in a still-developing economy is in order. Most theoretical and case studies have focused upon the need to accelerate growth while

[1] Edward S. Mason, *Economic Planning in Underdeveloped Areas* (New York: Fordham University Press, 1958), p. 19, does refer to the problem of balancing the increase in oil revenue with needed social and economic changes.

[2] See Ragaei El Mallakh, "Planning in a Capital Surplus Economy: Kuwait," *Land Economics*, November, 1966, pp. 425–40.

balancing requirements within an economy's resources to best achieve this objective. The crux of such a treatment of planning is not "balanced" versus "unbalanced" but rather increasing growth by any means. The intent here is to present a study of a contrasting condition—where growth has been rapid yet confined to one factor and hence the *raison d'être* in planning is to upgrade the performance of other factors and achieve an element of balance.

A blurring of the strict necessity of priority decision can occur when a capital surplus is sufficient to create a degree of complacency; then planning puts on a different cloak, assuming methods and objectives different from the role ascribed to it in most developing countries. Diffusion of the source, in this case oil, and the outlet of capital funds are the primary requirements. Second, a form of insurance is needed to cushion the fluctuations in prices and to offset the slow but ultimate depletion of the resource. Finally, expanding the absorptive capacity of the domestic market should be carried out simultaneously with the exploitation of all possible regional and international opportunities to utilize the surplus capital productively.

We should recall that the Kuwaiti economy still exhibits obvious characteristics of underdevelopment, specifically in its disproportionate dependence on a single commodity, in the existence of a clear differential between the export and other sectors, and in the inadequacy of indigenous skilled and unskilled labor, a serious restrictor. Under such conditions, and given the presence of these economic features, the applicability of the well-known growth theories of Harrod and Domar is greatly curtailed. Working against the simplification of these theories is the fact that in a capital-surplus economy like that of Kuwait's, the economy generates savings continuously and almost consistently but lags in adequate investment possibilities. This contrasts with the situation prevailing in developed countries, where it is expected that investment will naturally follow savings because the investment opportunities are present or easily created.[3]

The most critical aspect in the economic Kuwaiti personality is the problem of overspecialization, with a single source generating

---

[3] These theories were formulated for advanced industrial economies witnessing secular stagnation and, according to Hirschman, have but limited effectiveness in the general classification of developing countries. A. O. Hirschman, *The Strategy of Economic Development* (New Haven: Yale University Press, 1958), pp. 29–40.

94 per cent of the governmental budgetary revenue and over half the national income traceable to the exploitation of petroleum. The concern over the one-product economy may be seen in four areas. The first and most obvious is the question of depletion. Geologists have managed to give planners a schedule with the recent estimate that Kuwait, possessor of the largest proven reserves to be found in a single country, can look forward to 80–100 years of production at the present rate of over 100 million tons annually. Second, as a principal oil producer, Kuwait is naturally wary of developments within the field of energy itself, with nuclear energy as the major threat. The third consideration revolves around price fluctuations. As an export economy based upon a primary commodity the apprehension over the terms of trade is understandable. The 1959 and 1960 posted price cuts for crude remain as a vivid reminder of the extent of vulnerability. The fourth concern, as pointed out in chapter 2, is that the world oil industry is becoming more competitive with the entry of new suppliers and the pressure for increased output on the part of established producers. Thus, to the exporting country, the fluctuations in the volume of exports rank equally in importance with the changes in price.

Both types of fluctuations affect the level of export proceeds, which are vital to the economy of Kuwait. Such proceeds are reflected in the level of employment not only in the government, which is the largest employer in the country, but also in the private export business. A secondary effect of export fluctuations on the whole economy is contingent upon the share of export receipts in the national income. If the export receipts represent a large portion of the national income, the impact of export fluctuations will be great. The net effect will be equal to the amount of decrease in export receipts multiplied by the domestic multiplier. Considering that Kuwait has one of the highest propensities to save and that receipts from oil are dominant in the national income, the implications must be widespread.

Comparing Kuwait with other raw-material-producing countries, its overdependence on a single commodity shows the extremity of its situation, as pointed out in Table 1.

While there has been an amelioration of the condition indicated in Table 1 for most of these raw-material producers, the change for Kuwait has been minor. In 1965 oil still accounted for 97.2 per cent of the total value of exports. The reexports, listed as of second importance, consist almost completely of consumer goods which require little if any processing in Kuwait.

TABLE 1

COUNTRIES RANKED BY PER CENT OF EXPORTS IN THE THREE COMMODITIES OF HIGHEST VALUE[a]

	Total Per Cent of Highest Three	First	Second	Third
Kuwait[b]	100	Petroleum (98)	Reexports (2)	...
Venezuela	98	Petroleum (92)	Iron ore (5)	Coffee (1)
Colombia	95	Coffee (77)	Petroleum (13)	Bananas (5)
Iraq	93	Petroleum (88)	Dates (3)	Barley (2)
Egypt	83	Cotton (72)	Textiles (7)	Rice (4)
Burma	80	Rice (74)	Rubber (4)	Cotton (2)

SOURCE: J. D. Coppock, *International Economic Instability, The Experience after World War II* (New York: McGraw-Hill, 1962), p. 99; *Survey of Kuwait*, p. 227.

[a] For 1957.

[b] For 1958.

Another problem connected with overspecialization encompasses the possibility of creating a dualistic situation where one or more sectors develop at a much faster rate than the rest of the economy. Here a differentiation could be made between "capital deepening" and "capital widening." The former condition occurs when increased investment in those sectors leads to an increment in the capital-labor ratio. The latter takes place when increased investment is necessary to maintain a constant average capital-labor ratio.

It has been pointed out that most of the investment taking place in the developing countries is of a capital deepening nature.

> It is not capital shortage as such but the fact that the capital deepening tendency of new investments outweighs their capital widening tendency which is the most significant factor explaining unemployment.[4]

While Kuwait does not offer an example of unemployment, it does exhibit overstaffing and underemployment, particularly in the service sector. The oil sector, characterized by a high capital–labor ratio, employs 3.8 per cent of the labor force while producing 61 per cent of the gross domestic product. In contrast, the rest of the economy has a higher labor-capital ratio and is more likely to be less productive than the oil sector. In reality, however, the expansion of the oil industry has been responsible for raising demand

[4] S. Dasgupta, "Underemployment and Dualism," *Economic Development and Cultural Change*, January, 1964, p. 180.

for other economic activities and indirectly, therefore, has pulled along other sectors. The capital surplus which has accumulated because of the growth of the oil sector can support diversification efforts should these be desirable.

PROBLEMS OF BALANCED GROWTH

Conceptually, balanced growth could be defined by usage—nontechnical, general technical, and specific technical. The first refers generally to the type of growth which achieves equilibrium in an orderly and sustained manner, spreading the benefits throughout the society. The general technical usage is concerned with the balance between aggregate resources and aggregate demand or between intended savings and intended investment. Here the problem is to maintain investment without disruptive inflationary pressures. Within this second category is the question of external balance and the equilibrium of incomings and outgoings of foreign exchange. This is specifically applicable to countries suffering from foreign exchange shortage. Finally, the specific technical usage refers to the balance among the size of the market, the volume of supply, and the demand for capital. With reference to developing countries in particular, questions concerning balance concentrate on the relationship between different sectors such as industry and agriculture. The most pressing problem facing the developing countries which are anxious about imbalance is the need for concomitant action to expand markets through a multiple-front attack.[5]

In this sense the theory of balanced growth does not only emphasize the need for different sectors of a developing economy to be kept in step to avoid "supply" difficulties but also considers that the requirement of balanced growth is derived from the demand side. To make development possible, accordingly, it is necessary to begin at one and the same time a large number of new industries which will be each other's clients through the interpurchasing mechanism. Perhaps more significant and more suited to the problems of developing areas is the stress that theory puts on simultaneous expansion of the economic and social infrastructure, specifically

[5] Hans W. Singer, *International Development: Growth and Change* (New York: McGraw-Hill, 1964), pp. 39–41.

in health, education, transport, and housing. In health and education the development of the human resource must be included in the overall perspective of balanced growth, regardless of the pace achieved in any or all sectors. This facet might be of importance to countries which have developed rapidly in a short span of time, such as Kuwait, since the process of education requires a gestation period and by its accumulative nature is time-consuming. The raising of health standards is more easily accomplished, particularly if capital is available. It is precisely a shortage of capital which presents many developing countries with the dilemma of balancing social overhead capital versus directly productive activities. Obviously Kuwait need not be faced with this problem.

The question of balanced and unbalanced growth arises when an attempt is made to ascertain the most effective methods of allocating resources. The apparent choice lies between concentration of investment in a few leading sectors, as the unbalanced growth doctrine recommends, or the simultaneous expansion of the most important and related sectors of the economy, as enunciated in the balanced growth theory. The idea of balanced growth harks back to the classical economists. Adam Smith maintained that the division of labor was limited by the extent of the market. John Stuart Mill states that every increase in production which is carried out rationally without miscalculation will create its own demand.[6] More recently the same concept of balanced growth has been discussed with variations—the "big push," Schumpeter's "waves of investors," and the so-called "investment package."

One of the prominent exponents of balanced growth was Professor Nurkse, who considered the narrowness of the market and the lack of demand (traceable to the low per capita income) and productivity the key factors inhibiting growth in the developing areas. In order to stimulate investment, it is necessary to expand the size of the market.

> Even though in economically backward areas, Say's law may be valid in the sense that there is no deflationary gap, it is never valid in the sense that the output of any single industry newly set up with capital equipment can create its own demand. Human wants being diverse,

---

[6] R. Nurkse, *Problems of Capital Formation in Underdeveloped Countries* (Oxford: Basil Blackwell & Mott, Ltd., 1953), pp. 11–12. See also Allyn Young, "Increasing Returns and Economic Progress," *Economic Journal*, December, 1928.

the people engaged in new industry will not wish to spend all their incomes on their products.[7]

Thus Nurkse considered that balanced growth would assist in the solution to the small size of the market and would, therefore, increase the inducement to invest. People employed in a number of complementary projects become each other's customers.

Singer, on the other hand, recommends the balanced growth doctrine as a remedy to avoid deterioration in the terms of trade of the primary producing countries.[8] As specialization in the less-developed countries is usually in food production and raw materials for export to the developed nations, there is little incentive for technological advance. Emphasis is placed upon the weak relationship between investment in raw materials and investment in other sectors of the economy, a situation from which an enclave pattern could evolve.

In contrast to the balanced growth discussed above is Hirschman's argument for "unbalanced growth" as a starting point in mobilizing latent resources. In his opinion, economic development proceeds best through the creation of "pressures, tensions, disproportions and disequilibrium." The most scarce resources in developing countries are not natural resources, capital, or entrepreneurial ability. These can all be produced in the process of development. Development is typically held back, however, by the absence of centers of investment or development decision. The strategy of development then is to create such obvious investment opportunities that decisions to invest will be easily induced. One of the basic positions in the unbalanced growth doctrine is that the rate of growth in the developing economies is limited not so much by the availability of savings as by the ability to invest.[9] In short, unbalanced growth creates bottlenecks which will increase the inducement to invest.

Hirschman's criticism of balanced growth centers upon the demand and supply sides. In terms of the former, he believes that the exponents of balanced growth underemphasize the possibility

---

[7] *Ibid.*, p. 9. Say's doctrine, which maintains that supply creates its own demand, has been considered one of the early premises for structuring balanced growth.

[8] This is put forward by Hans W. Singer, "The Distribution of Gains between Invested and Borrowing Countries," *American Economic Review*, May, 1950.

[9] Hirschman, *Strategy of Economic Development*, pp. 35–40.

of breaking into the "underdevelopment equilibrium" at any one point. As for supply, Hirschman's main criticism to the balanced growth theory is that the underdeveloped countries lack sufficient financial resources to start their development in a balanced way and to maintain a considerable number of new industries at the same time.[10]

In stepping into the balanced versus unbalanced controversy, the Kuwaiti economy cannot adhere strictly to either grouping, just as it wavers between the developed and developing categorizations exhibiting characteristics of both. To meet the specific demands for its case, planning in Kuwait must be eclectic. For example, Hirschman's position that the ability to invest overshadows the actual availability of savings is clearly demonstrated in Kuwait. The abundance of capital has reduced the tensions and pressures, thereby decreasing the motivations to invest productively. Yet the one factor to be kept in mind is the physical narrowness of the domestic market, which acts as a very real constrictor to local investment. On the other hand, Hirschman's supply-criticism of balanced growth—insufficient financial resources to initiate balanced development and a multifront attack—simply does not apply to Kuwait as there is surplus, not just adequate, capital.

Turning to the doctrine of balanced growth, one finds that certain premises are inapplicable, specifically that narrowness of the market is primarily a symptom of low per capita income. While this assumption may hold true for most developing countries, it does not for Kuwait. If, however, the Kuwaiti economy is placed within or associated with a regional framework, then the supposition of a per capita income determinant of the market size would be valid. Regional balanced growth could then benefit from the addition of capital, enabling an expansion of the Kuwaiti as well as the regional market.

As for Singer's argument which views balanced growth as a method of ameliorating the deterioration in the terms of trade of raw-material-producing countries, its validity is limited for Kuwait, since, pragmatically speaking, a dependency of 97 per cent of export earnings cannot be lessened overnight. While such a goal should be pursued, the hindrances must be recognized; the near-total absence of resources other than oil, and the small population.

[10] *Ibid.*, p. 52.

The stress on social overhead capital by advocates of balanced growth is remarkably suited to the capital-surplus economy. The Kuwaiti accent in recent years on expenditures for education and health services in addition to economic infrastructure follows the line of balanced growth.

One should recognize the fact that balanced growth assumes a different form than that existing for most developing countries where agriculture is slighted in favor of industry. The cleavage in the Kuwaiti economy comes instead in the polarization between the oil and non-oil sectors and between the services and production sectors. In the former categorization there is an increasing degree of overlapping with the development of petroleum-based industries. In the latter situation an analogy can be drawn between the role and structure of services in Kuwait as compared to the place of agriculture in overpopulated but underdeveloped nations. Over-staffing is an admitted economic and social problem, and releasing the surplus portion for production of those engaged in services is not only desirable but also would require a more balanced economy in order to absorb it.

While extremely attractive, balanced growth cannot rapidly solve the problems imposed by the size of the domestic market. Could some form of economic regionalism work simultaneously with efforts toward balance in a way to raise the level of productivity and widen the range of choices acting in the Kuwaiti economy? The potentialities of such an approach will be discussed in the following chapter. We should look now at the possibilities of greater balance through industrialization.

INDUSTRIALIZATION: STIMULATING A SECTOR

In examining the relationship between industrialization and economic development, it is advisable to attempt some satisfactory definition of the former concept, for there are no common definitions agreed upon which could be used under different conditions and circumstances. For the purpose of our inquiry, industrialization can be defined as an increase in the amount of capital equipment and productivity per employed person, and an increase in the variety of goods. This also indicates that the process of industrialization emphasizes the expansion of manufacturing and other secondary production as contrasted to agriculture and other primary production.[11] According to such an interpretation, industrialization means more than the popular, narrow definition of simply having more factories.[12] If we accept the previously mentioned definition however, we are faced with the question of deciding whether or not to exclude mining from it. Here we have to adopt the second alternative and include that sector of production, especially after considering its vital role in the first stages of industrial production in developing countries. In Kuwait's case it has been the indispensable factor. Moreover, the usual rivalry for priority allocation between industry and agriculture has been greatly reduced in the Kuwaiti economic structure; industry, therefore, must be judged more on its merits rather than as a refuge for excess rural population. If should be kept in mind, however, that industrialization is not synonymous with economic development but is, rather, a means toward the latter. Industrialization could meet with varying degrees of success and failure and could also lead to misinvestment and misdevelopment. An assessment of the economic requirements in the process of industrialization will lessen the possibilities of maldirection.

Among the strategic requirements to be considered seriously are first, the assurance of a minimum level of efficiency in some principal sectors of the economy other than industry; second, a supply of labor suitable for modern industry; third, sufficient capital for the undertaking; fourth, a supply of entrepreneurial and managerial talent able to carry out the decisions involved in the processes of industrial change; and last but not least, adequate demand for domestically produced industrial commodities.[13] As for the first requirement, it is clear that the oil sector is the only leading sector which has achieved a high level of efficiency. It can provide goods of prime necessity but is more restricted in range than, say, agriculture. Nonetheless, petroleum offers a greater variety of processing possibilities than any other single raw material.

In the second requirement, an adequate labor supply for modern industry, Kuwait is deficit. Yet it can import and has imported a large portion of its present needs. While it is possible to attract

---

[11] Eugene Staley, *World Economic Development* (Montreal: Staples Press, 1944), p. 51.

[12] N. Buchanan, "Deliberate Industrialization for Higher Incomes," *Economic Journal*, December, 1946, p. 533.

[13] Simon Kuznets, *Economic Growth and Structure* (New York: W. W. Norton & Co., 1965), pp. 197–208.

well-trained technicians from outside because of the wage and salary levels and the social services, ultimately the country has to develop its own qualitative or structural requirements. The only restricting element in such development is time. The third need, sufficient capital, is completely met in strictly quantitative terms. Two difficulties cloud the picture: (1) the inability to move the savings into investment; and (2) possibly harder to overcome, the tendency, which accompanies overabundance of capital, to overlook or underestimate the effectiveness of the other requirements for industry.

The fourth prerequisite of entrepreneurial ability is partially met. The main obstacle here is the degree to which the traditional, Levantine-style promoters can be redirected into an industrial managerial group capable of handling the technological bases of modern industry. But the final requirement, sufficient demand for industrial production, will be the most difficult to meet in the Kuwaiti economy. Low purchasing power is not the negative element in keeping the market small. The numerical size of the population and the free trade policies which have led to acquired tastes for imported goods from every corner of the globe combined to narrow the demand for locally produced commodities. The hazards of industrializing for export purposes are discussed in chapter 5 within the context of possible advantages to regionalism. It suffices to point out that the cement industry in Kuwait, which acts as a gauge of capital development activities, suffered from a low volume of sales and below-capacity operation.[14] With these requirements in the background, we should now turn to an examination of the actual industrialization attempts in the Kuwaiti economy.

Manufacturing industries do not play a significant role in the Kuwaiti economy; the value added by industry in the gross domestic product is about 3 per cent. Small-scale industry predominates as a result of narrow market demand, shortages in raw materials other than oil, and in many areas a lack of skilled workers. Since most such workers come on a specific contract, this portion of the labor force is marked by turnover and a degree of uncertainty. Table 2 gives some idea of the labor force distribution and the size of the concerns.

From this table the smallness of the size of the industrial units is

[14] *IBRD Report*, pp. 63–64.

TABLE 2

NUMBER OF ENTERPRISES AND WORKERS (EXCLUDING OIL PRODUCTION), 1963

Activity	No. of Workers	Per Cent of Total	No. of Establishments	Per Cent of Total	No. of Workers per Establishment
Oil Distribution	470	2.2	1	...	470
Manufacturing Industries and Maintenance (more than 5 workers)	10,402	49.1	588	24.8	17–18
Manufacturing Industries and Maintenance (less than 5 workers)	4,265	20.1	1,755	74.1	2–3
Government Enterprise	6,062	28.6	26	1.1	233
Total	21,199	100.0	2,370	100.0	

SOURCE: Kuwait Chamber of Commerce and Industry, "The Industrial Situation in Kuwait," a paper presented to the U.N. Conference on Industrial Development in the Arab Countries, held in Kuwait, March 1–10, 1966 (Kuwait, December 30, 1965, mimeographed), p. 18 (in Arabic).

clear. Wide variations exist, however, according to the type of industrial activity. Apart from the oil industry, the government industrial units have the highest number of workers per unit, an average of 233. Most of the governmental establishments are concerned with water distillation, electric power, motor vehicle repair, food processing, metal products manufacture, printing and publishing, and the manufacture of salt, chlorine, and caustic soda. An interesting feature of industry in general in Kuwait is that 42 per cent of the total industrial labor force is engaged in maintenance.[15] This high proportion reflects the dependence of the economy on imports of industrial commodities. The private sector is represented in small consumption-oriented industries averaging about 18 persons per industrial unit. The activities include dairying, rubber products repair, shipbuilding, and soft drink manufacturing, among others.

It is apparent from Table 3 that the share of the Kuwaiti national income generated by the labor force is comparatively low, 39.7 per cent. Possible explanations could be the labor force's low level of productive ability, maldistribution of national income, and/or the size of the industrial labor force. Considering that the average wage in Kuwait is approximately double that offered in most neighboring countries and in many cases approaches the level of group three (Table 3), one is not inclined to consider the second possibility the dominant cause of the low contribution wages make to the national income. Judging from the size of the labor force and the fact that most of those engaged in industry are working in small-scale manufacturing and repair shops, the first and third reasons would seem to contribute to the situation. The share of investment directed toward industry in 1964/65 amounted to about 20 per cent of the $277.2 million total investment. Again one observes the stress upon small industries, which receive 6.5 per cent of the total investment and 32 per cent of all industrial investment.

Although industrialization is faced with numerous problems, not the least of which is the smallness of the market, the development of this sector will further the opportunities for development of additional sectors such as commerce and services, which have been associated more with government bureaucracy rather than directly related to the economy itself. Diversification in any measure should

[15] Kuwait Chamber of Commerce and Industry, "The Industrial Situation in Kuwait," a paper presented to the U.N. Conference on Industrial Development in the Arab Countries, March, 1966, p. 20.

serve to lessen the dependence upon oil as the production factor
and the reliance upon the government as the principal direct
employer. It should, moreover, offer an arena in which to reestablish
and strengthen the effort-and-reward relationship.

TABLE 3

WAGES AS PERCENTAGE OF NATIONAL INCOME, 1964

Kuwait, Ghana, Uganda, Cyprus, Greece, Peru	Less than 40%
U.A.R., Brazil, Chile, Colombia, Philipines	More than 40, less than 50%
Belgium, Japan, Denmark, Holland, Norway, Argentina	More than 50, less than 60%
Canada, Sweden, Australia, France, Switzerland, Germany (Western)	More than 60, less than 70%
United States, United Kingdom	More than 70%

SOURCE: Technical Secretariat of the Conference on Industrial Development in the Arab Countries, "The Industrial Labor Force in Kuwait," a paper presented to the U.N. Conference on Industrial Development in the Arab Countries (Kuwait, March 1966, mimeographed), p. 11.

There are two possibilities for industrialization, one geared
toward domestic consumption, the second primarily for export.
Within the first grouping we have seen that the domestic market
cannot support industries requiring large output to operate with
feasible costs. Thus the present small-scale type of operation is
likely to continue to dominate for some time, as the increase in
population, estimated to reach about 531,000 by 1970/71, still is
insufficient to offer ample marketing opportunities. Industries
with import-substitution content could be stimulated. Likely as
not, the initial output would be of lower quality and possibly of
higher price than the imports to which the Kuwaitis are accustomed.
Some form of government protection would be called for in such a
situation. Customs duties would be of questionable effectiveness,
however, as the average Kuwaiti's purchasing power is such that
it could take this increase in stride. Limiting imports holds the germ
of inflation, a condition which has not yet drastically touched the
commodity market in that country. The more viable policy probably
would include something similar to an import quota, which could
ensure at least a share of the domestic market, indicate the existence
of alternatives for domestic investment other than real estate, and
yet not severely hamper the consumer sovereignty in Kuwait. A
complementary government policy might be direct support to
bring down costs and prices to a level compatible with that of

long-standing industries abroad. Before such a subsidization approach is installed, a full assessment of the elements involved would be required, particularly including marketing studies. This policy should be directed on a pilot project basis with the understanding that the industry must eventually cease to receive support and must compete with the imported products within the local market. This would give a different twist to the "infant industry" argument for protection, with subsidies applied rather than tariffs because the government can afford the financing of the former and does not require the latter for revenue purposes.

It will be recalled that an industrial survey was carried out in 1963 to examine and assess the possibilities for development in this sector.[16] Among the industrial products recommended as potentially feasible in Kuwait were foodstuffs such as dried fish and meat; textiles and fabrics, specifically cotton and rayon; construction materials, including cement and plastic products; pharmaceutical products; and certain consumer commodities (batteries, tires, soap, and metal rodding). Domestic demand was deemed sufficient to support fully or partially medium-sized industries in the latter category. Earlier in 1961 a mission of the World Bank also suggested that most of these products might be investigated for possible introduction or expansion. The first IBRD report recommended a study of the possibility of establishing a glass industry. This industry would benefit from the presence of certain types of sand, and natural gas would provide a cheap source of energy. Because of the high freight costs of imported glass materials to Kuwait, the Mission thought this industry could survive on local demand. An assembly plant for the production of batteries was also put forward as a possibility. It is particularly interesting that sufficient demand is based upon the short life span of batteries in exceedingly warm climates. Finally, the Bank report referred to the need to guard against further proliferation of the already developed construction industries.

The sea offers a vast resource upon which a fishing industry and that of distillation and chemicals can be based. Large-scale distillation of sea water is not new, as Kuwait has been among the early pioneers in this endeavor. The chemical industry associated with this process began as a by-product but has been expanded to meet

[16] Ministry of Finance and Industry, *Industrial Survey 1963: By Industrial and Process Engineering Consultants, London*, vol. 2 (Kuwait, 1963, in Arabic).

industrial purposes and local needs. Among the commodities produced are caustic soda, chlorine and hydrochloric acid, soda ash, bromine, and magnesium.[17] Most of these products, particularly chlorine for the purification of water supplies, are consumed in Kuwait. Caustic soda is a surplus commodity and in liquid form, as it is now produced, is difficult to export, although present plans project its conversion into a solid-flake state. Schemes are contemplated for the export of this commodity to developing countries. With the expansion of these sea-based industries, the cost of production of chlorine and hydrochloric acid is expected to be slashed by almost one-third as a result of economies of scale, thereby reducing simultaneously the cost of distillation.

On the whole, products which aim at the local market are limited because of the size of the population, but four factors contribute to natural protection of industries such as glass, sea-water chemicals, and cement. These are (1) the availability of the basic raw material, (2) the unique requirements of the domestic market, (3) the high costs of transportation involved in imported materials in these lines, and (4) the availability of cheap energy sources.

A recommendation was also made that export industries be established which could utilize the available raw materials and be of sufficient size to reach optimum scale with lowest possible costs. Capital-intensive industries were a natural selection as financial resources are no problem in Kuwait. The vertical expansion of the domestic oil industry as well as the petrochemical industry falls into this category. The Kuwait National Petroleum Company has invested in downstream activities, thus seeking marketing outlets and additional refining experience (besides that provided by the refinery in the Shuaiba complex).[18] The rationale of the operation

[17] For details for the sea salt uses and chemicals see Ministry of Power and Water, "Extraction of Chemicals from Sea Water Distillation Units," a paper presented at the Conference on the Industrial Development in the Arab Countries (Kuwait, January 2, 1966, mimeographed), pp. 1–11 (in Arabic).

[18] The initial downstream effort involved KNPC's purchase of 5 per cent of the Central African Petroleum Refineries Ltd., located at Umtali, Southern Rhodesia. Other companies participating include BP, Shell, Mobil, Caltex, Compagnie Française des Petroles, and Aminoil. Because of Kuwait's compliance with the United Nations embargo on all oil shipments to Southern Rhodesia, KNPC has interrupted the implementation of its 5 per cent crude-supply right. Kuwait recently submitted a bid in the Haldia Refinery in Calcutta in partnership with the Indian Government. The possibility of participation in a West German refinery, pipeline, and station distribution system has also been put forward.

is premised upon the problem of product flexibility; i.e., in the consuming countries there are certain products in short supply with an imbalance existing between the patterns of product consumption and of the product mix derived from these refineries. An inadequate supply of distillate heating oil and diesel in European centers and kerosine in Asia illustrates the variance in product demand. As a barrel of crude cannot be refined into a barrel of a single product but breaks down into several, increased local refining in consuming countries would not solve the problem of surplus and deficit products. Presently this condition is met by the transport of a refined surplus product to meet the demand of another consumer. Thus, double transportation costs can be incurred for the market-located refineries, first in shipping the crude itself and second in moving the excess product to a demand area, often in another continent.

An export refinery in Kuwait enjoys two economic advantages. First, it is spared the cost of moving the crude for processing, and second, it is geographically centered between Europe and the developing countries in Africa and Asia. As mentioned earlier in chapter 2, the all-hydrogen refinery of KNPC is specifically geared toward the processing of high sulfur content crude. The sulfur is sharply reduced, with high-quality final products resulting. It should be pointed out that the KNPC product line would be complementary to rather than competitive with the present line of products from existing refineries in the Gulf area, owing to the differing levels of sulfur. The Shuaiba plant will be sufficiently large to achieve economy of scale in the output of premium products, the cost of which would be prohibitive to small market-located refineries.

Because of marketing requirements, KNPC is investing in storage and marketing facilities outside Kuwait. A fuel oil storage terminal is located in Copenhagen with a subsidiary company established there to operate the facility and engage in retailing. Additional offices are scheduled for opening in London and New York. KNPC's markets principally are internationally directed toward Europe and the developing countries in Asia and Africa rather than the Arab Middle East, which on the whole is expanding its own refining capacity.

A second logical direction in which to diversify would be in petrochemicals. The range of potential products derivable from natural gas and other petroleum sources is enormous. In U.S. production it has been found that 119 chemicals can be processed directly from natural gases, and 57 emanate from other petroleum sources.[19]

There are four features which characterize the petrochemical industry and make it attractive to Kuwaiti development. First, it is a heavily capital-intensive undertaking. For example, the cost of a petroleum refinery runs about $12–$20 a ton of annual output, while it costs $600 per ton for polyethylene. And refineries are considered capital-intensive! Second, technological advances are continuous, thereby reducing the production costs. As a newcomer Kuwait can benefit from the backlog of research and experience amassed by the more established producers. The third feature is that no direct correlation exists between the required investment and the productive capacity of this industry. Should the industry be expanded threefold, costs required might increase by only 20 to 45 per cent of their original level. In short, this industry has a core of increasing returns to scale. Finally, there are several indirect products, mainly gases, which usually accompany petrochemical operations. Although utilization would require further investment, it would, at the same time, raise the profits of the industry as a whole.[20]

With reference to the requirements of the industry, while Kuwait has abundant and cheap raw materials an obvious shortage exists in the availability of technicians and skilled workers, and there is the initial difficulty of breaking into the international market. The need for a proper labor force could be met in the short-run through the importation of skills, assistance from the oil companies and international agencies, and in the long-term through education and training. The marketing problem does not seem insurmountable at the present time.

Nearby India and Pakistan, with a combined population exceeding 550 million, consume only 500,000 tons or so of nitrogenous fertilizers, as compared with Japan's annual consumption of 670,000 tons for a population of 96 million.[21] The Arab world is also capable

[19] *IBRD Report*, p. 115.

[20] M. El-Halfawi, "The Petrochemical Industry in the Arab Countries: Its Future and Possibilities of Growth on a Regional Scale," a paper presented at the Conference on Industrial Development in the Arab Countries (Kuwait, January 30, 1966, mimeographed), pp. 3–4 (in Arabic).

[21] Charles Issawi, "Kuwait's Market Growth in Subcontinent," *Emergent Nations*, Autumn, 1965, p. 57.

of utilizing greater amounts. The U.A.R. alone is expected to double its consumption by 1970. A conservative figure of nitrogenous fertilizer needs of the Arab countries has been estimated at 1.13 million tons by 1970, with an absorptive level of 1,000 tons of ammonia daily. However, increased output of nitrogenous fertilizers by major oil and chemical companies has been projected to meet consumption demand by 1970, and the very real possibility of a surplus exists.[22] Whether this materializes or not is quite beside the fact that chemical fertilizers are an extremely competitive field and those countries which are likely to need it most are usually the least able to pay because of foreign exchange problems. Still, Kuwait has some advantages because of its low production costs. The conversion process involves a minimum number of steps from the natural gas into its main products of hydrogen, ammonia, and urea.[23]

Other petrochemical products include ethylene, synthetic rubber, and artificial fibers. Ethylene is an important intermediate item in the production of various chemical products. Kuwait has an advantage of producing ethylene at a lower cost than most other producers for two reasons. (1) Kuwaiti natural gas is relatively low in cost. (2) It is relatively rich in hydrocarbons which can be easily isolated and converted. Such characteristics give Kuwait a locational advantage. Ethylene is the base for such finished products as plastics and lubrication oils. Synthetic rubber is much in demand throughout the region. Imports to the Arab countries of this material alone amount to over $50 million a year, and with a rise in the standard of living consumption should likewise increase. Similarly, artificial fibers account for a like proportion of imports annually into the region.

[22] El-Halfawi, "Petrochemical Industry", p. 12. This projection is based upon a study carried out by the Tennessee Valley Authority for the Agency for International Development. It states that there will be a surplus of 13.6 million tons of this type of fertilizer by the beginning of the 1970's.

[23] The differential between Kuwaiti costs and European costs is seen in the table below. It is based on the quantity of natural gas used to produce the given commodities at Kuwaiti prices or Western European prices of the gas and would represent the following percentages of total daily cost including capital cost for depreciation, interests and maintenance.

	Hydrogen	Ammonia	Urea
Kuwait	11%	3–4%	3%
Western Europe	60%	30%	23%

SOURCE: Faisal Mazidi, *Natural Gas in Kuwait and Its Utilization: Kuwait as a Base for Petrochemicals*, p. 9.

While capital-intensive industries have been particularly suited to the export sector of Kuwait, it appears confined to petrochemicals. At this stage of development, the production of intermediates might be even more advantageous for and suited to the Kuwaiti economy. First there is the benefit of the availability of cheap fuel, which accounts for a major part of the intermediate costs. Second, the production of an intermediate does not require the same high caliber of research and technical abilities involved in final products. Third, there is an element of flexibility associated with the production of an intermediary, as such a commodity could be the input for several types of final products. Finally, it is easier to market a semifinished product which could be converted by the buyer into any of several finished requirements.

The core of the Kuwaiti petrochemical industry is presently the operations and development plans of the Kuwait Chemical Fertilizers Company (KCFC), a mixed venture in which Gulf Oil Company and British Petroleum each participates in 20 per cent shares, with the remaining 60 per cent held by the Petrochemicals Industries Company (see chapter 3, Table 5). Total investment in the existing complex is approximately $36 million. The present KCFC project comprises:

Ammonia Unit	400 tons/day
Urea Unit	550 tons/day
Ammonium Sulfate Unit	500 tons/day
Sulfuric Acid Unit	400 tons/day

With a negligible local market, the products are directed for export principally east and south of Suez where the competitive situation is favorable, particularly with regard to freight. In the fall of 1966 the initial shipment was made to Iraq by KCFC with contracts for future deliveries to East and West Pakistan, Turkey, Cyprus, Saudia Arabia, Qatar, Somaliland, Ethiopia, Jordan, Bahrain, Tanzania, and Sudan. Fertilizers are sold worldwide in a public tender market with the large competitors being American, European, and Japanese firms. The three factors which have allowed KCFC to compete have been (1) the low price of gas as a feedstock; (2) the low cost of electricity, which uses gas as a fuel; and (3) the geographical location of Kuwait, which lowers freight charges. Even when the KCFC f.o.b. price has been the highest, tenders were awarded to the company.

Expansion plans of KCFC envisage the construction of a new liquid ammonia plant with a capacity of 1,500 tons/day making it the world's largest. About half the output would be processed into urea in Kuwait with the remainder exported for conversion in market-located plants, thereby entailing some downstream investments. Such expansion would carry a price tag of about $100 million. Two additional projects under study are the establishment of an 800 tons/day methanole plant and a gas fractionation complex. The latter, involving a cost of $15 million, would process gas as a base of a more elaborate petrochemicals industry seeking to attract greater foreign investment.

With the development of large-scale petrochemical industries, the industrial characteristics of Kuwait are likely to undergo a change. First, the government will cease to be the main consumer of industrial output. Second, the construction industries cannot hope to sustain the high level of activities of the 1950's and early 60's. Petrochemical development is entering the industrial picture at an appropriate time. Finally, it is likely, therefore, that the export-directed industry will dwarf the small, domestic consumption industries and an intensified drive to secure markets will be launched.

AGRICULTURALIZATION: CREATING A SECTOR

It has been pointed out throughout this study that Kuwait lacks a viable agricultural sector of any significant size. The 100 acres or so under cultivation form the experimental farm system. This proportion makes Kuwait one of the least agriculturalized countries in the world. The dependence on imports of foodstuffs is almost complete. This state of affairs has had economic as well as sociological effects on the population. The urbanistic character of the indigenous population has been reinforced by the lack of farming opportunities. The withdrawal from economic activities related to the sea has further concentrated the population in urban centers. The non-Kuwaitis, who generally come from agricultural countries, find themselves somewhat estranged. In most affluent societies agriculture has become the employer of fewer people although it has grown in productivity. The agricultural sector in advanced countries of Western Europe and the United States absorbs less than 15 per cent of the population, contrasted to 70 to 90 per cent in developing economies. In the latter instance, the sector is labor-intensive and productivity is generally extremely low. In both the developed and underdeveloped nations, regardless of the portion of the population involved in agriculture there is a clear-cut attempt to raise productivity in this vital sector. Not only is such a drive motivated by the desire for adequate provision of foodstuffs but also by the need for materials for industrialization and as a means of increasing foreign exchange earnings.

Trying to find an alternative to agricultural development has proven difficult if not futile. Even England, which devised an elaborate exchange system of its nonagricultural products for foreign foodstuffs, still had to depend heavily upon its domestic agricultural resources in the early stages of its industrialization, from the 1750's to the second quarter of the nineteenth century. Today development economists have come full circle and recognize that agriculture cannot be visualized as an alternative to industrialization, thereby forcing a choice between the two, but rather as an integral part of the industrialization process.[24]

Despite the formidable obstacles in the path of agriculture, Kuwait must, in the long run, make a determined effort to utilize fully whatever potential exists in this sector. Among the measures directed toward creating a more favorable environment for such development are expanded desalination of water, intensified underground water surveys, and the realization of the Shatt-el-Arab project to move water from Iraq.

Already the price of distilling water in Kuwait has reached a comparatively low level. Production of sweet water by distillation in the Morro Bay Station on the West coast of the U.S. costs $1.96 per 1,000 gallons while the Kuwaiti expense in producing a like amount is $1.75. The natural gas energy base is the cost-lowering element in Kuwaiti production. Groundwater surveys have been extensive. In 1960 the discovery of the Raudhatain water field was made. By 1962 a 55-mile pipeline was bringing a capacity of 6 million gallons of sweet water a day to the city of Kuwait.[25] But current estimates place the span of utilization of this underground

[24] This realization has been clearly pointed out by W. W. Rostow, "Unsolved Problems of International Development," *International Development Review*, December, 1965, p. 15.

[25] United Nations, *Water Desalination in Developing Countries* (New York, 1964), ST/ECA/82, p. 181.

lake, at the present level of consumption, at one generation. Therefore, an economic decision may have to be made to seriously investigate the possibility of introducing atomic power for distillation
purposes, thus conserving the natural gas for the petrochemical
industry. Even though Kuwait is an oil producer such a study
should be made. Recent technical developments in the peaceful use
of atomic power are allowing the construction of a plant in another
area of the world which also suffers from a relative dearth of water
supply. In the Los Angeles region an installation is being built to
provide 150 million gallons of sweet water daily in addition to
electric power at competitive costs. Kuwait is in a financial situation
to consider such processes in order to diversify its sources of water.

Attempts to develop water resources to cope with agricultural
needs will ultimately help to revise the traditional conception of
water for sheer personal consumption and simultaneously will
provide for the growing needs of modern industry. Kuwait should
investigate the possibility of moving from the experimental to the
commercial stage of hydroponics. The historically urbanistic feature
of the Kuwaiti economy has alleviated the mass movement of
indigenous population from the farm to the city with the expansion
of the oil industry as, for example, in Libya. The development of
agriculture would require many of the prerequisites for industrialization. In Kuwait the availability of relatively low-cost capital
and the abundance of natural gas could be used to facilitate the
expansion of the desalinization and fertilizer industries. Another
purpose of the development of agriculture would be to encourage
truck gardening and grazing activities on such a scale as to relieve
Kuwait's overdependence on imports of food. The distance and
delays in transportation have caused waste and loss of nutritional
value. Most countries, including the United States, subsidize their
agricultural sectors in one way or another. While this is not a blanket
endorsement of such an approach, Kuwait can well afford some type
of support, even a temporary one, to attract private investment.
This would be slow in coming as a large portion of the population
would not think of agriculture as an investment outlet.

A side effect of agricultural development would be the improvement of the quality of the environment. Physical attractiveness is
something of a locational advantage, particularly as Kuwait
industrializes. Moreover, the creation of such a sector should serve
to increase the integration of the people with the land and widen

the range of production alternatives, thereby lessening the negative transit attitude which pervades a large share of the population. Agricultural expansion need not aim at self-sufficiency or export possibilities but should seek to supply a portion of the daily needs. The cost would not be substantially greater than that of imported foodstuffs, particularly vegetables and dairy products.[26]

Also included in the agricultural sector is the fishing industry, which is no stranger to Kuwaitis as an economic activity. As contrasted with agriculture proper and land reclamation, immediate returns are possible. Although pearling has declined, shrimp and other seafood are now being processed, the former for export and the latter for local consumption. Per capita domestic consumption is estimated at 18 kg. in 1965, which is higher than the United Kingdom's at 13 kg. but far below Japan's level of 30 kg. Besides the primary industry, there are manufacturing industries in this field which could be further stimulated: freezing, salting, drying and smoking, canning, and the production of fish meal. Small-scale fishing is still active, involving about 1,500 persons, with the private craft valued at $1.4 million. This group receives tacit protection from the government in order to maintain prices on the local market. Three larger firms operate—Gulf Fisheries, Kuwait National Fisheries, and International Fisheries Company—none of which has government participation in its capitalization.

Gulf Fisheries alone has a fleet of 42 ships and employs about 1,350 workers. The National Fisheries is much smaller, engaging about 200 employees. The third enterprise, International Fisheries Company, was established in 1965 and is still in the formative stage. All have packing plants and participate in shrimp fishing, with the United States their largest single customer. Recent suggestions have been made to coordinate fishing activities in the Gulf to insure national rights while working with the Food and Agricultural Organization of the United Nations to modernize and expand the industry.[27]

---

[26] An investigation of the cost of transporting vegetables and the degree of waste involved has been carried out by the World Bank mission. It was concluded that Kuwait could probably produce vegetables on a competitive basis as water costs become lower. *IBRD Report*, p. 130.

[27] Ministry of Trade and Industry, "The Utilization of the Fishing Wealth of Kuwait," a paper presented at the Conference on Industrial Development in the Arab Countries (Kuwait, February 5, 1966, mimeographed), pp. 3–15 (in Arabic).

HUMAN RESOURCE DEVELOPMENT

In the economics of balanced growth the distinction is often made between Social Overhead Capital (SOC) and Directly Productive Activities (DPA). The SOC, as defined earlier in this chapter, covers the elemental services on which primary, secondary, and tertiary productive activities are based including various areas ranging from education and public health to law and order and capital overhead in housing and transportation. Investment in social overhead is comprehensive, concerned with the general growth of the economy rather than being a form of economic activity. In many cases SOC investment could lead to the encouragement of investment in directly productive activities.[28]

Most underdeveloped countries are faced with the problem of a choice between the two forms of activities because of the scarcity of capital resources. A country like Kuwait must still make allocation choices between the two, but with greater leeway, as it is spared the compelling "either–or" decision facing many poorer nations. It is a question of degree and ease with which it can carry out its choice. In the previous chapter we noted that from 1963/64 through the 1966/67 budget estimates for health, education, and social services accounted for an average of over 25 per cent of total budgetary expenditures. In the latter budget, health and education together accounted for 21 per cent. It would appear there are two underlying factors in this relatively heavy emphasis on social overhead capital. One, as mentioned earlier, is the availability of funds; the second is that social overhead will facilitate investment in the directly productive activities.

An abundance of capital and the small size of the population has enabled Kuwait to make fast strides in education. The growth of primary and secondary education in the 30-year span from 1936 to 1966 corresponds to the rapid rise in wealth due to oil revenues. In the base year there were two schools, 61 in 1956, and 160 in 1966. Student enrollment falls into the same pattern: 600 in 1936, 30,412 two decades later, and 101,045 by 1966. The teaching staff rose from no more than 25 in the base year to 1,425 twenty years later, reaching 5,611 in 1966. Furthermore, the nonconstruction budgetary allocation for education rose from less than half a million

---

[28] Hirschman, *Strategy of Economic Development*, p. 83.

dollars in 1946 to almost $31 million by the end of the next decade and to some $56 million in 1966. What is obvious here is the direct relationship between oil revenue and educational activities.[29]

Compulsory education is now required from 4 to 16 years of age. Stress has been placed on adequate secondary education on the ground that a poorly developed education at this level could become a bottleneck upon which the success of both primary and higher education depends. Schooling is free to everyone residing in the country. In 1965 over 1,000 students were attending universities abroad under scholarships, which represents almost two of every 1,000 persons in the entire population. Education is broadening the labor force through the addition of trained women. In 1957 only two per cent of this force was made up of women, but this is undergoing change as over 42,600 girls are presently in school, i.e., about 40 per cent of total student enrollment.

Two major institutions of higher education and training were opened in 1966. The University of Kuwait, which is expected to draw and is drawing its students mainly from the State of Kuwait and the neighboring countries, is the first center. The questions may be raised why a country with less than half a million population needs to institute a University of its own and what standards and selectivity can be followed practically. On the other hand, how rapidly and to what extent would the new University absorb the ever increasing secondary school graduates and meet the development requirements of the nation? The estimated potential enrollment demands based upon high school graduates could rise from 500 in 1966/67 to 880 just two years later and to some 5,250 in 1977/78. Accordingly, in 11 years the University is envisaged as absorbing a freshman class of 3,500 to 4,000 new Kuwaiti students. With a modest addition to the 1977/78 enrollment of non-Kuwaiti students, the University capacity would reach about 15,000.[30]

The ramifications of these educational guidelines, the lack of tuition and fees for attendance, and the accessibility of free scholarships might have a negative impact. This could be a further lessening of the already weakened relationship between effort and reward. The younger generations have experienced only the post-oil

[29] Minister of Education, "Address on the Inauguration of the University of Kuwait," November, 1966, p. 3 (mimeographed).

[30] Abd-El Fattah Ismail, Rector of the University of Kuwait, "Address on the Inauguration of the University of Kuwait," November, 1966, p. 3 (mimeographed).

affluence and prosperity. It has been noted earlier in the analysis of the most recent census of Kuwait that among the Kuwaiti population there is a relatively low proportion engaged in gainful employment. The capacity of the government as an efficient employer has, in most cases, long been surpassed. Higher education could be viewed as a tool to strengthen the relationship between effort and reward through selectivity and by emphasis upon those disciplines which would most immediately affect the nation's economic and social development.

Another factor to be considered in the role of higher education in a country as small as Kuwait is the restricted socioeconomic milieu. Advanced students might benefit from exposure to other, more diversified environments, and hence fellowships for study abroad, particularly on the graduate level, assume a significant role and will need to be continued.

While the environment may be a restrictive factor in higher education, a positive element exists in a reduction of the financial constraints which usually face universities, especially in the early stages of development. The Kuwaiti institution can pursue both educational and research goals and, indeed, the latter may offer a means of diversifying the economy. The cost of advanced research in the physical sciences is often prohibitive to the developing nations because of expensive technical equipment. For Kuwait this poses no great problem.

The second educational center is the Kuwait Institute of Economic and Social Planning in the Middle East of which the executing agency is the United Nations Special Fund. Its objective is to act in a remedial capacity to train specialists in finance and economic and social planning. A program of practical and theoretical planning procedures will be extended to employees of Middle Eastern governments and members of the staffs of economic organizations. It will, moreover, serve as a center for advisory services in the fields of economic and social planning.[31]

---

[31] The Special Fund's contribution to the project was $904,000, of which $802,000 is directly from the Fund and $102,000 is Kuwait's contribution to the expenses for 1966–70. The Kuwaiti government has given $6,869,417 toward the establishment of the Institute. Moreover, the government and the Kuwait Fund for Arab Economic Development will make fellowships available. United Nations Special Fund, *Kuwait Institute for Economic and Social Planning in the Middle East*, SF/R.10/Add.31, November 16, 1964, p. 5.

Strides in health services have been quite rapid also. In a two-decade span facilities have increased from one hospital to 15 and from four physicians to about 500, or one doctor for almost every 750 persons in the country. As with education, all medical services are extended without charge to anyone in Kuwait. Training of personnel has gone forward, the first class having graduated from the new Nursing Institute in 1966.

Another area of human resource development is connected with the absorption of the stream of expatriates who have immigrated to Kuwait with the idea of participating in the country's growth and benefiting from the high wage and salary level, the social services, and the free market. There is no doubt that there has been a partnership here and that the non-Kuwaiti contribution has been substantial, accompanying the rapid pace of economic development within the country. There are some economic ramifications to this population mix.

We have pointed out that the savings-investment relationship is marked by a high level of the former but a low degree of transfer into the latter. An undeniable transit mentality exists among the non-Kuwaiti population. As they come on contracts of short duration and cannot participate fully in ownership, there is a tendency among some to save and transfer rather than spend in the domestic market and invest. It is difficult and actually useless to try to delineate the cause and effect of such a condition. Perhaps a solution along the lines of U.S. immigration and naturalization could be worked out whereby new entry for an extended period would be selective, based upon ability, education, and the human resource needs of the economy. With such limits to immigration, economic privileges could be extended under a permanent residency arrangement which would serve to attach the non-Kuwaiti to the country and its economy, minimize the "foreign" element among the non-Kuwaitis, and enhance continuity (and by extension, investment and economic growth).

In summing up the development of human resources, if one were to choose a single area of potential which could contribute ultimately to a more balanced economy, it would be education. The economics of education are still in the formative stages. The impact of education has yet to be fully assessed in terms of the process of growth, attitude changes, and increases in income and productivity it can bring about. The bottlenecks to investment domestically do not apply to education, the investment requirements of which are insatiable. Because Kuwait is limited in physical resources, development of its human capabilities could assist in economic diversification, with the possibility that in the future it could become a net exporter of skills and emerge as a research center.

THE FIRST FIVE YEAR PLAN, 1967/68—1971/72

Within the milieu of the peculiarities of the Kuwaiti economy, its imbalance, capital surplus, and its resource potential, the architects of planning in Kuwait constructed the first program for economic and social development. The initial plan was released in early 1966 but was revised and its final form published in April, 1967. However, the main lines of action and the objectives of the initial plan, which was to have spanned the years 1965/66 through 1970/71, were retained and remain valid in the most recent draft. The main difference between the two plans has been the tendency toward a more conservative and, in light of world oil developments, perhaps more realistic evaluation of revenue for the next half decade. In addition, the growth rate targets have been lowered with the rationale that such increments can be realized and, under favorable conditions, surpassed. It should be mentioned that in the absence of sufficient information in some areas, tentative estimates have been made in the Plan on the basis of historical background or with methods utilized by other developing countries which lack well established statistical data. In the next few pages an attempt will be made to describe the salient features and enunciate the broad guidelines advanced for development.

The Plan encompasses two sets of objectives, one of long-run implications and the other of a more immediate nature. The long-term goals deal with the basic structure of the society to actuate social and economic principles. Among these are (1) building a diversified self-sustaining economy, with emphasis on sectors other than oil; (2) raising the standards of education and training; (3) insuring a high rate of economic growth; (4) creating a geographical balance between cities and smaller municipalities through improved transportation and communication facilities, with such infrastructure development leading to external economies, similarly a main broad goal; (5) increasing the Kuwaiti population to return it to majority status; (6) assuring and raising the Kuwaiti proportion in the labor force; (7) creating employment opportunities; (8) limiting the use of labor from nonindigenous sources except in highly technical vocations, to be balanced and surpassed by the exit of certain numbers of unskilled non-Kuwaitis; (9) realization of a greater degree of social justice; (10) actuation of the principle that every citizen has proprietary rights which are inviolable; (11) working toward Arab economic complementarity.[32]

However, the more immediate goals of the First Five Year Plan are dealt with extensively. A total of eight targets was set up. First, in economic development, the Plan envisages an increment in the gross domestic product of 37 per cent during 1967/68—1971/72, averaging 6.5 per cent yearly. In absolute terms, the gross domestic product will increase from $2,251.2 million in the base year (1966/67) to a total of $3,085.6 million in 1971/72, that is, an increment of $834.4 million for the five years. Also projected are rises in the gross national product of about 6.9 per cent annually and 6.5 per cent per annum in the national income.[33] Making these targets will depend upon the continuous flow of oil estimated on average at a 6 per cent yearly increase. (The initial plan draft placed this output rise at 8 per cent.) Second, the development of the human resources base is to be advanced through education, training, and raising health standards, partly by implementation of the 1965 compulsory education law as well as extension of education to the university level.

The third goal deals with the social and economic opportunities for the population. The initial draft of the Plan placed the population of Kuwait at 541,000 by 1970/71; the objective of 10,000 less than this number is to be adjusted by the departure of 2,000 non-Kuwaitis annually over the five-year period. It assumes a 3.5 per cent increase per annum in the Kuwaiti population and 3 per cent for non-Kuwaitis. Participation by the Kuwaiti labor force is to be expanded. It is expected that the share of Kuwaitis in the labor force at the end of the plan period (1971/72) will be 26.6 per cent of the total force in contrast to its share at the base year of only 22.6 per cent.

[32] These objectives are enunciated in both drafts of the plan. The Planning Board, *The First Five Year Economic and Social Plan, 1966/67—1970/71* (Kuwait, 1966), p. 25 (in Arabic) (hereafter cited as *The Plan, 1966/67—1970/71*), and The Planning Board, *The First Five Year Economic and Social Plan, 1967/68—1971/72* (Kuwait, 1967), pp. 9–19 (in Arabic) (hereafter cited as *The Plan, 1967/68—1971/72*).

[33] *The Plan, 1967/68—1971/72*, pp. 66, 100.

According to population estimates, the increase in the labor force during the next ten years is to be about 51,000 additional workers. Such an assumption is based upon an increment of 21,000 in the Kuwaiti portion and the remainder to be filled by non-Kuwaitis.[34]

Improvement of the standard of living is the fourth objective. This requires the upgrading of the quantity and quality of the public services which are directed toward the low-income groups. The rise in population will require a corresponding increase in consumption goods, growing by 35 per cent during the plan period. If we take into account the rise in population, the net increase in consumption will be 24 per cent.

Of widespread economic implications is the aim of economic diversification. This fifth stipulation specifies two ranges. The short-run is directed toward a reduction in the high degree of dependence of the economy on housing, construction, and trade sectors. In the longer-term, the target is to diminish the predominant position of the oil sector in the makeup of the economy. As industrialization proceeds, it is anticipated that the relative importance of the oil sector will decline. In this connection it must be emphasized that diversification is time consuming, particularly in the growth of industry as returns are not always immediate in accruing. Thus, although the growth rate of 6.5 per cent for the whole economy is high compared to other nations, and in spite of the fact that it is anticipated on the basis of the expected continuation of the flow of oil at a rate of 6 per cent increase annually, nevertheless, the actual growth rate of the Kuwaiti economy will probably be more in the order of 5 per cent per annum on average. This may be premised upon the fact that if the Plan is to be undertaken aiming at the reduction of the relative importance of oil and construction contributions to the GNP, it is expected that this process of diversification will automatically be reflected in a slower rate of growth than achieved in the past, at least during the five-year span. According to the Plan, although construction is still given the largest percentage in total domestic investment (19.4 per cent), the emphasis in new building is to be shifted from housing to office and factory facilities (see Table 4).

The sixth goal, that of geographical balance between cities and small municipalities, was mentioned as a long-term target as well.

[34] *Ibid.*, p. 110.

The seventh objective, improvement of the infrastructure, involves social overhead capital. Finally, the redistribution of income and wealth is based upon a wage increase of 26 per cent for the five-year period.

TABLE 4

SHARES OF SECTORAL CONTRIBUTION IN GDP FOR BASE YEAR AND FINAL YEAR
AND INVESTMENT GOALS OF PLAN

Sector	Per Cent of Total Contribution		Per Cent of Total Investment
	1966/67	1971/72	1967/68—1971/72
Oil and Natural Gas	61.1	59.7	7.7
Commercial and Financial Services[a]	9.5[b]	9.7[b]	2.4
Public Administration and Defense	5.7	5.1	8.1
Construction	4.7	4.8	19.4
Industry	3.6	4.1	9.4
Transport, Communication, and Storage	2.8	2.9	24.9
Electricity, Water, and Gas	2.3	2.6	15.0
Agriculture and Fishing	0.5	0.7	1.3
Real Estate and Services	9.8[c]	10.4[c]	11.7
Total	100.0	100.0	100.0

SOURCE: *The Plan, 1967/68—1971/72*, pp. 43, 79, 80, 96.

[a] Including tourism.

[b] Wholesale commerce accounts for the lion's share in contribution, 8 per cent in 1966/67 and 8.2 per cent in 1971/72.

[c] Real estate is estimated to contribute 4.7 per cent in 1966/67 and 5.1 per cent in 1971/72.

The degree to which these goals can be met will largely depend upon a number of factors including the extent of cooperation and coordination between the private, public, and mixed sectors. With the rapid rate of growth in Kuwait, economic stability assumed a top priority. Here the Plan emphasizes the expected role of the Central Bank to regulate monetary policies and to adjust interest and rediscount rates to keep fluctuations in line.

Since the Plan is seen as the cornerstone of several plans to follow, one of the driving principles is that it achieves the institutional and organizational development to sustain future planning. First priority in investment is slated for those projects deemed the greatest contributors to social, educational, and communication facilities. Finally, the planners emphasized that consistency and flexibility to conform with actuality were basic in fashioning the Plan.[35]

[35] *Ibid.*, pp. 62–65.

In diversification efforts, the general policy of the Plan is one of encouragement of oil refining, the production of petrochemicals, and water resource development. Some $280 million is earmarked for channeling into the industrial sector; this is projected to increase the value added in industry from 3.6 per cent of the 1966/67 GDP to about 4.1 per cent of the gross domestic production in 1971/72. Table 4 gives an indication of sectoral contribution to the economy and the investment designated for each during the plan.

The appropriate measure for the determination of the volume of investment is the absorptive capacity of the economy, at present and for the future. Moreover, any serious changes in prices or shifts in the price structure will necessitate a corresponding change in the volume and distribution of investment. Additionally, if the assumed increment in efficiency cannot be met, further capital will be needed.

As for the distribution of the total volume of investment among different sectors, it should be noted that the Plan applies the net sectoral contribution to the increase in the GNP and national income. This can be done, as the Kuwaiti economy experiences neither foreign exchange difficulties nor an excess supply of labor. Employment and foreign exchange were omitted, therefore, as criteria for the distribution of investment. No reference has been made in the Plan indicating whether complementarity among projects in any given sector was assessed or not.

The process of distributing the aggregate volume of investment over the five years was left to be determined annually in order to absorb the alterations in social and economic conditions and the development achieved in the financial system. Estimates of distribution of the aggregated volume have been to allot about 55.6 per cent for the public sector and 37.8 per cent and 6.6 per cent for the private and mixed sectors, respectively.[36] Within these sectors, no priorities were established concerning specific projects.

The Plan clarifies that as the amount of realized savings has been much higher than the absorptive capacity of the domestic economy, Kuwaiti investment abroad should be encouraged rather than a policy of merely holding the excess savings. Table 5 offers a breakdown of savings into investment. The volume of savings is scheduled to increase on average by about 7.5 per cent annually during the plan period to give a total of $3,808 million for that span. As total

[36] *Ibid.*, p. 78.

domestic investment requirements are estimated to reach $2,553.6 million, the balance of $1,254.4 million represents the capital funds available for foreign use for the five years.[37] The Kuwait Fund for Arab Economic Development is to be supported and utilized to invest some of the governmental surplus. In setting up the level of investment within the overall Plan, the absorptive capacity has been emphasized as the base. Population, the level of income and its distribution, managerial abilities, labor skills, tastes, and finally, foreign markets all function as elements in determining this capacity.

TABLE 5
SAVINGS AND INVESTMENT IN BASE YEAR AND FINAL YEAR
OF PLAN (AT BASE YEAR PRICES)
(IN MILLION DOLLARS)

	1966/67	1971/72
Total Savings	610.4	876.4
Domestic Investment	420.0	582.4
Foreign Investment	190.4	294.0
Total Investment	610.4	876.4

SOURCE: *The Plan, 1967/68—1971/72*, pp. 53, 106.

In this respect it is interesting to note that total domestic investment will increase by 90 per cent over an earlier corresponding period (1961/62—1965/66) with the public sector undertaking the major role as investor. For example, in the five-year period just cited, the public sector accounted for 46.9 per cent with the mixed and private sectors contributing the remainder of the total $1,344 million. For the Plan years, 1967/68—1971/72, the public sector is to undertake 55.6 per cent of the total domestic investment of $2,553.6 million with the mixed and private share dropping to 44.4 per cent.[38]

The volume of investment during the Plan is expected to raise the GDP from $2,251.2 million in the base year to $3,085.6 million in 1971/72, as mentioned earlier. This is based upon the assumption that the capital-output ratio is 2 : 1 for the economy as a whole (5 : 1 in the non-oil sectors and 0.33 : 1 in oil). The high capital-output ratio in the non-oil sectors is attributable to the shortages of economic and social factors necessary for investment, the lack

[37] *Ibid.*, p. 107.
[38] *The Plan, 1966/67—1970/71*, p. 66, and *The Plan, 1967/68—1971/72*, p. 93.

of managerial talents, and insufficiency in skills and technical capabilities.

The governmental contribution in financing development in the Plan is primarily derived from oil receipts. Thus, the economic dependence on this source, from which more than 90 per cent of total revenues consistently emanates, will be continued, as seen in Table 6.

The estimates of the Plan indicate that while savings amount to 36 per cent of the GNP of the base year, in the final target year a level of 37 per cent of the GNP is projected. A factor influencing the level of savings would be fluctuations in consumption. From the initial and more detailed plan draft the marginal and average propensities to consume for the years 1966/67—1970/71 can be computed as follows:[39]

	1965/66	1966/67	1967/68	1968/69	1969/70	1970/71
Δy	...	50	53	57	62	68
Δc	...	20	17	33	27	25
C/Y (APC)	0.57	0.56	0.53	0.54	0.53	0.52
$\Delta C/\Delta Y$ (MPC)	...	0.40	0.32	0.57	0.43	0.35

It should be noted that while both propensities are relatively low, the average propensity to consume, in general, is diminishing whereas the marginal propensity shows no steady trend. This behavior could be attributed to other factors which affect the consumption rate of change to the change in income, such as the assets held by individuals, the demonstration effect, and the influence of social overhead.

Certain economic trends and attitudes can be discerned in the alterations made on the initial draft. First is the lowering of revenue estimates. This should not be regarded as a major departure from past fiscal policy, which is, indeed, characterized by a cautious revenue projection. Kuwaiti budgets show a consistent and substantial underestimation of expected compared to realized revenues. Also, the experience of the relatively low 1965 increase of 2.28 per cent in oil output, a drop from the previous year's increment of 10 per cent, reinforced the circumspect attitude toward revenues.[40]

Second, actual expenditures generally have fallen below those projected. For example, in reworking the initial plan draft, the

---

[39] Computed from statistics in *The Plan, 1966/67—1970/71*, p. 82.
[40] Output figures given in chapter 2, Table 2.

131

TABLE 6

Public Receipts during the Plan Period by Origin
(In Million Dollars)

Origin	Base Y 1966/67	67/68	68/69	69/70	70/71	71/72	Total	Annual Per Cent Change
Oil	648.76	687.68	728.84	772.80	819.00	868.28	3,876.60	6
Government Enterprises	14.56	15.40	15.96	16.80	17.64	18.48	84.28	5
Customs Duties	12.04	12.88	13.44	14.28	15.12	16.24	71.96	6
Others	19.32	21.28	23.24	25.76	28.28	31.08	129.64	10
Total	694.68	737.24	781.48	829.64	880.44	934.08	4,162.48	...

SOURCE: *The Plan, 1967/68—1971/72*, p. 120.

domestic investment goal was increased by 25 per cent. This could be viewed as an attempt to bridge the discrepancy by applying pressure for efficient allocation of capital. Yet based upon the absorptive capacity of the Kuwaiti economy reflected in recent investments and the level of infrastructure development both social and economic, it appears the Plan's investment target is ambitious, not for want of capital but for lack of sufficient domestic alternatives for productive utilization.

Considering the possibility that the Kuwaiti economy cannot absorb all the projected capital and since the Five Year Plan earmarks almost 33 per cent of total investment to be directed abroad, foreign investment opportunities will continue to play an important role in the entire picture of Kuwait's development. From the monetary standpoint, the movement of capital abroad could reduce the inflationary pressures which can arise when savings outrun the absorptive capacity of the economy. The government has enlisted the assistance of highly qualified, international financial experts to review and coordinate public policies on finance and to increase the efficiency of that sector's investment. The present members of the International Investment Advisory Committee include Eugene R. Black (former president of the World Bank), Claude Loombe of the Bank of England, Dr. Marcus Wallenburg of Sweden's Enskilda Bank, and Dr. Samuel Schweizer (chairman of the Swiss Bank Corporation).

In summarizing balanced development and planning in Kuwait, one notes that while capital surplus may increase the range of economic choice in planning, the strictly limited resource base in turn narrows the same range of choice. As we have seen, simply broadening the base of the economy is the pivotal concern in the Plan. Oil will continue as the leading sector and major source of revenue, but other economic opportunities must be fashioned to eliminate waste in human resources and redundancy of effort. In the following chapters we shall delve into some of the economic foreign relations at work regionally. We shall also assess the Kuwaiti aid program as a means of investment diversification.

Regional Economic
Cooperation: Motives,
Patterns, and Shortcomings

5

SOME ECONOMIC IMPLICATIONS OF SIZE

No single criterion exists in economic literature by which a nation can be labeled as simply large or small. Defining size is unavoidably multifarious. Actual physical size is perhaps the easiest method of such a delineation. Smallness may indicate that an area is less likely to possess varied and large-scale mineral resources and may hold less land for agricultural development. But this is not rigidly applicable. Another method of defining size is through population. Likewise there is ambiguity here. Not only is it a question of population in regard to actual numerical size but it is also a matter of density. Over half the membership of the United Nations is composed of countries with less than five million population; the same pattern prevails among the Arab states. Certain European nations such as Belgium and Switzerland are densely settled yet have numerically small populations. By such standards the United States, the Soviet Union and India may be considered large with the latter nation encountering economic problems arising from overpopulation and transportation difficulties. But one is again faced with the situation wherein a country may be large in land mass, as are Canada, Australia, and Brazil, yet small when categorized by numerical population and density.

Finally there is the economic aspect of the size of a nation. Such indications of an economy's size would be in the GNP, the national income, and the per capita income which in turn would reflect the purchasing power of the individual in the country as well as that of the whole nation. Certain other elements exist which weigh in efficiency, the rate of growth, and indirectly in the economic size of a nation. These include such aspects as the quality of the population, the totality of resources, and often the portion of the entire population which is involved in growth and developmental efforts. Now with such diverse factors in the definition of size, let us turn to the case of Kuwait.

In actual physical size Kuwait is, by all standards, a small country. It has a small population which is not dense, except in the capital city of Kuwait. Its population is urbanistic, which accounts for the entrepreneurial ability of the indigenous inhabitants, and it has a relatively high level of skills due to immigration from the surrounding area. Small though it may be, Kuwait exerts a pressure and holds a position far above what the physical measurements would indicate. Its per capita income is the highest in the world. In turn, the purchasing power of the economy is high. It is a capital-surplus country with a high propensity to save, and it is spared the need for imposing import restrictions as it is not faced with a balance-of-payments problem. Given the situation of Kuwait as a small nation with a sizeable financial and economic impact internationally, when viewed within the regional framework its position becomes even more powerful and significant. We should examine now the components of a "small" economy and the obstacles it faces.

Two factors could be pointed out as reflecting the conditions of economic smallness, one dealing with technological aspects and the second an economic facet. An economy may be considered technologically too small if its domestic market cannot provide adequate outlets for the full-capacity production of the most efficient plant in any specific industry. Thus an economy can be too small in this manner for some industries but not for others and, by extension, this factor may be considered a technological determinant of the composition of foreign trade. Not only is there the industry directly involved, there are intermediate industries necessary for the function of the primary one. A further question is whether the economy can supply optimal markets for full-capacity plants in these fields. It has been concluded that "the technological optimum size for an economy therefore may be very much larger than one might think at first."[1]

[1] T. Scitovsky, "International Trade and Economic Integration as a Means of Overcoming the Disadvantages of a Small Nation," in *Economic Consequences of the Size of Nations* (Proceedings of a Conference held by the International Economic Association), edited by E. A. G. Robinson (London: Macmillan & Co. Ltd., 1960), p. 283.

Involved as economic factors are competition and, by direct influence, efficiency. Using these measures an economy may be considered too small or unviable if it cannot provide the competitive conditions which are required for the most technically efficient plant. It is probable, therefore, that the technological optimum is reached much before the economic optimum. This may be an important factor in the emphasis placed by small nations on planning as larger economies may rely to a greater extent on domestic competition and the profit motive to push toward optimum efficiency.

Having presented some criteria for ascertaining what a small nation and small economy are, it is worthwhile to note the various aspects of vulnerability connected with smallness. Most often there is a high level of foreign restrictions. Second, the individual country is particularly exposed to the erratic and unpredictable shifts in the level and scope of such restrictions. Third, the economic functions in a small country may be greatly affected by the domestic policies of their partners in trade. Finally, bilateral trade and payments techniques, in which bargaining power is given precedence over price and quality competition in determining a small nation's pattern of trade, constitute yet another point of vulnerability.

What, then, are the advantages which the large nations have? These include polito-economic power in international markets by virtue of size and the scale of economy. "A small nation may, of course, exercise a domination effect on still smaller ones and occasionally even on a larger nation especially if that small nation's products are highly specialised and much in demand; but a permanent domination effect on a large nation is excluded."[2] Second, the size of the large nation's domestic market allows it to sell the greatest portion of its output at home and thereby reduce the economy's sensitivity to economic fluctuations on the international level. Third, it may take the greatest advantage of the economies of scale derived from mass production. The first two advantages of the large nations are not readily accessible to the individual small country.

Yet the third advantage of the large nation could be applied in a small economy. Implementation of economies of scale would be based upon the small country's ability to enlarge its outlets by

[2] G. Marcy, "How Far Can Foreign Trade and Customs Agreements Confer upon Small Nations the Advantages of Large Nations?" in *Economic Consequences of the Size of Nations*, p. 270.

expanding exports and/or by regional cooperation through a common market, free trade area, or some form of economic integration.

This stand is further reinforced by certain characteristics of export trade. First, for efficacy in mass production a relatively stable, large, and fairly homogeneous market is desirable. Generally speaking export markets cannot offer these qualities because of possible balance-of-payments restrictions and noneconomic reasons. Second, the effects of competition on the international basis are not always advantageous. Political considerations can and often do override economic factors. Third, the possibilities for the stabilization of export markets are limited. In some areas, this can be accomplished partially through long-term agreements, but unfortunately such action seldom can be realized for industrial and manufactured commodities. Finally, there appears a real danger when investment is made in mass production equipment when there is only the prospect, but with no real assurance, of expanding or creating a market.[3]

Assuming that a form of economic integration has been effected, the possibility of trade-diversion should be investigated. The two aspects, trade-creation and trade-diversion within the framework of regional integration, cannot be appraised by viewing the immediate trade concessions such an agreement requires. The longer-term and more indirect incentives and policy are of a wider significance in arriving at an objective judgment of the total impact of such a regional arrangement on future patterns of trade. The trade-diversion argument is sapped of much of its strength in the case where balance-of-payments deficits coincide with unemployment.[4] Such a condition is the norm for the Middle East and North Africa. Kuwait is an exception to the rule. The simultaneous drop in unemployment and lessening of balance-of-payments pressure would

[3] Scitovsky concludes that international trade, no matter how free, "would usually be considered too precarious to serve as the main basis for mass production" and that "thorough going economic integration would be required to solve these problems of too small an economy." "International Trade," p. 286.

[4] The experience of the European Common Market with reference to trade-diversion and trade-creation is worth noting. Statistical findings indicate that the trade-creating effect would be significantly greater than the loss to the national income from trade-diversion and that economic union would offer advantages in other areas such as balance of payments, employment and investment opportunities. "Discussion," *Economic Consequences of the Size of Nations,* p. 408.

then tend to reduce two major incentives for restrictions and discrimination against non-member countries. Care would be needed, however, when the favorable effects of trade-diversion on employment and the balance-of-payments situation reach an equilibrium as full employment nears. Then additional expansion of intraregional trade could be accompanied by over-employment pressures, price increases and reduction of exports from non-member nations. In this case there is the danger that economic union might develop into a high-cost area cut off from international competition by inflationary developments domestically behind ever higher barriers against imports from abroad.

A form of economic integration would offer beneficial results through freer trade and greater intensity of competition. Greater efficiency through freer trade or through economic union could come by rendering competition more impersonal. The existence of many small firms is not proof of atomistic competition. Instead, a system of oligopolistic control and a possible condition of overall lack of capital for any single small firm to expand will act as a depressant on greater competition in efficiency and economies of scale.

Finally, economic incentives to integration, in addition to smallness of size, are intimately connected with the degree of economic interdependence between geographical areas and the awareness of this interdependence by the countries involved. These incentives, along with political motivations, must be sufficient to overcome the bureaucratic stumbling blocks to the drawing-up of advanced commitments on policy, and to certain lines of action.

Kuwait, although small in physical size and population and having a limited range of resources, does possess important attributes in a geographically central position allowing it a greater economic position than its sheer size would warrant even before the oil era and present massive trade. Within a regional context the country assumes a much larger role than many of its Middle Eastern neighbors because of its high purchasing power. Measured by the standard of the per capita income of the Arab world (the average is still below $200 annually), Kuwait is in this respect equivalent to a country at least fifteen times its population. So far as the rate of growth of an economy is a function of its size, Kuwait shows that the growth rate need not be handicapped by smallness. On the contrary, the Kuwaiti economy for the past two decades has exhibited a growth rate among the highest in the world—not only among the developing but the developed nations as well.[5]

Kuwait is also minimizing the destabilizing effects of smallness by expanding those advantages which attend its size. (1) Greater decision-making power and rapidity of implementation are two benefits accruing to the small nation. Even with the democratic process in planning which might slow down decisions and implementation Kuwait's record remains enviably efficient in conceiving and realizing developmental projects. Domestically the establishment of the Shuaiba industrial complex in a remarkably short span of time indicates a high degree of decisiveness. The same characteristic marks the external aid programs. (2) Kuwait is taking full advantage of technological progress to offset location disadvantages of its small size. Examples include the determined and large-scale efforts to provide for sufficient water resources for urban and industrial use. Widespread installation of air conditioning and urban beautification have helped to increase Kuwait's locational offerings. (3) Finally, the disadvantage of a small population is being overcome by a liberal policy of immigration and employment openings to citizens of neighboring countries.

Size is a major determinant in the scale of a country's market. A small nation has to stretch its limited domestic market through the expansion of exports internationally and/or through increased trade through some form of regional coordination. A very real element in plans for industrialization or for general development throughout the region is the scale of the Arab market and the degree to which it has been fragmented. Although the Arab population of the area totals over 100 million, the distribution is uneven in that over half of the countries have five million or less and nations such as Jordan, Lebanon and Libya have less than three million. This fact alone limits possibilities for expanding production and marketing except through coordination. Such coordination is likely to involve the reduction or elimination of tariffs, quotas, and government subsidies to favored industries. In the case of regional economic cooperation, those industries which had previously been most highly protected or subsidized would probably suffer most with the initial removal of protective restrictions. Those nations which are largely dependent on foreign trade for marketing and

[5] *Ibid.*, p. 388.

follow low tariff policies will be in an early advantageous position.

In this respect the industries of some small economies which have functioned in an international and export milieu, less protected, would find themselves in a relatively more favorable position within a regional economic framework than those industries which have been sheltered in larger-sized countries where the production has been geared toward domestic sales. Kuwait is the epitome of a small nation which thrives on freedom of trade and international competition. Accordingly, those Kuwaiti industries existing and those planned under the influence of liberal trade would be advantageously positioned to encounter regional competition.[6] It should be kept in mind that a far-reaching regional cooperation among the Arab nations, unlike the pre–European Economic Community situation prevailing in that region where countries were highly industrialized and competitive, would encompass complementary economic aspects and, through planning, could avoid excessive duplication on the regional scale.

This complementarity is conditioned by (1) the relatively early stage of industrialization in most countries; (2) noncompetitive agricultural crops and raw materials (particularly in oil and non-oil producers); and (3) diversity in human resources (varying density of population, size and level of technical skills), climatic conditions, and geographical location, with outlets stretching from the Atlantic to the Indian Oceans, and a dominant position in the Mediterranean basin and inland Africa.

Given the premise that a small nation could function competitively in speciality industrial or agricultural products within a regional framework, would the constraints of limited capital, labor, and natural resources inhibit expansion? Although these are valid considerations, Kuwait is excepted from this implication through its abundance of capital, its diversified utilization of this capital, and a sufficient supply of its basic resource—oil—for a century to come. Through education and immigration its labor supply will probably be numerically sufficient and skilled to meet the developmental needs in expanding production.

---

[6] Nonetheless, not all protected industries need be inefficient. In the final analysis, those industries producing specialty products, the demand for which is relatively inelastic, will hold the most favorable position in the region.

ECONOMIES OF SCALE

Since diversification via industrial development is a prominent objective of the Kuwaiti economy and since markets for industrial output must be found, the concern over economies of scale looms large. Economic integration would influence the development of national industry and could increase the facility with which economies of scale can be realized. Economies of scale, which relate to the operation of individual firms, refer to internal and external economies. The former is concerned with efficiencies reached as a result of an expansion in the size of the firm while the latter deals with economies emanating from a more favorable locational concentration of firms in a geographical area. In industrialized nations the industrial system is interdependent in the sense that the growth of one industry is affected by the growth of other industries and the industrial complex as a whole. This interdependence entails consideration not only of the environment of the industry but of the functioning of and decisions taken in other industries.

The threads of interdependency are woven horizontally and vertically. Hortizontal linkage exists in the same firms which would benefit from external economies resulting from the expansion of the industry in general. Individual Arab states are limited in such horizontal linkage because of size and income. (In the Kuwaiti case, the latter is again not a formidable obstacle.) Once more regionalism would offer an escape. It would also make more feasible the establishment of auxiliary industries to provide by-products and by-services thereby making full use of the original industry. Here a minimum requirement of inputs is needed to warrant the efficient creation of such auxiliary firms regardless of capital needs.

Vertical linkage involves the interdependency of supplying and using industries, but not necessarily in the same state of production. It has been shown that in countries such as Japan and the United States, the intermediate primary production is characterized by a low ratio of interindustry purchases to value-added ("backward linkage"), while a high forward linkage is mirrored in the sales to other sectors.[7] As primary production represents a major portion of industrial output in Kuwait and other Arab countries (yet in

[7] Hollis Chenery among others has contributed studies on this characteristic of industrial development, with particular reference to these countries.

varied industries such as petroleum, natural gas, phosphates, iron ore, manganese, mineral salts, fisheries, and cotton, sugar and other agricultural products) the possibilities of efficient production in such industries would result in the supply of low price inputs to other industries on the same vertical lines.[8] Data should be collected on the regional as well as the separate national basis for computation along both lines to determine alternatives for optimal-use and economies.

In most Arab countries, including Kuwait, a lack of structural balance in the industrial sector, and the sectoral narrowness itself, renders the expansion of existing firms or the creation of new projects difficult. The benefits accruing to the large-sized firm include lower production costs, increased ability for improvement, and greater ease in securing investment for growth. Mass production operates on the principle of high turnover. Because of quantity output, and given correct estimates of price elasticity of demand, lowering prices can be an instrument for insuring capacity operation of a large firm.

The average consumer's elasticity of substitution between consumer goods is relatively low in Kuwait because of the exceptional per capita purchasing power and the diversified tastes acquired through quality imports of long-standing from varied sources. This situation, where the entire population shares such tastes and ability to buy the imports, instead of only a small, economically privileged group, is rare in developing countries. Thus the low-income nations surrounding Kuwait offer a potential market for Kuwaiti domestically produced items.

Another approach to the economies of scale as related to a free trade area and/or closer economic ties on a regional basis is to survey the capital and technical requirement of optimum plant size permitting production at lowest costs in various industries. A Bain-type[9]

[8] According to J. Marcus Fleming, "External Economies and the Doctrine of Balanced Growth," in *The Economics of Underdevelopment*, edited by A. N. Agarwala and S. P. Singh (New York: Oxford University Press, 1963), p. 285, conditions for a vertical transmission of external economies are far more favorable than for a horizontal transmission between industries at the same stage. "There is . . . a much stronger case for joint planning of development of industries at earlier and later stages of the same 'line' of production than of industries at the final stage of different 'lines.'"

[9] Joe S. Bain, "Economies of Scale, Concentration, and the Condition of Entry in Twenty Manufacturing Industries," *American Economic Review*, March, 1954, pp. 15–39.

series of investigations of optimal industrial plant requirements should be carried out by each Arab country on a national basis and within a regional framework. Such an approach would be extremely valuable as Kuwait and its Arab neighbors are still in the early stages of industrialization and there is little if any cost of displacing existing plants to realize external economies. These economies could be reached with the institution of new industries, as mentioned in chapter 4 with the treatment of industrialization in Kuwait. Economies of scale are generally less significant in mining industries than in engineering industries. The desired level of engineering industries has yet to be attained in most Arab countries. Present concern is geared toward industries such as refining, petrochemicals, and natural gas energy-based steel industries which require sizeable production and heavy capitalization.[10]

BALANCED DEVELOPMENT

Balanced development has been a widely accepted goal of developing countries, and the Arab nations offer no exception. But because of implications of size of the national economies and obstacles to economies of scale, difficulties in achieving balanced development have been encountered in the nature of economies, resulting from growth and expansion of markets with interdependence of various sectors of an economy. Distribution of production among major sectors in the Arab countries shows a high disproportionality regardless of national specialization based on indigenous resources whether it be agriculture, mining, or services. The fact that some countries are heavily petroleum-oriented and others lack this resource does not affect or improve the proportionality among the sectors of the national economies, as seen in Table 1.

The Arab countries striving to accelerate their growth rate through industrialization still depend heavily on raw material production whether agricultural or mineral. A sectoral examination shows, for example, that manufacturing industries play a modest role as a

---

[10] A discussion of the future of these industries may be found in United Nations, Economic and Social Council, *International Symposium on Industrial Development, Conference on Industrial Development for the Arab States* (*Kuwait, 1–10 March, 1966*). (Hereafter cited as *Conference on Industrial Development for the Arab States.*)

source of domestic product. Their share in the Arab economies never exceeds 20 per cent and varies between that level and 10 per cent of the domestic product. This ratio remains far below the 20 to 40 per cent share of the manufacturing industries in the domestic production of developed countries.[11] Moreover, the absorptive capacity of such industries in terms of employment opportunities varies widely from one Arab country to another. The labor force engaged in manufacturing ranges from 3 to 11 per cent of the total

TABLE 1

DISTRIBUTION OF PRODUCTION[a] AMONG MAJOR SECTORS IN SELECTED ARAB COUNTRIES

	Percentage of Production in		
	A	M	S
Algeria (1963)	11	50	39
Jordan (1963)	19	14	67
Kuwait (1965)	0.4	69.9[b]	29.7
Lebanon (1964)	18	15	67
Morocco (1964)	28	25	47
Sudan (1963)	52	14	34
Syria (1964)	38	21	41
Tunisia (1964)	25	26	49
U.A.R. (1961)	25	26	49

A = agriculture, forestry, fishing.
M = mining (including petroleum), manufacturing, construction and electricity, gas and water.
S = transport, storage, communications, wholesale and retail trade, banking, insurance, public administration, defense and other services.

SOURCES; U.A.R., Jordan, Iraq, Sudan, and Tunisia: United Nations, *Yearbook of National Accounts Statistics*, 1965; Morocco, The International Bank for Reconstruction and Development, *The Economic Development of Morocco* (Baltimore: Johns Hopkins Press, 1966), p. 314; Lebanon and Syria, *Middle East and African Economist*, January, 1966, p. 9, and February, 1966, p. 23; Kuwait, The Planning Board, *The First Five year Plan for Economic and Social Development, 1966/67—1970/71* (Kuwait: Government Printing Press, December, 1965), p. 60.

a Production is mostly taken to equal GDP at current factor cost except that for Syria and Lebanon production is taken to equal national income.

b The oil industry contributed 61 per cent of the GDP of Kuwait.

force. In comparison, the ratio in advanced economies is from 30 to 40 per cent.[12] These proportions indicate that while manufacturing industries exist in all Arab countries, the variance is great among them as well as between them and advanced nations. A glance at the manufactured goods share of total national exports shows that

[11] *Ibid.*, p. 5. This Conference offers an excellent source for up-to-date information concerning the level of industrial development in the Middle East and North Africa and reflects regional planning in this sector.
[12] *Ibid.*

the ratios vary between 5 per cent in certain Arab states and 40 per cent in others, which are exceptional cases. The two main reasons for this are (1) the concentration on consumer goods as import substitutions and (2) the obvious low volume of production coupled with the inability to compete in the world market.

Such statistics are further evidence of the great variations in the sectoral development of individual Arab economies. Although industrial development has been emphasized vigorously in overall developmental efforts within the national plans, the share of investment allocations directed towards the industrial sector ranges from 10 to 30 per cent of the total projected investment of outlays.[13] Not only does industrialization differ in degree of importance within a national economy, but countries also have specialized industries apart from some light consumer goods for local demand such as tobacco, household utensils, local beverages, and foodstuffs. Most agricultural countries have emphasized textiles, sugar, and other agriculture-based industries while petroleum-rich states are emphasizing industrial expansion in refining, petrochemicals, fertilizers, and the like. As stressed previously, only a few plants manufacturing assembled products of an engineering nature are scattered throughout the Arab world.

The lack of planned regional coordination and the fact that even in the most industrially advanced Arab countries industry, strictly speaking, is still underdeveloped have contributed to an inadequacy in developmental balance. Considering the resources of the Arab countries, room for expansion in industry exists, particularly taking into account the exceedingly low per capita share of industrial income in the majority of the Arab nations, totaling about $25 in 1963, approximately one-twentieth of the per capita share of industrial income in developed countries.[14]

The need to diversify is not confined only to the single-product economy (generally emanating from oil) but to other countries which find themselves heavily dependent upon a single commodity such as cotton in Egypt, Syria, and Sudan. The imbalance of most Arab economies is also due to the fact that in their agricultural activity the productivity is low and of a labor-using type, especially in areas where capital is scarce. Agricultural activities are not income-generating in comparison with modern industrial activities

[13] *Ibid.*, p. 6.
[14] *Ibid.*, p. 5.

and advanced agriculture in developed countries. The question is more than correcting sectoral proportions to achieve a balanced economy; it involves the issue of underdevelopment in the various sectors themselves.

A study of the distribution of the labor force in the Arab nations of Algeria, Iraq, Jordan, Syria, and the U.A.R. shows that agriculture, while contributing over one-half of the national product, employs about 85 per cent of the labor force. In other words, the largest single sector in these economies is the least productive.[15] The other side of the coin, however, is exhibited in countries such as Kuwait and Saudi Arabia where the oil sector, responsible for more than half the national product, can employ directly only 8,000 and about 10,000 respectively, or 1.6 per cent and 0.25 per cent.[16] The petroleum industry in its three stages of exploration, drilling, and production is capital-intensive and is itself limited in the number of total skilled and unskilled workers which it can employ. Any effort to reduce the cost of output will be made through increasing automation. Hence, expanding gainful employment in other areas must be considered a primary objective in the planning policies of the oil-dominant economies.

To those Arab states which are not substantial producers of oil, the position of the large-scale exporters among them can appear most desirable. This feeling is reinforced since many of the oil "haves," such as Kuwait, Libya, Saudi Arabia, Qatar, and the tiny Trucial States, are experiencing a condition of rapid capital accumulation and even capital surplus.[17] Nonetheless, these countries generally find themselves suffering from acute dependence on a single product with all the attendant problems. As primary commodity producers the economies of the petroleum-rich states are extremely sensitive to price fluctuations, depletion, competition

[15] Some of the Arab countries remain net importers of foodstuffs despite the preponderant role of agriculture in the region. In the United States, for example, agriculture is a surplus sector while it employs a minor portion of the labor force.
[16] The population of Saudi Arabia is given variously from three to six million. This figure was based upon a total population of four million.
[17] It is noteworthy that, according to United Nations projections, the total capital deficit for non-oil producing Arab countries for the decade 1960–70 was roughly estimated at $3.2 billion while the total capital surplus of Arab oil producers was figured to reach $5.3 billion for the same period. *Document Submitted by the Secretary-General, A/4121, June 15, 1959,* United Nations General Assembly, Fourteenth Session, in *Middle East Journal,* Summer, 1959, pp. 310–11.

from other oil producers and forms of energy, and the development of new sources of energy.

REGIONAL SECTORAL PLANNING

Balanced development on a regional basis requires coordination in sectoral planning and the safeguarding of capital movements. Although most of the limited progress achieved to date in the efforts towards greater economic cooperation in the Arab world occurred in the mobility of agricultural commodities, emphasis is lacking to achieve a degree of regional sufficiency in this sector. As a result of both the population growth and adverse climatic conditions, agricultural imports, specifically of foodstuffs, have increased at a more rapid rate than agricultural exports. Moreover, there has been a persistent deficit in the regional per capita caloric intake, which is well below the 2,400 minimum daily calories standard.

In specific cases, agricultural progress has been of a very limited nature. In the Arabian peninsula states, imports have more than doubled from non-regional sources during the period 1957–64. Yet the Arab world has a problem of surpluses in certain products. So far most of the regional planning has centered upon a reduction or abolition of tariffs. This has not proven an adequate answer to the needs of coordinated production in the area, particularly if it is recalled that many products in this sector previously had no substantial trade obstacles or were subject only to negligible tariffs. Continued increases in tariff cuts did not materially alter this picture. Planning for further improvements in regional agriculture might require measures of a more positive nature. The idea of establishing a common fund, to which national treasuries could contribute, to pay for price and export subsidies and to coordinate production in a way to encourage subregional comparative advantage and production specialization would be a possible step. Already the European Common Market has approved a scheme of this sort to improve its agricultural sector.

In the Arab world problems of shortages and surpluses in agriculture could be eased by providing adequate storage and creating better transport facilities, which in many areas leave much to be desired. Also, establishing uniform quality and market packaging could help to more evenly balance regional supply and demand. One cannot overestimate the importance of the agricultural sector to the development of the Arab world, not only in terms of employment but as a foreign exchange saver and earner. It is certain that that portion of the Arab world will never again hold the title "bread basket of the world," but it can and should furnish its own basic requirements in addition to growing specialty export crops.

Equally pressing is the necessity for concentrated and positive planning for industrial coordination on a regional basis. Three factors involved here are (1) the need to accelerate the rate of industrial development, (2) the scarcity of technical resources and specialists, and (3) market limitations which set severe limits to large-scale production.[18]

Industrial development is a dynamic process which requires constant designing, redesigning, and planning on a scientific basis. Such planning is especially important to developing areas as modern industry requires a higher amount of fixed cost than, for example, agriculture. Highly automated production can be supported only at or near capacity level, otherwise the fixed cost per unit becomes excessively high. These conditions make the availability of markets a near prerequisite for sustained industrialization. Let us take note of the more prominently discussed fields for industrial development in the region.

The manufacture of textiles still has considerable room for expansion on a regional scale. While the Arab world is a major producer and exporter of cotton, its total annual production of cotton textiles comes to only half the requirements for the area. Although it is not a prerequisite that textile industries be physically located near the raw material source, there should be a rational system based on nearness to large markets and labor supply governing the location of the industry in nonproducing countries.

In the steel industry, which is so far of an extremely modest nature yet of growing importance regionally, coordination among the various states could better exploit the available iron ore supplies through utilization of the area's abundant natural gas and petroleum resources. Recent estimates have placed iron and steel production in the Arab countries to reach a total of 7.5 million tons annually during the next decade.[19] It can be questioned whether investment

---

[18] *Conference on Industrial Development for the Arab States,* p. 38.
[19] *Ibid.,* p. 10.

in this industry throughout the region is truly economic as a world-wide surplus is dumping growing tonnage on export markets. Hence small producers and newcomers will find competition stiff.

Petrochemicals may prove a key industry in the Middle East and North Africa. The estimate was given earlier in this study that the amount of natural gas being flared off in production in the Gulf alone could furnish about 20 million tons of nitrogen compound a year. Algeria, Iraq, Kuwait, Libya, Saudi Arabia, and the United Arab Republic all are producers of the primary commodities—natural gas and crude oil—and most have embarked on ambitious industrial programs utilizing these resources. Before excessive duplication and possible fragmentation of effort can take place, coordinated planning must be quickly carried out. Fertilizers are needed within the region to raise its agricultural productivity, and an immense export market could be developed. Other by-products of the petroleum industry are so numerous as to be almost countless. Among the more important are synthetic fibers, plastics, and pharmaceutical products. Such a wide range of products should permit ample opportunity for specialization. Semi-finished products could be transported from supply sources to processing centers near large markets.

Through coordination the Arab states can become an extremely valuable market not only to the regionally produced industrial commodities but to the outside world as well. To this end investment in industry should be encouraged, and the creation of a collective Arab institution for guaranteeing Arab and foreign capital investment would quicken the pace of industrialization and facilitate balanced development. For a capital-surplus country such as Kuwait an agency of this type would offer the needed security to stimulate private investment throughout the region.

Since all Arab states fall into the category of developing economies, a final résumé of the benefits accruing to a developing area through economic coordination might prove helpful. First, the formation of an integrated area could bring about an improvement or at least halt the deterioration in the area's commodity terms of trade. Such improvement could be attributed to two causes: (1) the reduction of exports from the integrated region of a commodity due to greater interregional mobility, and (2) the decline in the demand for nonmember country imports as the possibilities for production within the area increase. Second, coordination might reduce fluctuation in export earnings because of the existence of a wider range of commodities possible in a larger economic unit and because the prices of various commodities tend to function independently. In addition, the formation of a larger economic unit could lead to a better bargaining position in the international market for a product, as the region's share of the total world output would be much greater than that of the individual country's. In the Arab states, the two most obvious primary commodities which could benefit from regional coordination are oil and cotton. Naturally this argument has its limitations as raw materials and their substitutes are too widely located about the globe to allow one region near monopolistic control. Nonetheless, it may be generally assumed that the larger the economic unit the stronger is its market position.

Besides the clear benefits of the economies of scale, regional cooperation could encourage healthy competition among the member states, with marginal operations compelled to either reduce costs or fall behind, thus reallocating resources from less to more efficient use and reducing the strength of original small unit monopolies which thrived on tariff protection. Not only could existing resources be better utilized but productive factors of entrepreneurial ability and technological advance would be enhanced by the wider scope of economic activities. It should be pointed out that economic coordination could be considered a method of rapid diversification, the lack of which has long plagued developmental efforts in the respective countries. Finally, as the vast majority of the developing nations suffer from capital shortage, a coordinated unit could simultaneously attract external investment because of its larger base and internal investment through greater mobility of capital resources. It should be emphasized that capital is but one factor of production, albeit an important one, which is unevenly distributed. Economic integration could lead to the exchange and better utilization of national specialties in entrepreneurial ability and technical skills as well.

Kuwait's position within collective efforts for regionalism has been advanced under the auspices of the Arab League, although Kuwait did not become a full member until its complete independence in 1961. Second, regardless of its dependent status, Kuwait participated in a number of coordinated economic ventures prior to independence. Finally, Kuwait's economic policy of extending public and private investments has complemented and supported regional collective measures.

COLLECTIVE MEASURES

Plans for coordination by the Economic Council of the Arab League have proceeded slowly in its sixteen years of existence since its establishment in 1950.[20] Three years after its inception, the Council formulated two major provisions for the mobility of goods and capital. These were (1) the Convention for Facilitating Trade Exchange and Regulating Transit Trade between States of the Arab League and (2) Settlement of Payments of Current Transactions and the Transfer of Capital.[21]

Briefly, the first convention provided for a 25 per cent tariff reduction on certain industrial imports between Arab states, full exemption from customs and duties for agricultural products and natural resources of Arab origin, the elimination of discriminatory excise duties on agricultural and industrial imports, preferential treatment concerning import and export permits among the Arab countries, and facilitating transit among them. In subsequent agreements, a gradual liberalization of trade exchange was carried out, particularly through lowering the percentage tariff reduction on industrial imports among the Arab states.[22]

The concurrent convention concerns the transfer of capital and settlement of payments allowed for permission to transfer capital

[20] The Arab League was created in 1945 to assist in the realization of Arab aspirations for political independence and economic progress. At that time various special committees were set up to deal with health, legal affairs, social problems, economic matters, and culture. The Economic Committee was to study commerical relations, customs and currency, and industrial and agricultural development. The bulky system of committees was streamlined and in 1950 the Economic Council was established, to be composed of the ministers of economic affairs of all the contracting states. It was to function in cooperation with the existing committees. Of importance was the stipulation that only a simple majority was needed, in contrast to the Arab League Council's requirement of unanimity on important questions.

[21] For the complete text see "Convention for Facilitating Trade Exchange and Regulating Transit Trade between States of the Arab League," *Basic Documents of the League of Arab States* (New York: Arab Information Center, 1955), pp. 27–35.

[22] Ragaei El Mallakh, "Trends toward Economic Unity in the Arab Middle East," in *The Arab Nation: Paths and Obstacles to Fulfillment*, edited by William Sands (Washington, D. C.: The Middle East Institute, 1961), pp. 93–107. This chapter gives further study of the ensuing modifications.

among Arab member countries within the limits of regulations for the safeguarding of capital. Again, the Economic Council introduced certain amendments such as the elimination of double taxation on transferred capital.[23]

The Economic Council has advanced other agreements concerning the unification of separate Arab policies toward petroleum affairs, tourism, and the classification of tariffs. In oil affairs, the Council adopted the recommendations of the Petroleum Committee which arranged for a system of consultation and interchange of views among members in the fields of conservation, export, and production of petroleum and its products. Under the Council's auspices the Arab Petroleum Congress was initiated, with its annual meeting commencing as early as 1959 in Cairo.[24] The Congresses are attended by formal representatives from the Arab countries and oil companies operating in the Arab world as well as by observer-delegates from the United States, Canada, Mexico, the Soviet Union, India, Indonesia, Venezuela, Rumania, and Yugoslavia, among others. Besides the discussion on the full spectrum of the petroleum industry, the Congresses have recommended fuller participation of the Arab countries within the industry, measures to insure the rights of the Arabs, and the advancement and support of stable relations between the companies and the host governments. Attention has been directed toward raising the level of technical institutes. Moreover, the Congresses have urged both the governments and the oil companies to follow tighter natural-gas conservation measures either by reinjection into reservoirs for future use or by fuller utilization. In general, this organization has focused attention upon the level of prices for crude oil, royalties and their use, general oil economics, legislation, labor affairs, and marketing, with a generous portion devoted to technical studies on oil extraction, petrochemicals, and other scientific research. The Sixth Arab Petroleum Congress, held early in 1967, was to study (1) prorationing and its effect

[23] It is of interest to note that resolutions and recommendations of the Council continue along the same general line, that is, belief in the necessity for expanded trade exchanges and cooperation. In the Eleventh Session held in December, 1965, further recommendations were made for drawing up a draft proposal for a unified petroleum law for the Arab nations, a draft agreement for an Arab Petroleum Company, and the establishment of an Arab Petroleum Research Institute. *Middle East Economic Survey*, January 14, 1966, Supplement, pp. 1–4.

[24] The Arab Petroleum Congress is discussed early in chapter 2 as one of the multilateral groupings of petroleum producers to which Kuwait belongs.

on price levels, (2) the technical methods for prorationing of oil production, and (3) the petrochemical industry and methods for its development within the region.

The goal of economic development throughout the Arab world has led to planning for an Arab development bank. In 1959 this agency, the Arab Financial Institution for Economic Development, was officially born when pledges for subscriptions to 75 per cent of the original capital of 20 million Egyptian pounds had been made. It was agreed that membership could be expanded and was open to non-League members.[25] One of the first non-League countries to indicate willingness to join was Kuwait, which at that time was not yet independent. The objectives of the Institution included assistance through loans in the financing of projects of governments, business firms, and/or individuals contributing to the economic development of the member countries and the promotion of investment of capital (private, foreign, and domestic), with the goal of insuring efficient utilization of economic potentialities in the members' economies. The preparation of technical studies on the projects to be supported was to be an additional function of the Institution.

One of the first collective economic measures to support a specific project was adopted in 1956 when representatives of the Arab states approved the agreement to establish the Joint Arab Potash Company, with an initial capitalization set at 4.5 million Jordanian dinars, for the commercial exploitation of the Dead Sea salts. Originally recommended in 1957 by the Economic Council, approval came four years later for the creation of the Arab Oil Tankers Company to transport oil from Middle Eastern producing centers to the consumption areas in Europe and the Eastern hemisphere. Its capital was set at 35 million Egyptian pounds. In 1960 the Oil Committee of the Economic Council approved the proposed plans for an Arab-owned pipeline linking Iraq, Kuwait, and Saudi Arabia with the Mediterranean Sea.

As early as 1959 the Economic Council made recommendations for a unified Arab Navigation Company and an Arab airline. Rather complete administrative plans were approved in 1962 for the navigation company, providing a capitalization of 5.3 million Egyptian pounds with the original shares distributed among the

---

[25] For complete details see M. F. El Khatib, *The Arab Financial Institution for Economic Development* (New York: Arab Information Center, 1957).

various Arab nations. In 1961 a final draft for the Arab Aviation Company agreement stipulated a capital of about 2.8 million Egyptian pounds, with operations to begin on a modest schedule. Another plan put forward was for an Arab Oil Company to which Iraq, Kuwait, Saudi Arabia, Syria, and the United Arab Republic, all oil producers in varying degrees, were to subscribe 50 million pounds and the other Arab states were invited to participate in raising an additional 50 million for capitalization. The Arab Oil Company was envisaged as a fully integrated firm, engaging in all oil operations from lifting to refining and even to final marketing on the local level. It was agreed that such a company would mesh with the national firms existing in individual Arab countries.

Another instrument to be used in forging greater economic cooperation came with the establishment of the Arab Council for Economic Unity by the Economic Council. The primary objective of the organization is to assist in the drive toward economic integration by providing freedom of movement to individuals with reference to employment, residence, and rights of property and to eliminate any discrimination in transit trade relating to kind of goods or nationality. Coordination of investment policies, facilitation of the exchange of Arab products, and freedom in the exercise of economic activity are the principal means by which the Council for Economic Unity hopes to realize its goals. Planning has advanced to the stage of a common market for the Arab world as designed by this Council's agreement, to which five countries have adhered as signatories— Iraq, Jordan, Syria, United Arab Republic, and Kuwait, with the latter's National Assembly voting to delay action. The implications of such an economic community for Kuwait and other Arab nations will be discussed in detail later in the chapter.

Besides the coordination under the auspices of the Arab League and its numerous agencies, subregional planning efforts for integration are being exerted. In the Maghreb, that is, North Africa, the Ministers of Economic Affairs of Libya, Tunisia, Algeria, and Morocco have been consulting regularly to strengthen the four-nation cooperation, stressing the place of agriculture and the possibility of joint marketing procedures. Approval was reached for the establishment of an industrial research center with financing by equal contribution. Similarly, transport and communications to connect the North Africa states are receiving regional attention, including plans to forge a road network stretching westward from the Gulf to the Atlantic, thereby linking the Arab world from east to west.[26] Yet the economic aspects of Maghreb unity remain in the blueprint stage only, with no plan of any real importance realized.

THE IMPLEMENTATION GAP

Despite an abundance of collective economic measures, implementation lags far behind planning. Such planning for Arab economic integration has placed emphasis on the negative aspects— removing trade barriers and obstacles to factoral movements—but bureaucratic and administrative restrictions have remained, thereby largely negating the impact of mobility reforms. The Arab payments convention, moreover, was never fully implemented, thus partially retarding the effect of the liberalization of trade. Accordingly trade among the Arab states did not expand to its potentially high level. Inter-Arab exports for the period 1951–60 among Egypt, Iraq, Jordan, Lebanon, Saudi Arabia, and Syria increased from 8.3 per cent of their total exports to 17.4 per cent, while the proportion of inter-Arab imports for the same years grew only from 7 per cent to 8.5 per cent of their total.[27] These figures show not only the minor change in inter-Arab trade but also that the most pronounced impact of the trade convention was in the agricultural sector, as seen in the rise in exports (which are mostly agricultural commodities in the developing areas as a whole) as compared to the share of imports (manufactured commodities which generally are supplied from advanced countries). Yet another hindrance to attaining a greater degree of exchange has been the short duration of both bilateral and multilateral trade arrangements, usually for only one year, which caused uncertainty and lack of continuity.

The implementation gap is best illustrated in the fact that most of the schemes for economic integration remain in the blueprint stage. With the exception of the Arab Potash Company,[28] a

[26] Intra-Bank, *Monthly Bulletin*, April, 1966, p. 2.

[27] Muhammad A. Diab, *Inter-Arab Economic Cooperation 1951–1960* (Beirut: Economic Research Institute, American University of Beirut, 1963), p. 64.

[28] An additional impetus in the development of the Arab Potash Company was the decision by the Kuwait Fund for Arab Economic Development to assist in financing the project. Further financial assistance is being sought from the International Bank for Reconstruction and Development.

relatively modest undertaking, there are no actual operations to date of the Arab Financial Institution for Economic Development, the Arab Navigation Company, the Arab Oil Company, the Arab-owned pipeline, and the Arab Oil Tankers Company. The Arab Common Market is having growing pains as well. In 1966, the Permanent Economic Committe of the Arab Council for Economic Unity, noting the low level of inter-Arab trade, stressed that the bilateral quotas and exchange arrangements between the various member states of the League do not always comply with the Arab Common Market stipulations.[29]

There has been a lack of awareness that serious economic integration in any form is a dual-prolonged process of abolishing discrimination barriers among a group of states and the deliberate introduction of coordination with the objective of establishing a level of economic cooperation whereby the optimal development and functioning of the total economy is achieved. The essence of such a policy is the combination of the negative element involved, that is, the elimination of tariffs, exchange controls, and administrative obstacles to economic freedom, and the positive aspect of instituting a coordination program, particularly in the agricultural and industrial sectors. Thus, the goal is not only to eliminate obstacles but to create incentives for development.[30]

Economic integration as such should not be motivated solely by the drive for self-sufficiency but should encourage and stimulate growth of agriculture and industry on a more rational basis than can be affected on the nation-state level. It should also be geared to increasing the gains from trade, whether in trade-creation by

[29] Apparently the gap between plans for economic integration and implementation is a characteristic of developing areas and their planning processes. For the experience of one region in Latin America see John W. Crow, "Economic Integration in Central America," *Finance and Development* (Quarterly Publication of the International Monetary Fund and the International Bank for Reconstruction and Development, Washington, D.C.), March, 1966, pp. 58–66.

[30] Among the publications on economic integration the following books and articles are of interest: R. L. Allen, "Integration in Less Developed Areas," *Kyklos*, 14, 3 (1961): 315–34; Bela Belassa, *The Theory of Economic Integration* (Homewood, Ill.: Richard D. Irwin, Inc., 1961); Bela Belassa, "Towards a Theory of Economic Integration," *Kyklos*, 14, 1 (1961): 1–15; James E. Meade, *Problems of Economic Union* (Chicago: University of Chicago Press, 1953); R. F. Mikesell *Intra-Regional Trade and Economic Development* (Washington, D.C., 1958); Gunnar Myrdal, *International Economy* (New York: Harper, 1956); Jan Timbergen, *International Economic Integration* (Amsterdam: Elsevier, 1954).

replacing high-cost producers within the integrated region by low-cost producers and thus increasing the benefits of division of labor with the shift of resources into more efficient production, or by trade-diversion, which would lead to greater interregional trade, replacing trade between integrated members and nonmembers. The ramifications of trade-diversion and creation as studied earlier in this chapter are potentially both beneficial and adverse depending upon the factors of employment and balance of payments. On the whole, the structuring of integrated regions should assist in accelerating development through the provision of benefits gained from intensified competition. Compartmentalization of industry, fragmentation of resources, and immobility of factors of production could be either avoided or counteracted through economic integration. This countervailing stance requires planning and could not be left to accident or to *ad hoc* measures.

Economic integration need not be visualized as "all or nothing". Various Arab attempts at coordination have suffered from this attitude. The tendency is to think in terms of complete economic unity rather than of a gradual process of closer coordination and cooperation. The range extends from the formation of a free trade area to total economic integration. The least intricate designs for coordination are those advocating a free trade area and a customs union, the core of both being trade. In each form quantitative restrictions and tariffs against each other in connection with commodity movements are abolished although in the free trade area member states retain their respective restrictions and tariffs vis-à-vis nonmembers. A common tariff policy is adopted when integration in the nature of a customs union is achieved. The next and more sweeping type of integration is that of a common market which shares with the customs union a common tariff against nonparticipating nations and a lack of interregional tariffs and trade restrictions but embodies as well the abolition of discriminatory and restrictive measures against factoral mobility among the members. The fourth form of integration, the economic union, surpasses the scope of the common market through the partial adoption of a unified and multilateral economic policy. Total economic integration is the ultimate evolution of the preceding positions. It involves not only trade and factoral coordination but unifies monetary, fiscal, countercyclical, and socioeconomic measures while requiring a regional decision-making mechanism and administrative system to implement the binding policies throughout the entire economic unit.[31]

While the free trade area appears an uncomplicated and relatively easily instituted system, it is limited in its effectiveness. Without a common tariff policy, nonmember country exports can enter through the lowest tariff nation and from there filter throughout the area. This bears particularly upon the Kuwaiti situation where the lowest tariffs and most liberal trade policies in the Arab world are to be found. Such a system is purely negative in that it concerns itself with removing existing trade barriers within the region. With a customs union, common market, economic union, and total economic integration positive action begins with the formulation of a unified tariff policy, economic coordination, and the final step towards supranational economic planning. Nonetheless, what appears clear and concise in theory often fails to function with such clarity in reality. The five stages of economic integration defined and discussed here need not necessarily follow in order but can overlap and bypass each other without a precise delineation. Noneconomic factors obviously enter into either the acceleration or retardation of the economic coordination and cooperation processes. In the Arab Middle East there has been wide-scale overlapping of plans. Since 1960 a common market has been discussed, but until 1965 no action was taken. Even today only four countries have proceeded to enforce the agreement for such an economic grouping.

There have been three principal causes for the implementation gap. First is the lack of coordination between regional and national plans and among the regional plans themselves. Second, there is a shortage of capital caused by either indigenous national scarcity in some cases or in others by the flight out of the area, due in large measure to immediate pre- and post-independence instabilities. Third, is the existence, as in most developing areas, of what has been described as a confusion between flexible planning and having a plan or series of plans.

> Those who equate a development plan with development planning—and they are many—confuse what should be a product of the planning process with the process itself. A plan can play an important part in the planning process when it makes explicit the basis and rationale for

[31] See Belassa, *Theory of Economic Integration*, p. 2.

planning policies and measures. But if a plan is prepared before the process has begun in earnest or is unable itself to generate the process, it is likely to have little significance for development.[32]

The conceptual problems facing economic coordination in the Arab Middle East include the lack of awareness that serious economic integration must include positive features as well as the negative aspect of removing restrictions and discriminatory measures, particularly in trade. Likewise there has been a tendency to either stand aside from concrete though seemingly small attempts at coordination in the economic sphere or to support overly ambitious plans which envisage a high level of integration and would prove difficult to implement among any grouping of nations, developed and developing alike.

In the final assessment of the collective measures advanced and the degree to which they have been implemented, it is of the utmost importance to point out the following elements in planning for economic coordination in the Arab world: (1) There is an abundance of plans, largely concentrated on the abolition or reduction of tariffs, the results of which have been limited. (2) Implementation of integration projects has not kept pace with planning. (3) Existing plans must be constantly scrutinized in order that their applicability remains valid. (4) Economic integration is not inevitable. The fact that the Arab world shares a common culture, history, and language is no assurance that coordination is predestined. Yet the prospects for economic cooperation are good because of these similarities in background and the complementary potential in human and natural resources. What is lacking is a determined and well-designed multilateral effort to effect this end.

BILATERALISM

Apart from the multilateral arrangements, usually under the guiding hand of the Arab League, Kuwait has concluded bilateral agreements which have regional implications. The following selected examples indicate the increasing role of bilateralism. In 1966 a sweeping agreement was concluded between Kuwait and

[32] Albert Waterston, "A Hard Look at Development Planning," *Finance and Development*, June, 1966, p. 86. This confusion of which Waterston speaks extends to regional and national planning alike.

the United Arab Republic which encourages capital movement and investments between the two countries. Among the more important terms to be implemented through a joint-committee type of organization are: (1) Kuwaiti national banks under gaurantee from both governments are to provide the Central Bank of Egypt with some $42 million (at 6 per cent repayable over ten years). This facet of the agreement will be discussed further in the chapter concerning Kuwait's foreign aid programs. (2) The Kuwait Company for Foreign Trade, Contracts and Investments[33] and the Kuwait Fund for Arab Economic Development will participate in various projects in the U.A.R., specifically in the establishment of a complex for phosphates production and a shipbuilding yard and in the realization of a land reclamation project. Feasibility studies will determine the eventual degree of Kuwaiti participation. (3) Provision is made for the creation of a jointly owned contracting and construction company to operate in Africa and the Middle East. (4) Bilateral cooperation will be established in civil aviation and shipping, and technical advisory offices will be set up to facilitate tourism and trade exchanges. (5) Perhaps of greater potential impact is the section of the agreement which arranges for investigation of the possible coordination of Kuwaiti production of liquid ammonia and the U.A.R. project for the manufacture of nitrogenous fertilizers. The implementation of this stipulation would be the first coordination in this field throughout the Arab world and offers the opportunity to study the budding petrochemical industry with an eye towards controlling duplication. (6) Finally, all investments resulting from this agreement are to be guaranteed against nationalization.[34]

A second cooperative measure between Kuwait and the U.A.R. involves the establishment of an Arab Printing and Publishing Organization, capitalized at $7 million, to be located in the newly created Port Said free zone.[35] Its purpose is to serve as a facility

[33] The Kuwait Company for Foreign Trade, Contracts and Investments was formed early in 1965 with a capital of $56 million of which 80 per cent was subscribed by the Kuwaiti government and the remaining 20 per cent by private Kuwaiti investors.

[34] At the same time it was agreed that the most-favored-nation treatment would be extended to Kuwaiti investments which have been affected by nationalization in the United Arab Republic. *Middle East Economic Survey*, February 4, 1966, pp. 2–3.

[35] The Port Said free zone is exempt from the nationalization laws of the U.A.R., and businesses located there will not be affected by United Arab Republic fiscal laws either at present or in the future.

through which African and Arab authors can publish their works, books can be translated into and from Arabic, and the number of volumes of school and university textbooks available for Africa and the Middle East can be increased.

In May, 1966, Kuwait ratified the economic cooperation agreement it had concluded with Iraq in October, 1964. In this accord exemptions are sought from customs duties and internal tax on all agricultural goods, industrial, animal, and natural resources products. The bilateral arrangement aims at encouragement of the movement of capital and investments between the two nations and the establishment of joint investment enterprises. Investors would eventually be allowed to transfer profits, interest, capital compensation, and liquidation funds in the same currency in which the invested capital was imported. Iraq and Kuwait further agreed to facilitate freedom in travel, entry of passenger and cargo vehicles, residence, work, and employment and business ventures in which the respective citizens participate. Some five permanent committees are to be set up to implement the various sections of the agreement. Worthy of note is a committee for the coordination of industrial and petroleum projects.[36] Thus Kuwait has taken positive steps for coordination of petrochemicals with two of its major Arab neighbors, Iraq and the United Arab Republic, which could offer sharp competition in petroleum-based industries, specifically fertilizers, but could also offer a potential market for these Kuwaiti products.

As Kuwait exhibits the characteristics of a highly export-oriented economy, the three major lines along which expansion could be made are (1) expanded traditional exports of primary products, in this case, oil, (2) substitution of imports with domestic production, and (3) development of home production to generate new exports of manufactured goods. The first alternative has limited applicability to Kuwait and the region in general as Kuwaiti oil is marketed largely in Europe and Japan and the marketing channels within the oil industry are not flexible. Implementation of the second alternative is likewise curtailed by the narrowness of the Kuwaiti market and its accessibility to foreign trade on a world wide basis. Finally, the third avenue might offer the brightest prospects for expansion of the export-directed economy through the development

---

[36] *Al-Kuwait Al-Youm*, May 29, 1966.

of petrochemical fertilizers and other petroleum-based industrial activities. It is within this sphere that bilateral agreements could have a marked impact regionally.

It should be pointed out, however, that bilateralism as seen in the Kuwaiti-United Arab Republic and Iraqi-Kuwaiti accords overlaps the collective measures of the Arab League. Moreover, Kuwait has shown a more active interest in securing safe capital movement and investment guarantees in its bilateral arrangements, while the collective measures primarily have stressed and achieved greater success in the application of freer movement of trade, particularly in the agricultural sector. Had implementation of the multilateral plans kept abreast of the initiation of such schemes, then bilateralism would have become redundant in most cases. In conclusion, while Kuwait's bilateral agreements seem able to assume a key role in both domestic and regional economic development, the level of final implementation of these accords will determine the degree to which such potential will be fulfilled. It is yet too early to evaluate the results of the bilateral efforts.

REGIONALISM AND TRADE

With the economy of Kuwait highly dependent on foreign trade, a study of the country's commercial ties with the rest of the Arab world may be of value in assessing the degree of regional cooperation. Both the relatively small size of the domestic market and the low level of import duties coupled with an exceptionally high per capita income contribute to the rapid rise in Kuwaiti imports. While presently Kuwait enjoys the highest per capita level of imports in the world, its non-oil exports are low. Such a relationship reflects an unfavorable balance of trade if oil is not included in the trade figures. Since oil is practically excluded from regional exchange and is exported mostly to Europe and Japan, any discussion of regional implications of trade must confine itself to trade in other commodities.

It is obvious from the percentages in Table 2 that the Arab world is but a minor source for Kuwaiti imports. Europe has been the traditional supplier with both the Western Hemisphere, that is, the United States, and Asia, primarily Japan, steadily increasing their shares at the expense of the European region. In 1965 the

United States became the largest single source of Kuwaiti imports.[37]

Turning to Kuwaiti imports from Arab countries, we find that they play only a small role in this trade sector, representing an average of 6.8 per cent of the total over the period 1960–65. Among the Arab exporters to Kuwait, Lebanon ranks first; its share has been consistently higher than one-third of the total. Iraq, Syria, the United Arab Republic, and Jordan follow in that order. Imports from these five states represent over 90 per cent of the total imports to Kuwait from the Arab world. Lebanese exports are mainly in the form of foodstuffs, specifically fruits and vegetables. Iraq is a

TABLE 2

REGIONAL SUMMARY OF KUWAITI IMPORTS, 1960–65

Year, Total Value (In Million Dollars)	Percentage of Total Kuwaiti Imports				
	Europe	Western Hemisphere	Asia[a]	Arab World	Africa[a]
1960 (242.2)	53.4	19.8	18.4	7.6	0.8
1961 (248.9)	51.5	21.7	20.0	6.3	0.5
1962 (285.3)	50.6	23.5	18.4	6.4	1.1
1963 (323.7)	49.2	23.0	20.0	7.0	0.8
1964 (323.1)	49.4	18.2	25.3	6.5	0.6
1965 (477.2)	46.5	22.0	23.5	7.0	1.0

SOURCES: 1960–63, *Survey of Kuwait*, p. 207; 1964, Kuwait Currency Board, *Fifth Annual Report for the Year ended 31st March 1966*, (Kuwait: Government Printing Press, 1966), pp. 21–22; 1965. The Planning Board, *Yearly Summary of Foreign Trade Statistics 1965*, pp. 1–5.

[a] Excluding Arab countries.

principal supplier of cement (over one-third of the total value of Iraqi exports to Kuwait), barley (20 per cent of the total value), and livestock. Syrian exports are largely of textile fabrics, accounting for 42 per cent of the total value of Syrian exports to Kuwait, and foodstuffs generally vegetables, fruit, and barley. Publications are

---

[37] Affluence and freedom of trade have combined to bring an unprecedented diversity of products to Kuwait—Japan's Sony electronic items, Italian knits, French perfumes, and from the United States, Parker pens and frozen Sara Lee coffee cakes. Most of the products retail at a lower price than in the country of origin because of the low tax policy of Kuwait and competition in the marketplace.

the largest single item from the U.A.R., amounting to almost 20 per cent in 1963 of that country's export trade with Kuwait, followed by cement, canned foods, tires and movie films. Vegetables and fruits make up two-thirds of Jordanian exports while dairy products account for most of the remainder. Saudi Arabia and other peninsula states are insignificant sources of Kuwaiti imports, as seen in Table 3.

TABLE 3

SHARE OF INDIVIDUAL COUNTRIES IN TOTAL ARAB IMPORTS TO KUWAIT, 1960–65

Year, Total Value (In Million Dollars)	Percentage of Total Arab Imports to Kuwait						
	Lebanon	Iraq	Syria	U.A.R.	Jordan	Saudi Arabia	Others[a]
1960 (18.5)	34.4	15.0	18.5	16.5	5.3	0.4	9.9
1961 (15.65)	44.3	13.5	15.3	12.7	9.2	1.6	3.6
1962 (18.15)	43.0	14.7	17.3	9.6	13.0	0.4	2.0
1963 (22.76)	40.5	18.8	15.0	10.0	10.2	0.6	4.9
1964 (21.11)	40.2	17.1	15.8	9.1	13.4	0.07	4.3
1965 (22.69)	41.7	17.9	16.3	6.4	14.3	0.7	2.7

SOURCES: 1960–63, *Survey of Kuwait*, p. 207; 1964, *Kuwait Chamber of Commerce and Industry Bulletin*, March, 1965, pp. 15–18; 1965, *Yearly Summary of Foreign Trade Statistics 1965*, p. 1.

a Includes all other Arab countries in Asia and Africa.

An examination of Kuwaiti non-oil exports reveals that more than half the total value is channeled into the Arab world. This proportion has remained relatively stable. Table 4 indicates the regional shares in Kuwait's exports.

In the trade among the Arab countries, Kuwait's immediate neighbors, Saudi Arabia and Iraq, consistently account for approximately two-thirds of total exports. Saudi Arabia has kept the leading position as the main importer of Kuwaiti non-oil exports, and Iraq remains second, although its share has shown a marked decline since 1964.[38] Lebanon and Jordan follow as buyers of Kuwaiti

[38] Iraq has kept its second ranking as a market for Kuwait except in 1962 when it imported only 5.3 per cent of the total value of Kuwaiti exports. This can be explained by the strained political relations between the two countries caused by the Iraqi government's behavior under Abdel Kerim Kassem.

exports, and the small Trucial states and Arabian countries such
as Oman, Qatar, and Bahrain when massed together represent a
substantial market, reaching as high as 25 per cent of total exports.
The other Arab nations, Sudan, Syria, the U.A.R., and North
African countries, share but little in the Kuwaiti export picture,
as is evident in Table 5.

TABLE 4

REGIONAL SUMMARY OF KUWAITI NON-OIL EXPORTS, 1960–65

Year, Total Value (In Million Dollars)	Percentage of Total Kuwaiti Non-Oil Exports				
	Europe	Western Hemisphere	Asia[a]	Arab World	Africa[a]
1960 (21.68)	1.2	0.4	41.5	56.8	0.2
1961 (23.84)	7.0	1.2	44.6	47.0	0.2
1962 (22.28)	5.1	2.7	27.6	64.1	0.5
1963 (28.86)	3.9	1.0	28.1	66.9	0.1
1964 (33.04)	8.6	1.7	20.4	68.4	0.9
1965 (39.48)	6.0	5.0	34.0	54.0	1.0

SOURCES: *Survey of Kuwait*, p. 226; *Kuwait Chamber of Commerce and Industry Bulletin*, December 1965, p. 11; *Yearly Summary of Foreign Trade Statistics* 1965, pp. 1–5.

[a] Excluding Arab countries.

More significant in the analysis of Kuwaiti trade, however, is
the composition of exports rather than the total value. Kuwait's
non-oil exports are almost exclusively in the form of reexports of
commodities and manufactured goods which require little or no
processing in Kuwait. Included in this grouping are automobiles,
automotive parts, tobacco products, tea, rice, flour, and appliances.
As an exporter of these commodities to Arab countries, Kuwait
has been favored traditionally by four factors: (1) its geographical
location on the Gulf between Iraq and Saudi Arabia, with commercial contacts with the Indian subcontinent; (2) the liberal trade
policy making Kuwait something of a free zone and a substantial
transit base despite its size; (3) the wide diversification of sources of
imports to Kuwait, ranging from Mainland China and the U.S.S.R.
to its main suppliers, the U.S., Great Britain, Japan, and Germany,

(no other Arab country has such access, either because of commercial restrictions, exchange controls, balance of payments, or political
limitations); and (4) the exceptional entrepreneurial skill of the
indigenous population, stemming largely from the mercantile-
oriented life of the pre-oil years. This latter element is qualitative
and should not be underestimated. It has furthered the diversification of Kuwaiti tastes, and in recent years this tendency has been
reinforced by the stream of Arab and non-Arab immigrants.

TABLE 5

Share of Individual Countries in Total Kuwaiti Exports to the Arab
World, 1960–65

Year, Total Value (In Million Dollars)	Percentage of Total Exports to Arab Countries						
	Saudi Arabia	Iraq	Lebanon	U.A.R.	Syria	Jordan	Others[a]
1960 (12.31)	35.8	26.5	6.3	2.1	3.4	1.8	24.1
1961 (11.34)	37.9	30.7	6.7	2.9	2.3	2.2	17.3
1962 (14.28)	29.7	5.3	8.9	19.0	2.6	10.5	24.0
1963 (19.38)	34.2	22.5	6.2	3.2	1.3	6.3	26.2
1964 (22.54)	44.1	16.5	7.8	2.0	1.6	1.9	26.1
1965 (21.59)	45.8	14.0	9.7	2.9	1.0	2.0	24.6

Sources: 1960–63, *Survey of Kuwait*, p. 232; 1964, *Kuwait Chamber of Commerce and Industry
Bulletin*, March, 1966, pp. 15–18; *Yearly Summary of Foreign Trade Statistics 1965*, p. 1.

a Includes all other Arab countries in Asia and Africa. However, two countries contribute more than
half or more of this amount annually. Qatar's percentage of Kuwaiti exports has ranged from 1 per cent
to over 10 per cent; Bahrain accounts for around 5 per cent.

A breakdown of the major exports to Saudi Arabia for the period
1960–65 shows that cigarettes and tobacco represented over 40 per
cent of the total while textiles occupied second place with almost
20 per cent. For the same half-decade Iraqi imports from Kuwait
were mainly in the form of sugar and rice (over 70 per cent of the
total value) while tobacco products accounted for about 16 per cent.
Similar proportions are to be found in Kuwaiti exports to Jordan.
An overall examination of Kuwaiti exports to other Arab countries
indicates that the pattern of reexport of consumption goods and
capital equipment remains the same.

In conclusion, Kuwait has a favorable balance of trade with
the Arabian peninsula states including Saudi Arabia, Bahrain,
Oman, Qatar, and Abu Dhabi, yet, with the exception of 1964

during the 1960–65 period, Kuwait's balance with the Arab world as a whole was unfavorable, particularly with Jordan, Syria, and the United Arab Republic.

THE ARAB COMMON MARKET

A breakdown and evaluation of Kuwait's trade patterns with those countries participating in the Arab Common Market are important in order to visualize the background into which the Kuwaiti position fits with regard to this regional economic grouping. Imports from the United Arab Republic have amounted to an average of almost five times the value of Kuwaiti exports to that country from 1960 through 1965, with the exception of 1962. The identical proportions existed in the Kuwait-Syria trade relationship. While the variance from year to year was not so great in exports from and imports to Jordan, Kuwaiti imports from this source were approximately eight times the value of its exports to that nation. Among all the Arab Common Market countries, Kuwait's trade with Iraq was the most nearly balanced during the first half of the 1960's. Table 6 gives recent data on the extent of Kuwait's negative trade balance with the four member states.

TABLE 6

KUWAIT'S TRADE WITH ARAB COMMON MARKET MEMBERS, 1965
(IN MILLION DOLLARS)

	Value of Imports	Value of Exports	Balance of Trade
Iraq	4.063	3.016	− 1.047
Jordan	3.237	0.442	− 2.795
Syria	3.693	0.210	− 3.483
U.A.R.	1.442	0.616	− 0.826
Total with Arab Common Market Countries	12.435	4.284	− 8.151
Total with All Arab countries	22.690	21.582	− 1.112

SOURCE: Central Office of Statistics, The Planning Board, *Yearly Summary of Foreign Trade Statistics 1965* (Kuwait, 1966), p. 1.

One might ask the question would Kuwait be able to increase its exports and offset its deficit in the balance of trade with those countries composing the Arab Common Market. While it is true that the Arab Common Market agreement of 1965 encourages the exchange of commodities among the members, yet it restricts the reduction of tariffs to agricultural commodities and to those industrial products in which the Arab share of costs in terms of labor and materials should not be less than 40 per cent.[39] In agriculture Kuwait's capabilities of exports are severely limited, with only 0.4 per cent of its GNP emanating from this sector (see Table 1). Kuwaiti industrial exports at the present time are almost completely reexports originating in advanced countries. The Kuwaiti share in processing these commodities is negligible. Kuwait's position in the exchange of such commodities takes on the characteristics of "middle man" and can be attributed to the native Kuwaiti's merchant-entrepreneurial bent. As Kuwait industrializes in petrochemicals and other locally-based production, however, the Common Market stipulation of 40 per cent Arab processing should loose its restrictive effect. Also, this would in no way hamper the exchange of semi-finished products, as the 40 per cent figure is the minimum level of the total Arab share, that is, more than one member country could contribute to the two-fifths Arab participation. The Prime Minister, Sheikh Jabir al-Ahmad al-Sabah, formerly Minister of Finance and Industry in 1965, supported Kuwait's entrance into the Arab Common Market.

> Kuwait, with its small population, will have to export the products of its industrial projects and the Arab countries offer a big market for them. We believe that it is in the interests of Kuwait to join the Arab Common Market, particularly when the products of its factories are ready for export.[40]

Interestingly, Kuwait's role in the reexport business has been recognized in the Common Market agreement but in a different and presently less important area. Kuwait is exempted from the Common Market regulation which prohibits the reexport of Arab agricultural and industrial products among thé member states and with nonmember nations unless industrial processing is carried out in the reexporting country. The purpose of this restriction is to safeguard the foreign exchange position of the country of origin. Kuwait's heavy dependence on trade and its limited industrial output at the time of the agreement have led to its exception from this stipulation providing two requirements are met: (1) that the

[39] Division of Foreign Trade Relations, Ministry of Trade, *Economic Unity and the Arab Common Market* (Kuwait: Government Printing Press, 1965), p. 19.

[40] *Middle East Economic Survey*, October 29, 1965, p. 3.

original producer be informed of the reexports, and (2) that the resale price should not be lower than the price charged by the country of origin. Such an exception should have greater beneficial effects as the level of industrialization rises in the Arab world.

Let us examine some of the relevant arguments concerning the benefits and disadvantages which could arise with the full functioning of the Arab Common Market as it is now envisaged. First, and perhaps of greatest importance for Kuwait at its present stage of development is that a common market implies a common tariff. Could a common tariff be compatible with Kuwait's traditional posture as a reexporter? Any realistic answer depends on two elements, (1) whether the new level of tariffs would be higher or lower than that existing in Kuwait—which is extremely low, and (2) whether Kuwait would be given special deferment until compensatory economic factors, specifically through industrialization, could be developed; in other words, when a sizeable shift could be made from reexports to exports. Otherwise Kuwait could be placed in a disadvantageous position vis-à-vis its reexport business, which stems from a liberal national trade policy. Even though Kuwait's non-oil exports by comparison account for a small portion of the GDP, yet it must be recognized that we are dealing here with an ingrained and sensitive economic characteristic of the local population and historically of the country itself. For all practical purposes, the total lack of an agricultural sector and the geographical location focused interest seaward and toward trade. Thus the reexport business is something of a "vocation" and must be measured in more than quantitative terms in value of millions of dinars (equivalent to $39.2 million in 1965), as it employs directly or indirectly much of that portion of the labor force not attached to either the oil industry or the government.

Another area of discussion revolves about the comparatively high cost of production in the common market area as most of the Arab countries, even the most advanced, are newcomers to industrialization in the modern sense of the word, most still being dependent upon imported equipment and raw materials. In addition, the low purchasing power of the majority of the population and the low productivity in the Arab Common Market nations are factors contributing to high production costs and lower quality. For the Kuwaiti consumer, who possesses the highest per capita income in the world, there is little allure to an Arab-produced commodity as compared to that exported from Western Europe and the United States to which he is already addicted. However, such an argument loses some of its strength when one considers the dynamic aspects of development and industrialization. While self-sufficiency in industry is neither realistic nor particularly desirable, certain Arab specialty products such as textiles and other consumption goods could compete effectively with non-Arab commodities through greater efficiency and wider markets.[41] Although the desires or requirements of the Kuwaiti consumer may be subjected to a period of adjustment and substitution, the Kuwaiti producer of industrial products would, in turn, benefit from the broader arena the Arab Common Market could provide.

Although the variation among the populations of the individual members of the Arab Common Market is great (the U.A.R. with 30 million to Kuwait at about half a million), the total population of the five members is approximately 50 million, which makes the grouping modest in size compared to the EEC and Latin American market. The region as a whole offers, through monetary complementarity, a substantial balance-of-payments surplus. This is primarily caused by oil exports and the improving balance of payments of Jordan and Iraq. If the surplus of Kuwait is added, the region's total surplus can be computed at over $1 billion. The most significant reservation of the Arab Common Market, however, is the limited role of inter-area trade, which represents less than 5 per cent (excluding Kuwaiti exports) of the region's total trade. This low proportion indicates that there exists an inadequate degree of complementarity among the products of the countries participating in the grouping. The inter-trade figures show that the total Kuwaiti exports to member countries in 1965 amounted to only $4.284 million while its imports from them in the same year amounted to $12.435 million. (See Table 6). These figures are, of course, prior to the Common Market's implementation and drive toward inter-trade expansion.

Yet another ramification of the Arab Common Market operations has been the concern over the development of industrialized "center" economies as opposed to nonindustrialized "periphery" economies. One can question whether the position of Raul Prebisch could be valid in the case of the Arab grouping, i.e., in an economic

[41] *Economic Unity and the Arab Common Market*, p. 15.

union of the common market type a duplication could take place on a regional scale of the international trade pattern between raw material producers and the industrial production centers. While it is true that among the five member countries the level of industrialization varies because of earlier modernization of industry, a closer look at the member economies would show that they either have or could develop definite specializations based on natural resources and geographical location. There is no reason why complementarity could not be emphasized rather than competitiveness.

For example, in Jordan, one of the least industrialized members, the Dead Sea mineral salts are a unique resource in the Arab Middle East and offer a specialized industrialization base. Kuwait's vast oil and natural gas resources and the abundance of capital would make a rapid development of the petrochemical industry a natural economic decision. Petrochemical potential exists in Iraq as well but not so enhanced by the vastness of reserves, availability of capital, and singleness of purpose as in Kuwait. Moreover, as Iraq has an agricultural sector, fertilizers could be marketed locally.

The greatest competitiveness in the Arab Common Market will probably exist between Syria and the United Arab Republic.[42] Both emphasize textiles, sugar, cement, and consumer goods. The major industries shared by these two nations is that of textiles. The Egyptian industry is older and more diversified than its counterpart in Syria, employing over 200,000 as compared with less than 50,000 in Syria. However, there is a degree of specialization in the quality of the cotton itself which dictates the type of finished product. An exchange of raw materials in this case could supply the U.A.R. with its needs for coarse textiles from Syria, and Syria could meet its requirements for finer-quality textiles.[43] It should be recalled that Jordan, Iraq, and Kuwait as well as Syria are still net importers of cotton textiles from outside the Arab Common Market area and that a rise in the standard of living in the member countries

[42] See Ragaei El Mallakh, "Economic Integration in the United Arab Republic: A Study in Resources Development," *Land Economics*, August, 1960, pp. 252–65.

[43] According to the Arab Common Market Secretariat, the best example of the wider prospects for further expansion in inter-Arab trade is cotton textiles, putting the Arab countries' requirements of cotton at approximately $20.7 million annually. Intra-Bank, *Monthly Bulletin*, July, 1966, pp. 1–2.

will further increase demand for textiles. In the sugar industry, too, there is a form of specialization based on the raw material used, sugar cane in Egypt and sugar beets in Syria. Investigation into the economic feasibility of manufacturing sugar from dates is being carried out in Iraq. All Arab countries remain net importers of sugar.

Sufficient local demand is likely to continue to reduce the sharpness of duplication and excessive competition. Thus the latter two factors, in contrast to complementarity, could not be assumed without a thorough study of demand and specializations within an industry. In industries such as cement which closely mirror construction and capital development in a country, demand and cost of production in relation to optimum plant size allow a wide geographical dispersion which need not mean wasteful duplication.[44] All Arab nations, including the U.A.R., which had a head start in this industry, are net importers of cement. Other industries which are compatible with smaller-scale, widely distributed plants are flour and fish and meat packing, all of which are flourishing industries in Kuwait.

Finally, there is the question of the freedom of mobility of labor in the Arab Common Market agreement and the concern that it might lead to mass shifts from the lower to the higher per capita income countries, an aspect relevant to Kuwait. Nonetheless, contrary to the popular belief in the West, that the Arab is nomadic, a strong attachment to the land and village is a sociological and economic facet of the majority of the Arab population. An example which could be cited here is the lack of any significant population movement between Syria and Egypt during their period of national union (1958–61). Second, because Kuwait's immigration policy has been the most liberal in the Arab world, there would be no need for radical change. Even though employment opportunities should ideally govern the movement of labor, certain intergovernmental arrangements could be made to head off and control any trend toward massive disequilibrium.

[44] One of the most influential studies in this area is that of J. S. Bain, "Economies of Scale, Concentration and Entry," *American Economic Review*, March, 1954, pp. 15–39. Although the findings are based upon U.S. industries, they offer a general criteria of locational advantages of selected industries. Bain concluded that one optimal cement plant need represent only four-fifths to one per cent of the national capacity in that industry; a flour plant need represent only one-tenth to one-half of one per cent of total flour industrial capacity to be optimal.

On the whole, the immediate returns to Kuwait in joining the Arab Common Market are not substantial, but since industrialization is proceeding at a rapid rate the economic benefits from such cooperation should not be long in materializing. Because of the unique features of the Kuwaiti economy, exceptions should be negotiated to safeguard the mutual interest involved and allow for a smooth transition.

INTERDEPENDENCE

Population

In no other Arab country can one find such a proportion of nonindigenous Arabs in the population as in Kuwait, where non-Kuwaiti Arabs account for 40.2 per cent of the total population and 76 per cent of all non-Kuwaitis. (See Table 7). Moreover, this section of the population represents nations stretching from Morocco on the Atlantic to Sudan and Yemen in the South and eastward to Muskat and Oman on the Gulf, although the majority come from the Middle East rather than North Africa. The economic impact of such a population mix is reflected in three areas. The first is the direct effect on the Kuwaiti economy through the provision of technically skilled and unskilled labor. Jordanians, Lebanese, Syrians, and Egyptians are primarily in professions such as medicine, education, and engineering, and serve as specialists on social, legal, and economic affairs. The non-Kuwaiti Arab females contribute most of the nurses, teachers in elementary and secondary schools, and administrators in welfare services.[45] Most of the unskilled Arab labor is drawn from the neighboring Gulf and South Arabian states, particularly from Oman and Yemen.

It is noteworthy that regionalism plays a dominant role in the number and origins of the non-Arab, non-Kuwaiti population. In the 1965 census, of the 54,504 Asians, all but 280 come from Iran, India, and Pakistan. In addition, the number of Iranians is over half the total number of persons from Asia and they form, after the Jordanians, the second largest non-Kuwaiti group in the country. Workers from Iran form the backbone of the unskilled labor force. Mercantile contact with the subcontinent of India has been

[45] For example, the U.A.R. agreed to lend Kuwait 750 teachers for the 1965–66 school year. "Chronology," *Middle East Journal*, Spring, 1965, p. 202.

strong traditionally and continues as the Pakistanis and Indians participate with Kuwaitis in trade and retail businesses.[46] It should also be noted that 67.2 per cent of the nonindigenous population are males of productive age, the majority between 15 and 65 years.

The second regional ramification of this Arab population is the transfer of funds throughout the area by remittances of almost $100 million annually, as a conservative estimate. Jordan, with the largest number of citizens employed in Kuwait, has benefited the most. These transferred funds, while largely applied to the maintenance of dependents remaining at home, contribute indirectly to the alleviation of balance-of-payments problems in the recipient Arab nations.

TABLE 7

NON-KUWAITI ARAB POPULATION, 1961, 1965

Country of Origin	1961 Census	1965 Census
Jordan	30,990	77,712
Iraq	27,148	25,897
Lebanon	16,241	20,877
Syria	...[a]	16,849
United Arab Republic	16,716	11,021
Oman	13,857	19,520
Saudi Arabia	4,544	4,632
Others[b]	11,647[c]	11,415
Total Non-Kuwaiti Arabs	121,143[c]	187,923

SOURCES: 1965, Central Statistical Office, The Planning Board, *Annual Abstract for 1966, Section Two*: Population and Vital Statistics, p. 23; *IBRD Report*, pp. 24–25.

[a] In 1961 Syria and Egypt were merged in the United Arab Republic.

[b] Includes Sudan, Bahrain, Qatar, Yemen, Aden, Muskat, Abu Dhabi, the Trucial states, and North African countries.

[c] Estimates.

Third, the presence of Arabs from the Middle East and North Africa has stimulated Kuwaiti entrepreneurship geared toward the Arab world through the human network existing between the immigrants and their home countries. There is a simultaneous double exposure arising from this situation. The non-Kuwaiti Arabs generally lack capital but are skilled and exhibit venturesome and inquisitive characteristics. They bring with them not only new ideas but con-

[46] Kuwaiti ties with India include the Indian government's plans to purchase petroleum products and petrochemicals from Kuwait. In May, 1966, a joint Kuwait-India Technical Committee was formed to discuss industrial ventures and trade expansion. "Chronology," *Middle East Journal*, Summer, 1964, p. 334; Summer, 1966, p. 370.

tacts. These Arabs in turn transmit to their countries of origin the recently acquired and diversified tastes encouraged by Kuwait's international outlook and liberal trade policy. On the other hand, the non-Kuwaiti Arabs provide the indigenous population with background knowledge which assists in the regional private investment by Kuwaitis. The 1962 total private Kuwaiti investment in the Arab countries was placed at about $280 million. Nonofficial estimates put Kuwaiti investments in the U.A.R. by 1966 at about $140 million, which is far below the much publicized investments in Lebanon, particularly in real estate in Beirut, and the more recent increase in Kuwaiti investment in Jordan.[47] This offers a general idea of the rise in Kuwaiti investment in the Arab states. The impact of commercial ties in the Arab world is reinforced by the indigenous Kuwaiti trait of mobility, particularly shown by travel to more hospitable climates during the harsh summers at home.

Yet another example of regional cooperation to the East is the proposition under consideration to establish a Pakistan–Kuwait investment corporation to finance joint industrial products.[48] The population mix of Kuwait, then, has assisted in the development of the country domestically through the addition of skilled and unskilled labor to a state which for developmental purposes is basically under-populated, and through the contribution these people make in spreading knowledge, funds, commercial contacts, and acquired tastes throughout the region. We should now examine other areas in which Kuwait is regionally interdependent.

Waterways and Water

The Suez Canal is well known as a major foreign exchange earner for the U.A.R., bringing in over $200 million annually in recent years.[49] Yet we are interested in looking at the Kuwaiti position respecting that waterway. Kuwait has contributed more

[47] Ministry of Guidance and Information, *Kuwait-Arabia 1963* (Kuwait, May, 1963), p. 23 and *Middle East Economic Survey*, February 4, 1966, p. 3.

[48] Intra-Bank, *Monthly Bulletin*, December, 1965, p. 5. Specifically mentioned was Kuwaiti capital investment in petrochemical industries and refineries in Pakistan. Moreover, technical skills from Pakistan include the visit by 100 Pakistani farming and fishing experts to train Kuwaitis in these fields. "Chronology," *Middle East Journal*, Summer, 1966, p. 370.

[49] *Middle East Economic Survey*, July 1, 1966, p. 7.

than any other single country to the traffic through the Canal, mainly by the shipment of northbound crude oil and petroleum products. In 1965 Kuwait's share of this traffic amounted to 64 million tons of crude alone, of a total of 155 million tons, the latter figure representing 84.5 per cent of all northbound traffic through the Canal. In other words, the Kuwaiti share was one-third of the total traffic. This constitutes almost all of Kuwait's oil shipped to Europe and the Western hemisphere. The dependence of Kuwait on this waterway is obviously coupled with the dependence of the Canal on the dues charged on Kuwaiti oil itself. In recent years a threat to this interdependence has developed through the constant evolution toward ever larger supertankers which, because of size, are forced to bypass the Canal for the sea route around Africa.

Out of the present total world tanker capacity (about 85 million tons) one-fifth is of oversized tankers which cannot transit the Suez Canal. This share of oversized vessels unable to utilize the waterway seems to be growing because of the orders for construction of such large-scale tankers. Two major alternatives have presented themselves to the Canal Authority. The first is the usual solution of widening and deepening the waterway.[50] In 1964 the Kuwait Fund for Arab Economic Development concluded an agreement with the Suez Canal Authority for a loan of over \$27 million to partially finance an overall improvement project, not only to deepen and widen the waterway but also to enlarge the Port Said harbor and upgrade the shipyards at Port Fouad. This tack has been furthered by the announcement in the summer of 1966 of a new six-year plan for the Canal which envisages accommodating vessels with a draft of up to 48 feet, enabling the Canal to handle fully loaded tankers of up to 110,000 tons, partially loaded tankers of up to 125,000 tons, and tankers in balast of up to 180,000 tons.[51] Ambitious as this plan is, however, with a total estimated cost of \$230 million, it would not provide a complete answer to the super-tanker threat wherein some vessels are to be as great as 300,000 tons deadweight.

[50] The Suez Canal Authority's efforts to improve this waterway have been sustained at a high level, with the costs representing 23 per cent of the Canal's total revenues over the last decade. For further details concerning the improvement projects see Ragaei El Mallakh and Carl McGuire, "The Economics of the Suez Canal Under U.A.R. Management," *Middle East Journal*, Spring, 1960, pp. 125–40.

[51] *Middle East Economic Survey*, August 5, 1966, p. 3.

A second alternative to meet the challenge is the construction of a pipeline running parallel to the Canal from Suez to Port Said. The plan, which has been formally advanced by M. Yunis, U.A.R. Deputy Premier for Oil and former Chairman of the Suez Canal Authority, is designed to allow the supertankers which cannot transit the Canal to unload at Suez and pump the oil through the pipeline for pickup by other tankers at the Mediterranean exit, Port Said. This project also entails the construction of larger tanker berths and storage facilities. Calculations made have indicated that such a method of transporting oil and petroleum products is economically feasible and less costly than the trip around the Cape, particularly if one considers that the most significant importer of Kuwaiti oil, Italy, is located in the Mediterranean.

With European oil imports expected to double by 1975, there is concern about the saturation point for tanker passage of the Canal, regardless of the element of size. There will be about 2.6 million barrels per day crude more than the existing methods (the Canal and Tapline) are able to transmit. With this growing discrepancy between present transport capacity and Middle East production, a Suez pipeline would be a needed complementary element to the functioning of tanker traffic via the Canal.

Three points should be considered with regard to the Canal and the proposed Suez pipeline. First, the trend toward more and larger tankers in the shipping industry is already in motion and would be difficult if not actually impossible to reverse. The economies of tanker transport are considerable; the cost of transportation of crude oil by tanker is presently two-third the cost of the 1940's. The recent commissioning of supertankers by the Kuwait Tankers Company and the Gulf Oil Corporation, mentioned earlier, are indicators of the seriousness of this trend. For example, by having Mediterranean and Gulf fleets of supertankers in operation, the one-month loss of use in the return trip to Kuwait via the Cape could be reduced substantially. The savings from increased and more efficient usage of giant tankers would offset the handling costs of offloading and reloading processes at both ends of the Canal pipeline.[52]

---

[52] It should be pointed out that for the most part the larger the tanker, the faster it can be loaded. For instance, experience has shown that it takes about five and a half hours to load ships up to 20,000 tons deadweight but only about ten hours for an 80,000 tons deadweight supertanker.

Second, the Suez Canal pipeline is economically feasible as it would be but 100 miles long with maintance problems shared and reduced by the proximity of the Canal itself. Moreover, technological advances and new nonconventional methods of dredging and deepening berths would reduce the cost. Third, the implications for Kuwait are large, particularly since it would be better served by tanker expansion than by the construction of a costly, second overland Tapline-like pipeline to the Mediterranean which requires the approval of all countries involved and which has not yet materialized although the proposal for the line's construction was made in 1960 by the Arab League.[53] Kuwait is also expanding its commitment to establish its own tanker fleet. Furthermore, the two largest importers of Kuwaiti oil are Italy and Japan. The latter is definitely dependent upon tanker transport, and the former could benefit from the Suez pipeline. As Kuwait already has the largest and most efficient loading facilities, only a relatively small expense would be needed to make any additional enlargement.[54]

A second vital area of economic interdependence in the region will materialize with the conclusion of an agreement between the State of Kuwait and Iraq to enable the former to draw water from the Shatt-el-Arab, the estuary of the Tigris and Euphrates rivers. To riverless Kuwait, the realization of this scheme would offer unprecedented amounts of sweet water for commercial and individual consumption, some 120 million gallons of fresh water daily. About one-half of the Shatt-el-Arab water will be treated for personal consumption, and the remainder is earmarked for irrigation purposes, thereby opening the door for agricultural development other than on an experimental and strictly limited basis. The economic feasibility of the project has been established by international experts including General Raymond Wheeler. The present plans call for a 100-mile pipeline from Iraq to Kuwait

[53] For details see Ragaei El Mallakh, "Trends toward Economic Unity in the Arab Middle East," in *The Arab Nation: Paths and Obstacles to Fulfillment*, edited by William Sands (Washington, D.C.: The Middle East Institute, 1961), pp. 100–101.

[54] Preparation for berthing facilities for the 300,000-ton tankers is underway with sea-bed surveys. *Middle East Economic Survey*, July 15, 1966, p. 5. Likewise, consuming nations are already committed to construction of suitable berthing and storage facilities including Gulf Corporation's expansion of Bantry Bay in south Ireland.

to be completed within five to seven years at an estimated cost of $123 million, excluding appropriations for the acquisition of property. The transfer of water from Iraq to Kuwait has a precedent in the water trade plied by the Kuwaiti fleet of dhows, which at their peak year brought an average of 80,000 gallons per day to the city of Kuwait. Nonetheless, the cost of such movement was high and service often erratic.

Although the addition of a generous supply of water from Shatt-el-Arab will be beneficial in developmental efforts and will increase Kuwait's economic ties with Iraq, Kuwait is likely to continue its already advanced desalination processes and further its surveys of underground water potential. New technology and innovation in underground resource development and the possibility of nuclear power for desalination are being actively studied. The Kuwaiti attitude in exploring all alternatives in expanding water resources can be attributed to (1) the five- to seven-year time gap before the finalization of the Shatt-el-Arab project, (2) greater demand as industrialization increases, and (3) the desirability of diversification of source supply and of balance in dependence on various sources of this vital commodity.[55]

CONCLUSIONS

In reviewing regional cooperation, the Kuwaiti stance has been conditioned by continued support for collective measures (even prior to its gaining full independence), which has been intensified greatly since 1961. Interdependence is reflected in the trade-oriented economy; the population admixture, which offers a balance between demand and supply of labor and technical skills; the vital interest in transportation routes in the region; and the need for expanded and diversified water resources and supply. However, regionalism as designed by the early resolutions of the Arab League has proven, on the whole, to be of extremely limited impact. These measures have concentrated on the negative aspects through abolition of trade restrictions with emphasis on customs duties. Such efforts have had but a slight effect on the Kuwaiti trade structure in general and imports specifically as Kuwait has

[55] Intra-Bank, *Monthly Bulletin*, December, 1965, pp. 4–5, and *Middle East Economic Survey*, August 26, 1966, pp. 2–3.

always enjoyed the benefits of an exceptionally liberal trade policy on a worldwide basis. Nonetheless, there has been a steady if small increase annually in Kuwait-Arab nations trade. The major objectives of regionalism in terms of stimulating the establishment and expansion of manufacturing industries on a more efficient basis, increasing the gains from trade and providing advantages from intensified competition, have not materialized to a sufficient degree.

It could be argued that regional cooperation is more difficult to achieve by those nations which have a high proportion of foreign trade to their domestic production and a low proportion of their foreign trade with one another.[56] The Arab countries and particularly Kuwait fit this description. Equally relevent to the region is the level of industrialization, which is admittedly low. In this case closer economic ties are not likely to cause sizeable gains resulting from more efficient use of resources unless industries have expanded and need wider markets than the individual domestic economies can offer. In short, narrowness of the local market is not a major stimulus to regional economic cooperation until a certain level of industrialization has been achieved. This is valid for most of Africa and the Middle East. Yet with the rapid pace of industrialization in Kuwait and with the special products based on its petroleum resources, which have almost no demand locally, the extreme narrowness of the market soon must become a progressively vital factor in regional ties. Such potential exports as fertilizers would be rationally directed toward the predominantly agriculture-sectored economies in the area, with which Kuwait now has an unfavorable balance of trade. This, of course, is from the viewpoint of demand.

Other problems apply to the supply side. As regionalism proceeds however, and there is greater mobility of labor, entrepreneurial ability, goods in finished and semi-finished form, and capital, sharper competition should result with its attendant benefits, including lower input costs. As mentioned earlier, Kuwait has utilized already the regional labor force and skills. Finally, the greatest constrictor of expanded regional economic cooperation has been the inability to implement the Arab League's basic agreement for settlement of payments of current transactions and facilitating

[56] Cf., R. G. Lipsey, "The Theory of Customs Unions: A General Survey," *Economic Journal*, September, 1960, pp. 507-9.

the transfer of capital. This, in turn, has impeded the exchange of commodities and lessened the gains from increased and freer trade. As a capital-surplus economy Kuwait has initiated a public policy of facilitating capital movement. It is a principal lender in Africa and the Middle East through its newly developed and now firmly established foreign aid program.

Foreign Aid: A New Factor　6

KUWAIT'S ENTRY INTO THE DONOR LIST

The entry of Kuwait into the limited list of foreign aid donors comes at a time when the needs of the developing countries are increasing and the amount of assistance funds from the developed nations has not kept pace but remained stable. The net outflow from the advanced to the less-advanced countries has stabilized at about $9 billion annually throughout the 1960's to date.[1] The Development Assistance Committee (D.A.C.) of the Organization for Economic Co-operation and Development (OECD), which includes the United States, Canada, Western European states, and Japan, accounts for the largest portion, about $8.3 billion in 1963–64, of the total economic aid extended by all donors.[2] On the other hand, in order to halt the widening gap between "rich" and "poor" by increasing the amount of assistance so that the growth rates of developed and less-developed nations would be equal, it has been projected that an initial capital transfer of between $15 and $25 billion would be needed, with an annual increment thereafter.[3]

---

[1] The Development Assistance Committee's *gross* disbursements of loans of more than 5 years' maturity rose by $222 million, or about 10 per cent, but there was a much greater relative increase in amortization on receipts on earlier loans, from $394 million in 1963 to $588 million in 1964, with the result that *net* loan disbursements rose by only $28 million. Organization for Economic Co-operation and Development, *Development Assistance Efforts and Policies of the Members of the Development Assistance Committee: 1965 Review* (Paris, 1965), p. 34. (Hereafter cited *Development Assistance Efforts and Policies, 1965.*)

[2] *Ibid.*, p. 20.

[3] Wassily Leontief, "The Rates of Long-Run Economic Growth and Capital Transfer from Developed to Underdeveloped Areas," mimeographed preliminary text of the paper presented at the Proceedings of the "Semaine d'Etude sur le Role de l'Analyse Econometrique dans la Formulation de Plans de Developpement et l'Etude des Fluctuations Economiques," Pontifical Academy of Sciences, October, 1963, p. 9.

At the current levels, aid accounts for up to one-fourth of the gross investments of the less-developed nations and up to one-third of their imports. With such demands for assistance funds by the underdeveloped areas, which have about two-thirds of the world's population yet produce only one-seventh of the world's output of goods and services, foreign aid has become "virtually a separate factor of production."[4]

Since the end of World War II and the actual beginning of foreign economic assistance, the general trend has been away from grants and toward loans. Grants and grantlike aid as a proportion of total official assistance commitments continues to decline. In U.S. aid, which accounts for the major part of world aid, the percentage has dropped from 64 per cent in 1962 to only 56 per cent in 1964. Therefore, in addition to the gap between the commitments of economic assistance and the needs of the recipients, the situation of the developing countries has been worsened by the rapidly rising debt burden, reaching the $30 billion level in 1965 and projected to reach $90 billion by 1975. The impact of this increase in terms of export earnings, which perhaps play the most strategic role in launching new productive development, is such that repayment is expected to take over 14 per cent by 1975.[5] With the increase in the debt and the debt service ratio to export earnings, the terms or "quality" of aid has assumed and will continue to assume a weight within assistance programs nearly as great as that of the amount extended. The terms of aid are becoming more difficult for the borrowers as a result of interest hikes to an unprecedented level on a worldwide basis and shortages of loanable funds. Besides these retarding factors which affect both private and public borrowing, current programs by major donors such as the United States and Great Britain have been restricted on the grounds of balance of payments, whether or not economic assistance has been a principal negative element in bringing about the situation. Moreover, the U.S. program for fiscal year 1967 has taken a different approach by

[4] Hollis B. Chenery and Alan M. Strout, "Foreign Assistance and Economic Development," *American Economic Review*, September, 1966, p. 679.

[5] On the whole it has been estimated that at the present terms, to enable a continued level of 1963 net lending would involve an increase in the share of the outstanding debt from about 11.3 per cent in 1963 to almost 23 per cent in 1970 of the GNP of the developing countries. Agency for International Development, U.S. Department of State, *A Study on Loan Terms, Debt Burden, and Development* (April, 1965), pp. 7, 12.

limiting the number of countries to which development loans can be made to only ten.[6] Under such conditions the entry of a new source of assistance funds is of consequence and cannot be overlooked. Of greater import here is that the funds are directed primarily toward one geographic region, largely underdeveloped, often overpopulated, and capital-deficit—the Arab Middle East and North Africa.

The share which Kuwait expends on economic assistance is unequaled by any other donor—almost 10 per cent of its national income annually. Itself a developing country, Kuwait has committed in the past four years or so over half a billion dollars. Four methods have been used in extending aid although the actual institutionalization of Kuwaiti foreign assistance was initiated in December, 1961, with the establishment of the Kuwait Fund for Arab Economic Development (KFAED) as an autonomous organization with the status of a jurisdicial entity.[7] It exemplifies the first national institution the goal of which is lending for regional development. The organization follows the general lines of the International Bank for Reconstruction and Development in business-like procedures, careful financing practices, and project lending. The General Authority for South Arabian and Arabian Gulf States, formerly known as the Gulf Permanent Assistance Committee (GUPAC), coordinates Kuwaiti financial assistance, which is mainly in the form of grants to the immediate region. A third agency, newly established in 1964 and in which Kuwait was a joint founder, is the Arab-African Bank, designed for "the development of Arab and African economies and the consolidation of economic cooperation between the peoples of the two areas."[8] The fourth source of Kuwaiti assistance has been the substantial loans granted from the

[6] Such limitations may give regionalism a boost as much of the aid to Africa is expected to be disbursed regionally, perhaps through the African Development Bank. Although development loans are restricted to 10 recipients, 40 nations may receive bilateral technical assistance. *Survey of International Development* (Society for International Development, Washington, D.C.), September 15, 1966, pp. 2–3.

[7] Publications by the author on various detailed aspects of Kuwaiti aid include: "Economic Development through Cooperation: The Kuwait Fund," *Middle East Journal*, Autumn, 1964, pp. 405–20; "Kuwait's Economic Development and Her Foreign Aid Programmes," *The World Today* (Royal Institute of International Affairs, London), January, 1966, pp. 13–22; "Kuwait's Foreign Aid," *International Development Review*, December, 1965, pp. 24–26; "Kuwaiti Aid to Africa," *Journal of Modern African Studies*, 3, no. 3: 439–41.

[8] *Arab-African Bank: Acts and Statutes* (Cairo: C.B.E. Printing Press, 1964), p. 2.

state reserves, reaching by mid-1966 total commitments of $348.74 million. Credits through this channel have been the most extensive and least institutionalized. It has been characterized by program rather than project lending. Of all the Kuwaiti aid efforts the KFAED has become the most firmly grounded and fastest growing; it is becoming the most influential assistance agency within Kuwait's overall programs and within the region.

THE KUWAIT FUND FOR ARAB ECONOMIC DEVELOPMENT

Developmental Lending and Creditworthiness

Presently the capital of the Fund is KD 200 million ($560 million) with authorization to borrow and issue bonds up to 200 per cent of the capital, if and when needed, raising the total potential to a staggering $1.68 billion.[9] To assess the drive toward developing and expanding the KFAED, it is necessary only to review the rapid increments in the capital base. The initial KD 50 million ($140 million) was doubled during the first year of operations. This $280 million subscription by the government represented more than one-quarter of the 1962/63 national income of $1.036 billion. The redoubling of the Fund's capital to the $580 million level was authorized by the National Assembly in June, 1966, with the second KD 100 million based upon an annual percentage of the governmental revenues. This percentage is to be specified each year in the law relating to the annual budget of the state. The budgetary allocation is to begin in fiscal 1967/68 and the amounts allocated will be transferred to the Fund's account in the year following that in which the KFAED's commitments reach half of its capital.[10] By linking the additional Fund capital to revenues, which, for all practical purposes now means oil revenue, the mutuality of interest in Kuwait's sustained prosperity has been consolidated between donor and recipients, between Kuwait and the region.

---

[9] "The Fund may borrow money and issue bonds within the limit of twice the amount of its capital plus its reserve." *Law No. 35 for the Year 1961 for the Establishment of the Kuwait Fund for Arab Economic Development as Amended by Law No. 9 of the Year 1963* (Kuwait Fund for Arab Economic Development, State of Kuwait), Article 24. (Hereafter cited as *The Charter*.)

[10] KFAED, *Fund Press Release No. 9*, July 7, 1966, "Increase of Fund's Capital to KD 200 million."

The objective of the Fund is to contribute to the economic development of the region through the extension of short, medium, and long-range loans and the provision of guarantees. In the KFAED's operations two financial aspects are dominant: (1) lending for development processes only and (2) the strict adherence to internationally accepted standards of creditworthiness in terms of recipient countries and the supported projects. This concern over project creditworthiness is especially vital to the success of the Fund as its capital is to be revolving. Needless to point out, a sound credit rating in the international market is necessary, should the KFAED wish to exercise its right to borrow or issue bonds. Thus the Fund has had to balance its prerequisites for borrowing with a responsible and responsive policy to changes in the world credit market and in the development of the recipient economies.

A close similarity exists between the World Bank and the Fund in the handling of submitted projects. The schemes are first given close scrutiny, with the sending of missions to investigate the economic and financial facets and the technical feasibility of the projects. According to the Charter, the economic appraisal must include an evaluation of the priority the proposed project holds within the general developmental plans of the borrower and the assurance that the supported project would not be in conflict with the economic interests of Kuwait or any other Arab state. The latter condition has dual benefits in reducing the possibility of wasteful duplication and the encouragement of regional planning by making the borrower function, to a certain extent, within the economic framework of the area.

The financial aspects of the appraisal policy require the linking of a credit to one specific project. The scheme must be profitable and revenue-yielding as well. Limits have been set as to the share and total amount which can be advanced—no more than 50 per cent of the foreign exchange requirements of any project, and not to exceed 10 per cent of the authorized Fund capital itself. Such stipulations seek to increase the responsibility of the borrower and at the same time stimulate participation by local capital. KFAED's 10 per cent restriction on its own share of financing safeguards the institution from assuming too heavy a commitment, which would reduce its scope of operations in favor of depth. Throughout the loan period the Fund is to receive progress reports and its representatives have the right to inspect the project.

KFAED can scarcely be accused of giving "hand-outs"; rather its attitude reflects the seriousness with which the financial arrangements are undertaken. A final financial factor is the guarantee assumed by the borrower that all Fund assets and income are exempted from any measures of nationalization, confiscation, and/or seizure. This is particularly suited to the Arab world, where economic experiments involving sizeable changes in the relative share of the public and private sectors have been carried out and which have resulted in financial, monetary, and economic instability.

An additional facet of the Fund's lending policies is the promptness with which loan applications are processed, made easier by the unilateralism of the KFAED's decision-making and the regional scope of its lending activities. If compared with regional financial institutions which were designed to carry out developmental lending activities in either part or all of the area in which the KFAED functions, mainly the Arab Financial Institution for Economic Development and the African Development Bank, the Fund's scale of operations is impressive. The Arab League's Financial Institution and the African Development Bank, established in 1959 and 1963 respectively, show slow progress, with the former unable to launch any loan operations and, for all practical purposes, existing only on paper.

The Quality of Aid

The quality of aid in this study refers to the terms and conditions of loans. Indeed, terms are determinants of the aid content in public lending. A rough method of ascertaining the degree of assistance in a loan transaction is based upon the difference between the terms available from the "aid" source and from normal commercial or financial sources or, for that matter, from other official bilateral or multilateral sources. The "aid" element might be calculated by subtracting from the face value of the loan the discounted value of interest and amortization in the lending arrangement, the rate of discount based upon either private market conditions, including risk allowance, or the rates and conditions of a loan emanating from another official lender.[11]

---

[11] See Raymond Mikesell, *Public International Lending for Development* (New York: Random House, 1966), pp. 27–28 for a discussion of this question of loans as aid.

With the pressures of debt burden and the inability to borrow in world markets, developing nations are in a double squeeze. External indebtedness in the Middle East has increased more than twofold since 1955 and is still rising. Total debt service payments have been requiring an expanding ratio of external receipts, exceeding 15 per cent on the whole.[12] Other pressing factors which continue to impede the ability to borrow include the difficulties of transferring savings, a relatively high capital output ratio, a low marginal savings ratio, and the unabated deterioration in the terms of trade of most Arab countries. Such an admixture of economic and financial conditions calls for a greater degree of flexibility in the terms of developmental financing. Over and above these deterrents is the foreign exchange shortage among the Arab borrowers, which has reached an acute and in some cases alarming stage; their demand for external credit is becoming increasingly inelastic.

Since payments on foreign loans can be derived either from the borrower's external or lipuidity reserves, or from current receipts in free foreign exchange, liquidity factors are a key indicator of a country's ability to repay loans and meet debt service demands. Liquidity reserves include, in addition to the gold and convertible currency holdings, the "gold tranche" position with the International Monetary Fund, that is, the amount that can be drawn from that international agency.[13] A sufficient level of reserves is intimately connected with fluctuations in export earnings and the capacity of a nation to cut its imports without a markedly adverse effect on its economic welfare and rate of economic development. It should be recalled that most Arab countries are primary commodity producers whose products and crops have been subject to negative changes in terms of trade. Moreover, many Arab states are heavily dependent upon a single product, and simultaneously

[12] Robert E. Asher, *Grants, Loans and Local Currencies* (Washington, D.C.: Brookings Institution, 1962), p. 39. See also A. J. Meyer, "Economic Modernization," in *The United States and the Middle East*, ed. Georgina Stevens (Englewood Cliffs, N. J.: Prentice-Hall, Inc., 1964), p. 66, where it is estimated that by the mid-1960's $300 million annually will be the combined Middle Eastern debt service charges, Arab and non-Arab nations alike.
[13] A country's gold tranche position with the IMF is defined by Mikesell as the member's quota minus the International Monetary Fund's holdings of the member's currency. If a member has no net drawing from the Fund and has paid into the IMF an amount equal to 75 per cent of its quota plus 25 per cent in gold, its gold tranche position would be equal to 25 per cent of its quota. Mikesell, *Public International Lending*, n. 27, pp. 211–12.

their ability to reduce imports is quite limited because of their reliance on imported goods such as capital equipment to maintain the level of domestic investment, and on consumption goods, particularly foodstuffs, to sustain the already low per capita caloric intake of their expanding populations. The seriousness of the liquidity factors is clearly illustrated in Table 1 wherein all Arab countries, with the exception of Saudi Arabia and Iraq, two major oil producers, show total liquidity resources equal to only 60 per cent or less of their annual imports. The position of Libya, however, is rapidly becoming more favorable with the speedy expansion of the oil industry in that nation.

TABLE 1

RATIO OF INTERNATIONAL LIQUIDITY TO IMPORTS
(SELECTED ARAB COUNTRIES, 1963)[a]

	Ratio of Gold and Foreign Exchange Reserves, plus IMF Gold Tranche[b] to Imports (c.i.f.)	Ratio of Gold and Foreign Exchange Reserves, plus Total IMF Tranche[c] to Imports (c.i.f.)
Iraq	93.4	98.1
Jordan	45.6	52.0
Libya	52.6	59.0
Lebanon[d]	57.7	60.0
Morocco	27.5	39.4
Saudi Arabia	162.1	183.9
Sudan	36.5	41.7
Syria	13.6	14.4
Tunisia	28.4	28.4
United Arab Republic	25.0	25.0

SOURCE: *International Financial Statistics*, November, 1964.

[a] Reserves, IMF Gold Tranche and IMF Total Tranche as of the last quarter of 1963; imports are for 1963.

[b] IMF Gold Tranche equals member's IMF quota minus Fund's holdings of member's currency.

[c] IMF Total Tranche equals Gold Tranche plus Credit Tranche, that is, additional amount member may draw.

[d] 1962 data used.

An examination of the KFAED's policy toward the terms of lending—interest and maturity—indicates a flexibility in the type of project supported. The credits for agricultural schemes carry consistently lower interest rates and longer maturities than loans extended for projects in any other sector: 3 per cent (which includes all service charges) for an average of 22.5 years.[14] Should the

[14] All the figures given with regard to KFAED loans are based upon the 12 loans given as of August, 1966. (The I.D.O. loan is counted as one credit although it eventually was re-lent to three projects with varying terms.)

borrowing involve an activity of an economic overhead nature, such as highways and power, which are not of a direct or immediate profit-making character, the rate of interest averages about 4 per cent and the average maturity of 15.3 years is somewhat longer than that for industry, mining, and tourism, which averages 12.25 years at 4 per cent. The terms also make an adjustment for the situation wherein the KFAED credits are reloaned by inter-mediaries to local agencies or authorities, allowing for charges to the second lender and moderate rates to the ultimate borrower. For example, the fourth KFAED loan was to the Industrial Development Organization (I.D.O.) of Jordan for the support of small industrial projects, with the Fund's rate calculated to be one-half of one per cent less than the interest charged by the I.D.O. to each of its borrowers (but not to be less than 3 per cent). The final KFAED charges to the I.D.O. of 3, 3.5, and 4 per cent were figured on the rates extended to three individual projects which I.D.O. assisted through reloaning the Fund credit. Moreover, the Fund's rates have been below the prevailing interest charged within the recipient countries.[15]

The rate of interest on KFAED loans has been comparatively low, consistently around 3 per cent and never higher than 4 per cent. These rates include all service charges and compare favorably with other institutions such as the United States Export-Import Bank, which charges from 3.5 to 5.75 per cent. Another comparison can be drawn with the terms offered by the largest grouping of aid-extending countries, the Development Assistance Committee (D.A.C.) of the Organization of Economic Co-operation and Development, whose members include the United States, Japan, Canada, and Western European nations. In 1964 the average D.A.C. terms, excluding those of the U.S., were some 16.9 years maturity at 4.2 per cent while KFAED, in the same year, extended credits at an average interest rate of 3.75 per cent for 14 and three-quarter years. In the preceding year, the Fund's terms averaged 20.5 years at 3.5 per cent in comparison with 16.1 years maturity and 4.6 per cent for D.A.C. average loans, excluding the United States portion. The KFAED's lending terms for all loans granted through July,

---

[15] The following short-term lending rates in selected countries will give some idea of the prevailing charges: U.A.R., 6%; Iraq, 8–12%; Jordan, 7%; Lebanon, 5.5%; Morocco, 7%; Dubai, 8%. *Middle East and African Economist*, May, 1966, p. 67.

1966, have averaged 3.6 per cent and range from 10 to 25 years maturity with up to six years' grace period covering the time needed for construction of the project, with overall terms contingent upon the type of project. In Table 2 the breakdown of terms of D.A.C. members' commitments indicates the liberal extent of Fund loans. Only three countries, Belgium, France, and the U.S., charged lower rates of interest in 1964 although that year marked the beginning of the trend toward softer terms.

TABLE 2

TERMS OF OFFICIAL BILATERAL LOAN COMMITMENTS OF D.A.C. COUNTRIES IN 1964

	Weighted Average Maturity (Years)	Weighted Average Interest Rate (Per Cent)
Austria	9	5.2
Belgium	20	3.0
Canada	25	4.7
Denmark	19.1	4.0
France	15	3.1
Germany	18.1	3.9
Italy	9.5	4.7
Japan	9.7	5.9
Netherlands	...[a]	...[a]
Norway	...[b]	...[b]
Portugal	19.8	3.8
United Kingdom	24.0	3.9
United States	33.4	2.5

SOURCE: OECD, *Development Assistance Efforts and Policies, 1965*, p. 138.

[a] Not included in data.

[b] Grants or grantlike terms only.

The quality of aid is a composite of the interaction among terms of lending, the debt burden, and the total amount extended, thereby affecting the actual amount of capital for investment in steady developmental progress among the borrowing nations. The greatest effectiveness of assistance in the development programs in the recipients' economies is directly related to the required level of *net* rather than *gross* lending. Under commercial "hard" terms rather than the so-called "soft" or developmental terms, an upward spiraling outflow of funds from the donors would be required to maintain a steady annual level of net inflow to the borrowers. If the terms of the U.S. Export-Import Bank are used for purposes of illustration, the gross lending needed to maintain a net flow of $10 million would have to increase to $16 million by the fifth year and to some $30 million (or 200 per cent) by the eleventh year.

Under such conditions repayments surpass outflow from the Bank in eight years.[16] (It comes as no surprise, then, that the Export-Import Bank recently revised and liberalized its terms.) Thus, maintaining a constant level of gross lending with hard terms could lead to a condition where there would be no net inflow to finance development, as shown in Chart 1. Realization of this condition led to the D.A.C.'s adoption in July, 1965, of a recommendation to reduce interest rates and extend maturities. A guideline was drawn up whereby a goal of 3 per cent for 25 years is to be met by 1968. Whether such a "softening" of terms can be achieved remains to be seen, as it will involve drastic change by certain D.A.C. members.[17]

Adaptability to the borrower's capacity of repayment under the stringencies of foreign exchange has been assured through the Charter of the Fund. The Fund also allows participation in projects in currencies other than the Kuwaiti dinar with repayment, interest, and other charges to be made in the same currency. Should the demands of financing any specific project be compelling enough, the Board of Directors of the Fund has the right to overrule the 50 per cent project participation limit mentioned earlier. Furthermore, in most KFAED loans the schedule of repayment has been set to take into account the high interest rate in the earlier years and the income effect of the projects; thus, earlier payments have been made relatively low. Yet another element in the quality of aid is rapidity in processing loan applications. Economic development is an urgent process. Timing is a key factor to countries struggling to raise their standards of living while their populations increase and their measures toward diversification and industrialization languish for need of funds. Avoiding delays helps to curb uncertainty and discouragement which might lead to the dropping of existing or potential plans requiring external financial participation.

Finally, Kuwaiti aid in general has been free from such conditions as procurement-tying and thus has allowed the borrower to benefit from the channels of international competitive markets. In fact,

[16] While the Export-Import Bank was not established for developmental lending but rather for the promotion of U.S. exports, most of the loans have been concluded with developing countries and accordingly have affected their level of indebtedness.

[17] Details of the D.A.C. recommendation for softening of financial terms may be found in *Development Assistance Efforts and Policies, 1965*, pp. 119–20.

Chart 1
Decline in Net Flow of Resources if Gross Lending Is Maintained at an Annual Fixed Level

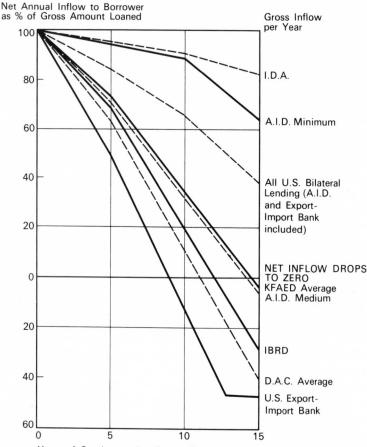

Net Annual Inflow to Borrower as % of Gross Amount Loaned

Gross Inflow per Year

I.D.A.

A.I.D. Minimum

All U.S. Bilateral Lending (A.I.D. and Export-Import Bank included)

NET INFLOW DROPS TO ZERO
KFAED Average
A.I.D. Medium

IBRD

D.A.C. Average
U.S. Export-Import Bank

Years of Continuous Lending at Fixed Amount

Based upon 1963 terms as follow: International Development Association (IBRD affiliate), ·75 per cent, 50 years including 10-year grace; Agency for International Development (U.S. Department of State), minimum terms of 2·5 per cent, 40 years including 10-year grace at 1 per cent, medium terms of 3·5 per cent, 20 years including 3-year grace; Development Assistance Committee (OECD), weighted average, 16 years, 3-year grace, 4·8 per cent; Kuwait Fund for Arab Economic Development, 3·5 per cent, 20·5 years; IBRD, 5·5 per cent, 20 years including 5-year grace; U.S. Export-Import Bank, 5·5 per cent, 13 years, 3-year grace.

KFAED encourages purchases of goods and services through competitive international bidding by making funds available in any currency required, other than the borrowers' local currency, to meet payments. Most other donor countries have been forced to introduce and maintain procurement and project-tying restrictions either because of temporary or structural weaknesses in their balance of payments. Another consideration in Western countries is the political aspect wherein tying aid funds gains wider public support for assistance programs by stimulating the donor economies.[18] Sino-Soviet lending has long been characterized by almost complete tying. Tied aid can lead to two developments. (1) On the recipients' side it can create a gap between the apparent amount of aid borrowed and the value of aid and ultimately can influence the recipients' use of its own resources. (2) A rigid geographic pattern of assistance and trade can be established through aid-tying which eventually can be reflected in world trade and patterns.[19]

KFAED Operations

In carrying out its objective of assistance in financing developmental projects in the Arab world, the Fund may grant loans or furnish guarantees and may partially finance study or research required for the preparation of a loan application. Although it is allowed a full range of functions by its Charter, the KFAED has restricted itself largely to the role of lender. The projects which the Fund has supported are varied and touch all economic sectors. Before discussing the impact of the KFAED policies, it would be helpful to enumerate and review the loans and the projects which have been supported. In studying the schemes which were successful in obtaining Fund assistance, one is struck by the standards of serious and detailed research involved in establishing the creditworthiness of the projects, their priority in individual and regional development plans, and the economic and technical feasibility.

---

[18] U.S. credits are 85 per cent tied while Japan's aid is virtually 100 per cent tied and Germany, which suffers from no balance-of-payments problems, tied 58 per cent in 1963 as compared to 9 per cent the previous year. See John White, *Japanese Aid* (Overseas Development Institute, Ltd., London, 1964) and White, *German Aid* (Overseas Development Institute, Ltd., London, 1965).

[19] For example, in 1963 total bilateral official gross disbursements by the D.A.C. nations to developing countries corresponded to about 25 per cent of D.A.C. exports to those areas. OECD, *Development Assistance Efforts and Policies: 1964 Review* (Paris, 1964), p. 51.

Just three months after its creation, the KFAED concluded a loan agreement with the Republic of Sudan in March, 1962, to help cover foreign exchange requirements for the second phase of the seven-year construction and renovation plans of the Sudanese railways.[20] The first phase of this long-range program was completed with the assistance of a World Bank loan made in 1958. The $19.6 million Fund credit was figured to furnish about 38.6 per cent of the total foreign exchange cost. The loan, with a maturity of 15 years at 4 per cent per annum, actually provides a little over one-fourth of the total cost of the entire project. For the economic development of Sudan there could scarcely be a more vital and timely project than the modernization and expansion of the railroad system. The Republic of Sudan is a vast country, more than one-third the size of the United States, and the largest nation in Africa and the Middle East. Its railways forge a critical network of transport and communication, and the only sufficiently large network between the rural agricultural producing areas and the urban market and processing centers, carrying some 80 per cent of Sudan's freight traffic, mostly foreign trade. A glance at the map will suffice to show how the railroads serve to link the north with the south and the Nile River with the principal port (actually the only Sudanese port of any size on the Red Sea), Port Sudan. Exports and imports flow along the Sudanese system in an ever increasing volume, expected to rise by some 52 per cent between 1962 and 1968.[21] The modernization project includes as well the improvement and enlargement of the facilities at Port Sudan, with the construction of two new berths and additional equipment for increased capacity in cargo handling.

A month later Jordan became the second country to reach agreement for a KFAED loan which covered three principal projects: (1) development of the phosphate industry, (2) the Yarmouk River multipurpose scheme, and (3) small industrial development with specific projects to be agreed upon at a later date. Phosphates have been a major contributor to the Jordanian export sector, and

[20] Details given in *Loan Agreement between the Republic of the Sudan and the Kuwait Fund for Arab Economic Development Dated March 25, 1962* (Kuwait: Government Printing Press).

[21] *Kuwait Fund for Arab Economic Development: First Annual Report 1962–1963* (Kuwait: Government Printing Press, 1963), p. 6. During the five years (1957–61) the growth averaged 5 per cent per annum.

expansion of this industry could be considered a method of improving the balance of trade and, by extension, the balance of payments situation. The Fund credit allocated $8.4 million at 3 per cent interest per annum for 10 years to assist in the financing of the newly started mines at Al-Hasa. The output from the expansion of these mines is projected to be 1.5 million tons per year.[22] At full capacity, the Al-Hasa complex would raise Jordan's phosphate output threefold and, more strategically, should increase that country's foreign exchange earnings by $14 million a year. In March, 1966, the Al-Hasa phosphate project was merged with the Jordanian Phosphate Mines Company. The Jordanian government is making the KFAED loan available to the Company, partly in the form of equity participation and in part as a loan.[23]

The second project supported in the Jordanian agreement of April, 1962, was for the development of the Yarmouk River. This scheme, with a total cost estimated from $112 to $140 million, involves the construction of a dam, the generation of hydroelectric power, and agricultural development of the newly irrigated and reclaimed 108,000 acres of land.[24] The Fund is but one of the lenders on this project. The first stage of the program, the East Ghor Canal, was financed by the U.S. Agency for International Development (A.I.D.) and completed in 1964. The terms of the $11.2 million KFAED credit are 3 per cent annual interest for a duration of 20 years. The repayment schedule begins with markedly lower payments (one-seventh) than the level of the two final installments. The Yarmouk River irrigation program now falls under The Jordan River and Tributaries Corporation, established to undertake the overall plan of water resource utilization and expansion. In September, 1965, a contract for the construction of the Mokhaiba Dam

[22] *Loan Agreement between the Hashemite Kingdom of Jordan and the Kuwait Fund for Arab Economic Development, Dated April 3, 1962* (Kuwait: Government Printing Press). (Hereafter cited as *Jordan Agreement*.) In the entire project $1.4 million has been allotted to the existing mines of the Jordan Phosphate Company at Rusaifeh. An identical portion of the credit is earmarked to finance the feasibility study, including a marketing study, as required by the Charter of the Fund. A final $1.4 million is provided for repayment of a credit advanced by the American Development Loan Fund.

[23] *Kuwait Fund For Arab Economic Development: Fourth Annual Report 1965–1966* (Kuwait: Government Printing Press, 1966), p. 13. (Hereafter cited as *Fourth Annual Report*.)

[24] Again, a portion of the credit, some $1.96 million, was allocated to assist in the financing of preparatory studies. *Jordan Agreement*, Article 3.

and its tunnel was let, with work begun in May, 1966. The implementation of this project will be the basis for the creation of a consolidated power system and distribution grid for the entire country. The remainder of the Fund's credit will finance the irrigation system and downstream network of the Mokhaiba Dam, with the final selection of a plan in mid-1966 to cover the agro-economic optimal water and land usage of the Jordan Valley.

The final section of the loan agreement with Jordan involved the allocation of $1.4 million to the Industrial Development Organization of Jordan for the development of small industries. This agency was to re-lend the funds to industrial projects approved by the KFAED. In April, 1964, two agreements were signed by which the Jerusalem Electric Company and the Jerusalem Intercontinental Hotel received loans from the Fund's credit to the I.D.O. Some $490,000 was extended to the Holy Lands Hotels Company at 4 per cent for 11 years for utilization by the hotel, located on the Mount of Olives, on which construction was completed in 1964.[25] About half its total cost of $3.36 million was met by a loan from the U.S. Export-Import Bank. The rising tourist trade to Jordan has focused attention on the need for more and better facilities. Moreover, tourism is a significant foreign exchange earner in the Jordanian economy; estimates are that this project would yield an annual sum of $1.26 million in foreign exchange, or an amount approximately equal to 8 per cent of Jordan's visible exports. The second scheme, which received $672,000 from the I.D.O. allotment, was that of the Jerusalem Electric Company for provision of an adequate supply of power to the Ramallah and Jericho areas. The interest charge by the Fund to the I.D.O. on this allocation was 3 per cent with a maturity of 17 years.[26] The KFAED loan covered the entire foreign exchange cost of the project. One of the by-products of the expanded electrical facilities for Jerusalem, Jericho, and Ramallah is the expected increase in the attractiveness of these cities and the growth of tourism.

The third project which received support from the I.D.O. was the Al-Urdon Hotel in Amman, the capital of Jordan, for which

---

[25] *Loan No. 4B, Loan Agreement (Jerusalem Hotel Project) between the Hashemite Kingdom of Jordan and the Kuwait Fund for Arab Economic Development, Dated February 5, 1964* (Kuwait: The Modern Printing Press, 1964).

[26] *Loan No. 4A, Loan Agreement (Jerusalem Power Project) between the Hashemite Kingdom of Jordan and the Kuwait Fund for Arab Economic Development, Dated February 5, 1964* (Kuwait: The Modern Printing Press, 1964).

approval was received from the Fund in June, 1965. A sum of $238,000 at 3.5 per cent interest for 14 years has been allocated for the reconditioning and upgrading of the existing hotel.[27] The loan will be used to make those changes, repairs, and installation of equipment that are necessary to bring the hotel up to the first-class, international standard. Thus, although the original loan to the Industrial Development Organization was made in 1963, the final allocation of the sum to various projects was not completed until 1965.

The KFAED and the Republic of Tunisia concluded two loan agreements in December of 1963, totaling $16.8 million. The two credits are designed to assist in the Tunisian plan of economic development through an allocation of $11.2 million for the expansion of the general program of the National Power Authority, Societé Tunisienne de l'Electricite et du Gaz (STEG). The National Power Authority is an autonomous governmental corporation which was created in 1962 to coordinate and operate the electrical power system of the country. The loan will cover the estimated foreign exchange component for the La Goulette power generation and distribution project, and the remaining part of the total cost for the plan, $7.8 million, will be provided by STEG from its own resources and reserves.[28] Moreover, the Fund will assume, according to the agreement, the responsibility of obtaining for the borrower the various currencies needed for the realization of the program. The terms of the loan stipulated a total interest charge of 4 per cent with 16 years maturity. The role of the National Power Authority has been an increasing one with an annual increment of about 8 per cent in the consumption of electrical power, and it is of vital importance to the expansion and growth of the country's economy.

The second Tunisian project which received support from the Fund is for the irrigation and land settlement plan of the Medjerda Valley. This scheme forms part of a three-year public investment plan (1962–64) and is expected to bring approximately 19,200 acres of land under irrigation and improve about 10,800 acres under

---

[27] *Loan No. 4C, Loan Agreement (Al-Urdon Hotel Project) between the Hashemite Kingdom of Jordan and the Kuwait Fund for Arab Economic Development, Dated June 3, 1965* (Kuwait: Al-Assriya Printing Press, 1965) (in Arabic).

[28] *Loan No. 5, Loan Agreement (LaGoulette Power Project) between the Republic of Tunisia and the Kuwait Fund for Arab Economic Development, Dated December 21, 1963.* The actual credit of the Fund was advanced to the Tunisian government, which in turn re-lent it to the National Power Authority.

"dry farming." The program envisages the creation of some 1,000 new farms with intensive agriculture. The Fund's loan of $5.6 million is to cover the foreign exchange requirements and carries 3 per cent interest with a duration of 25 years.[29] It is hoped that ultimately some 144,000 acres will be irrigated through this project, which involves the improvement and extension of the existing primary and secondary canal networks, the opening of new access roads, the construction of farm houses and public utilities, and furnishing agricultural extension service. In 1958 the Medjerda Valley Authority, Office de la Mise en Valeur de la Vallee de la Medjerda, was established as an autonomous governmental agency to handle this entire project, which stands as one of the more ambitious developmental programs of its type in the African continent. The technical aspects of the project include the construction of six sizeable dams, the financing for which has been arranged through development loans and grants from the United States and Soviet Union. By mid-1966 the project for which the KFAED credit was advanced was practically completed.

The credit to Algeria in 1964 by the Fund was especially timely as that country faced not only the task of development but rehabilitation and reconstruction as well, following seven years of open conflict. The loan of $21 million at 4 per cent with an amortization of 15 years is linked to the construction of the Haoud El Hamra-Arzew crude oil pipeline, the third in the country.[30] The 500-mile-long pipeline connects the Hassi Messaoud field to Arzew, an industrial complex on the Mediterranean. The 28-inch diameter pipeline is the longest on the African continent, and, with the other two lines being fully utilized, the addition of another transport line for crude oil is of the most pressing nature in order to fully exploit the vast petroleum resources of the nation. The Haoud El Hamra-Arzew line, the first such line fully government-owned and operated, was put into use in the spring of 1966. Construction was carried out under the auspices of the recently set up government corporation, Societe Nationale Algerienne de Transports et de Commercialisation des Hydrocarbures, at a total cost of around

---

[29] *Loan No. 6, Loan Agreement (Medjerda Agricultural Project) between the Republic of Tunisia and the Kuwait Fund for Arab Economic Development, Dated December 21, 1963.*

[30] *Loan No. 7, Loan Agreement (Haoud El Hamra-Arzew Oil Pipeline Project) between the Democratic and Popular Republic of Algeria and the Kuwait Fund for Arab Economic Development, Dated June 23, 1964.* The other two pipelines terminate at Bougie on the eastern Algerian coast and La Skhira in Tunisia.

$106.6 million of which about 80 per cent was in foreign exchange. The Fund's loan provided about 27 per cent of these requirements and the balance was acquired through arrangements with foreign banks. The pipeline has an initial capacity of 10.1 million tons/year crude oil with potential expansion to a 22-million-ton capacity. New discoveries in the area assure sufficient demand for the pipeline and, in fact, Algeria is already pushing ahead with the second and third phases of its total program, including additional berths at Arzew, storage and loading facilities, and pumping units as well as reaching the 22-million-ton level. An initial agreement has been concluded for an additional KFAED credit of $7 million. Increased oil exports mean increased foreign exchange for Algeria and a stronger balance of payments situation. It has been estimated that at full capacity the yield from this third pipeline would double the Algerian government royalties from the 1964 base of $64 million. Moreover, the revenue to the government from the dues for oil transportation has been expected to reach up to $20 million annually depending upon the rates fixed.[31]

For the United Arab Republic the Suez Canal is its largest foreign exchange earner; therefore, the continued successful functioning of this waterway is of top priority in the nation's economic planning. In July of 1964 the KFAED concluded a loan agreement with the Suez Canal Authority (and with the United Arab Republic as guarantor) extending $27.44 million for the purpose of physical improvement of the Canal and the Port Said harbor. The credit carries 4 per cent interest for a 16-year period.[32] Constant repair and improvements have been made on the Canal since 1956, increasing the depth from 35 feet to 38 feet to enable larger ships and oil tankers passage and to facilitate a greater volume of traffic. The earning power of the Canal and Kuwait's usage, via tankers, have been discussed in the preceding chapter, which pointed out the ever pressing need for continued development of the waterway. The Authority plans to increase the depth of the Canal to 40 feet maximum draught, thus allowing the passage of oil tankers of about 55,000 tons dead weight fully loaded. The project also includes the deepening and widening of Port Said harbor,

---

[31] *New York Times*, April 11, 1964.

[32] *Loan No. 8, Guarantee Agreement (Suez Canal Development Project) between the United Arab Republic and the Kuwait Fund for Arab Economic Development, Dated July 5, 1964.*

the construction of deep quays, and the expansion of the Port Fouad shipyard to enable the building of two 12,000-ton ships simultaneously. The Fund loan assisted in financing the second phase of a long-term program, the first stage of which was financed by a credit from the IBRD.

Sudan received a second loan from the Fund in 1965, this time directed toward an industrial project, the Khashm El Girba sugar plant. The government of Sudan will re-lend the $4.76 million to the Industrial Development Corporation, a government-owned agency charged with the execution and operation of the project. The loan has a duration of 14 years at 4 per cent interest.[33] Included in the scheme is the establishment of a sugar cane plant with a capacity of between 67,000 and 81,000 tons of refined sugar and the cultivation of sugar cane on an area of about 19,500 acres. The total cost of the project is estimated at $21.84 million and was, interestingly, born of the necessity of resettling the inhabitants of Wadi Halfa as a result of the Aswan High Dam's construction. A dam has been built near the area on the Atbara River to provide water for the eventual agricultural development of about half a million acres. The KFAED loan will be used for the procurement of varied industrial and agricultural equipment, intermediate goods as part of the working capital of the entire project, and in the construction of housing and public buildings. The plant began operation in March, 1966, and is expected to show a modest output. Expectations are for 1966/67 production in excess of 40,000 tons, and by the following year the designed capacity will have been reached. The Sudanese railway, through the KFAED loan made earlier for its expansion and modernization, was able to lay down a 45-mile extension from the Khashm El Girba dam on the Atbara River to the newly developed agricultural area involved in this second project.

In May, 1966, Morocco joined the ranks of borrowers from the KFAED with the signing of two loan agreements. The first credit, equivalent to $20.58 million, will assist in financing the Tessaout Agricultural project in central Morocco. The Tessaout Perimeter covers an area of 124,800 acres of which slightly over half is under cultivation. The traditional system of agriculture predominates and a lack of regular water supply has further inhibited productivity.

---

[33] *Fourth Annual Report*, pp. 17–18.

The objective of the plan is to provide cultivated sections with a dependable supply of water and to concentrate upon the intensification of agriculture through modernization of farming techniques. Principal construction includes a storage dam, diversion dam and tunnel, irrigation canals, and land improvements including extension services. The terms of the credit are for 25 years at 3 per cent interest.[34] The project should be completed in 1972.

The second Moroccan scheme is for further agricultural development of the Tadla Plain, also in central Morocco, through the extension of irrigation. An ultimate total area of about 336,000 acres is envisaged to be under cultivation in the plan. In order to insure sufficient water, the project is involved with main canal extension and the necessary irrigation and drainage networks to service the area. Also included are assorted land reclamation activities, flood control, road construction, and extension services. The scheme will press for intensive agriculture such as the production of industrial crops, mainly cotton, beets, citrus fruits, and dairy products. The loan carries a 3 per cent interest rate over a 20-year amortization period, with the project scheduled for completion in 1970.[35]

A KFAED credit equivalent to $6.72 million at 4 per cent for 13 years was extended in the summer of 1966 to the Litani River Authority, guaranteed by the Lebanese government.[36] The first phase of the Litani River Project was completed in 1965 with the construction of a dam at Karoun, the diversion of the Litani waters, and the building of two hydroelectric power plants. The second phase, the Joun Power plant to which the Fund loan is directed, will include such items as technical studies, the building of ac.ess roads, transmission lines and substations, the actual construction of the power plant itself with two units each of 24,000 kW capacity, and required diversion works. The scheme is programmed

[34] *Fund Press Release No. 7, Signing of Two Loan Agreements between the Kingdom of Morocco and the Kuwait Fund for Arab Economic Development,* May 29, 1966, pp. 1–3.

[35] *Ibid.,* pp. 3–5. Both loans are made to the Government of Morocco which re-lent the funds to the Office of Agricultural Development, L'Office de Mise en Valeur Agricole, a government institution charged with agricultural development throughout the country. In both areas this institution will furnish extension services as well as providing agricultural equipment on a basis something like that of a co-op system.

[36] *Fund Press Release No. 8, KD 2,400,000 Loan for Joun Power Plant Project in Lebanon,* July 4, 1966.

for completion before the end of 1968. The power requirements of Lebanon have been increasing rapidly, particularly with the boomlike conditions prevailing in Beirut and the greater metropolitan area. Such infrastructure development is sorely needed to keep abreast of the demands which accompany a rising standard of living.

As the result of a loan application from Yemen, the Fund has undertaken the financing of a preliminary economic resource survey as a prerequisite for the support of any Yemeni project. This is a new approach for the KFAED, yet it is compatible with the intentions of its Charter. As one of the least developed Arab countries, planning in Yemen is hampered by a near-total lack of statistics and economic and natural resource surveys. In short, it is impossible to establish developmental priorities if one has not the vaguest idea what the nation's potential is in human and physical resources. The Fund has been able to secure the participation of the highly respected Netherlands Economic Institute in a reconnaissance mission to Yemen. It was the decision of this Mission that an economic survey would be both possible and useful and should be carried out. The KFAED has, therefore, assumed the financing of such a survey to be done by the Netherlands Institute, with the final report expected early in 1967. Such an evaluation is of inestimable value for drawing up a national plan and ascertaining the feasibility and priority for projects within the general development program.[37] Moreover, the Fund has agreed (in principle) to finance, with the United Nations Special Fund and under the auspices of the Food and Agricultural Organization, a part of the first stage of the Wadi Zabied development. This phase is, by and large, a survey to weigh the possibilities for development, the construction of badly needed roads, the launching of some experimental farms, and training of Yemeni personnel.[38]

[37] *Fourth Annual Report*, pp. 5–6.
[38] *Kuwait Fund for Arab Economic Development: Third Annual Report 1964–65* (Kuwait: Al-Assriya Printing Press, 1965), pp. 17–18.

KFAED loans either since concluded or pending include: (1) $12.88 million for 14 years at 4 per cent to Tunisia to assist Stage B of the previously supported La Goulette II Power Project; (2) $7 million at $3\frac{1}{2}$ per cent for 14 years to Algeria for the second and third stages of the pipeline project aided earlier; and (3) a $14.196 million loan to Sudan ($2\frac{1}{2}$ per cent, 20 years) for the extension of three existing agricultural schemes including Khashm el Girba. With these loans Fund commitments total $179.536 million.

Assessing the Fund's Impact

In reviewing the KFAED's record to date, there are three economic characteristics which mark its lending operations. First, the sectoral distribution has seen concentration on infrastructure development, specifically power and transportation, which, as noted in Table 3, accounts for almost 60 per cent of total KFAED commitments. This emphasis is caused by the fact that public utility requirements of capital are substantial and have to be obtained at relatively low cost and easy terms. Also, power and transport are recurrent bottlenecks in most Arab economies. It is only in a few instances that overheads of power and transport have been provided in advance of demand. Among Arab states which lack major oil and natural gas resources, expanding hydroelectric power becomes a prerequisite for industrialization and development. Loans to Jordan, Tunisia, Lebanon, and Morocco to finance power generation and distribution projects lay the groundwork for later industrialization. On the other hand, in a country like Algeria the need is to move its energy resource to a center for processing, use, and/or export.

Commanding second place in the distribution of KFAED loans is agriculture, with over 30 per cent of total Fund commitments. This compares favorably with the world project aid level for agriculture of only 12 per cent.[39] Agriculture has not been given its due share in international lending despite its undeniable importance in developing economies where overpopulation and narrow markets reinforce the dominant position of this sector. The difficulties agriculture faces in attracting its proportionate share are complicated by the outlook that most of the expenditures needed are of a current nature and of little importance in content. Fortunately, both lenders and recipients are realizing the real necessity of a sound agricultural base for development. In this sense, KFAED has shown an awareness of this realistic and current trend.

With reference to industry, the Fund has extended 9.5 per cent of its lending toward that sector. This may appear inadequate but it should be recalled that the KFAED is mainly geared to loan rather than equity capital and that industry in most instances requires retail rather than wholesale financing—more a form of

[39] United Nations, Conference on Trade and Development, *Financing for an Expansion of International Trade*, E/CONF. 46/9 (Geneva, 1964), Table 22.

TABLE 3

Major KFAED Loans Classified by Purpose and Country as of August, 1966
(In Million Dollars)

Purpose	Total	Per Cent of Total	Algeria	Jordan	Lebanon	Morocco	Sudan	Tunisia	U.A.R.
Total development loans extended	145.46	100	21.00	21.00	6.72	28.14	24.36	16.8	27.44
Electric Power									
Generation and Distribution	18.592	12.8		0.672a	6.72			11.2	
Transportation	68.04	46.8							
Railroads	19.60						19.60		
Ports and Waterways	27.44								27.44
Pipelines	21.00		21.00						
Agriculture		30.9							
Irrigation, Land Reclamation, Flood Control	44.94			11.2		28.14		5.6	
Industry	13.888	9.5							
Mining	8.40			8.40					
Industry (including Tourism)	5.488			0.728a			4.76		

a Allocations of the $1.4 million loan to the Industrial Development Organization of Jordan.

equity than loan capital. The Fund is moving away from participation in smaller industrial projects for which financing can be
secured from other sources. The primary obstacles confronting
the financing of industry in the Arab world are (1) the absorptive
capacity and (2) inadequate financial and technical capacity.

The capital absorptive capacity refers here to the capacity of an
industry to employ financial capital in a way which will result in
an increment to the net product the discounted value of which is
equal to the amount of that capital employed. Assuming no
diverting of resources, employing capital for high priority projects
in the recipient industry would create a net addition to capital
formation. In most of the Arab countries there is a dearth of studies
relating to the absorptive capacity of industries, particularly with
reference to the profitability in disposal of the products. Smallness
of the domestic market and low purchasing power are the great
constrictors which have yet to be eased. Still, the Arab countries
share with the developing group as a whole the fixed image of
industrialization as the panacea for underdevelopment and
synonymous with development itself. The refuge of high tariffs is
an appealing method of avoiding competitive marketing on a
regional and international basis.

A few exceptional cases may be noted in the Arab world where
attempts have been made to coordinate marketing policies of such
products as phosphates. In Algeria, Libya, and Morocco a coordinated program in the processing and marketing of paper and other
commodities of esparto grass has been established. The KFAED
has been critical of the lack of thorough planning and studies which
has accompanied the applications for support of industrial projects.
It has itself been presented with and has been unable to accept
such proposed programs as a textile project which would be
noncompetitive and heavily dependent upon excessive tariffs, and
a sugar industry of questionable profitability, the inputs of which
were overpriced to support the cane farmers. In most cases there
has been a common problem of failing to estimate realistically
the time and conditons needed for a plant to reach capacity.[40]

Technically the Arab nations suffer from a shortage of scientific,
detailed studies which could help in the implementation of projects

[40] These difficulties have been discussed in a study by the Fund, "Shortcomings
in the Preparation and Implementation of Industrial Projects in the Experience
of KFAED," *Kuwait Chamber of Commerce and Industry Bulletin*, April, 1966, pp. 21–23.

related to such vital areas as water distillation, petrochemicals, and engineering industries. As for financial planning, in the last decade the Arab Middle East has been facing not only a lack of capital but an inability to attract it as well. A circle has evolved whereby capital insufficiency has led to shifts and juggling, most often between the public and private sectors, resulting in instability and loss of business confidence, which in turn reduces the ability to borrow and ends with aggravating the capital shortage situation. Two additional negative factors emanate from this spiral. There is capital flight in some cases from a nation experiencing such conditions, which forces industries to borrow at excessively high rates of interest from commercial banks or at relatively steep rates from nonspecialized agencies such as export-import institutions, because of the risk involved. Moreover, in financial planning there are the specific problems arising from the tendency to underestimate initial capital requirements and current and maintenance needs. A squeeze condition can thus occur, pushing the industry to take additional loans with unfavorable terms to salvage the project. In the drawing up of applications for the Fund, there has been a technical slackness in evaluating the importance of external economies to the specific projects in question.

The third economic characteristic of the Fund is the diversity of recipients represented on three fronts. One is the numerical aspect. In the relatively short period since its establishment, the KFAED has supported 14 projects in seven countries in Africa and the Middle East. Considering that the Fund is regional in its lending scope, the total number of recipients compares well with worldwide lending by the United States and the Sino-Soviet bloc. In recent years the U.S.S.R. has pursued a relatively selective policy. For example, only four countries received more than half of the cumulative total of Sino-Soviet loans to the beginning of 1964. These were India, the U.A.R., Afghanistan, and Brazil. In 1964 one nation alone, Algeria, accounted for about one-half of the total Sino-Soviet commitments. In the case of the United States, the development lending policy has steadily narrowed the numerical recipient base of loans. For fiscal 1967, the U.S. restricted to ten the number of countries to receive development loans. Kuwaiti lending, however, has followed a pattern of widening the scope of recipients and even in the case of the seven borrowers (excluding the survey work being carried out in Yemen), they represent more than half the total Arab states. Among the remaining nonrecipients, Saudi Arabia and Libya are oil-rich and capital-surplus.

Not only have the KFAED loans been spread numerically among the nations of the region, but the distribution by amounts has not been lopsided. The two borrowers of the largest sums, Morocco and the U.A.R. (about 19 per cent each of total KFAED commitments), are the most populous in the area. Sudan's two credits account for 17 per cent of Fund lending based upon its need for infrastructure, its present level of overall development, which is lower than that of many Arab states, and its potential. Algeria and Jordan have each received $21 million, or 14 per cent of all KFAED loans to date. Although Jordan is one of the smaller Arab countries, it is faced with large-scale problems resulting from population transfer.

The lending policy of the Fund—wide divergence in recipients rather than deep commitment to a few borrowers—has followed its founding objective to act as a catalystic financial force throughout the Arab world. The KFAED is not set up as a replacement for local capital but is to function in a supplementary manner; internal resources must be mobilized by the borrowing nations. The Fund participates in relatively large projects which have other sources of financing, bilateral and multilateral, as in the Suez Canal and Sudanese railways, which also had IBRD loans, and in Jordan and Tunisia, where the U.S. Agency for International Development was a co-financer. The KFAED's participation in Yemen with the U.N. Special Fund and F.A.O. is yet another example. Should the Fund extend a credit to the Arab Potash Company in Jordan, presently under consideration, it would be financing the $75 million project in cooperation with the IBRD and the United States A.I.D.

Most of the infrastructure projects supported by KFAED loans have regional as well as national implications. Ramifications in the former area are clearly shown in the case of the Suez Canal, where loans will enhance the capabilities of that waterway to handle an increased volume of traffic, specifically in the tanker fleets moving Middle Eastern oil. A more efficient and modern railway system in Sudan, and an improved Port Sudan, should facilitate greater trade in general and regional trade in particular. Because of Sudan's geographical position vis-à-vis the Arabian peninsula, greater and more rapid movement of Sudanese exports, especially foodstuffs, should enable Sudan to expand its trade with its neighbors.

Finally, credits have been extended by the Fund for support of projects among countries where the form of government and/or economic ideology vary widely with regard to the public sector, from monarchies such as Morocco and Jordan to republics including Tunisia, Algeria, and the U.A.R. Political problems receive generous newspaper column space. The success of economic aspects in overcoming political considerations injects a positive note into Arab affairs. Likewise, cooperation by the Fund among recipients whose economies stretch along the spectrum of public-private sectoral ratio, from socialistic Algeria to "laissez faire" Lebanon, is pragmatic.

ECONOMIC AID THROUGH GRANTS

Long before its independence, Kuwait was already an aid-extender, with a program consisting of outright grants to its immediate neighbors on the Gulf. The small sheikhdoms perched along the edge of the Arabian peninsula have been extremely poor, isolated, and forgotten except when the prospect of petroleum has brought some interest from abroad. Prior to oil-searching activities and as early as 1952, Kuwait opened the first modern school in Sharjah. In 1962 the grant program was institutionalized with the creation of the Gulf Permanent Assistance Committee (GUPAC) which was to recommend and administer economic aid to the seven Trucial coast states Dubai, Sharjah, Himriyah, Umm al Quwain, Ajman, Ras al Khaimah, and Fujairah as well as extend certain services to Yemen. The GUPAC has followed a dual approach to development efforts for the area. One is of a short-term nature to deal with problems of health and illiteracy. The second program adopts long-range measures for the financing of resource surveys, soil analysis, and evaluation and development of water resources; in short, assessment of the economic potential of the area. Before any development plans can be structured, economic knowledge is a prerequisite and the Trucial states have been deficit in this commodity for some time. The economic survey program of GUPAC has emphasized possibilities for industrialization and diversification such as an appraisal of iron ore deposits which could form the base for a steel industry and an assessment of the availability of raw materials which could be utilized in the manufacture of cement products. Road development is being studied, as are water potential and actual planning for a distribution system.

The original short-range program of the Permanent Committee included the construction of eight schools (four each for boys and girls) on the elementary and secondary levels; the furnishing of 40 teachers and the allocation of funds needed for school equipment; the setting up of three clinics with hospital annexes for Dubai, Sharjah, and Ras al Khaimah and smaller clinics in Ajman, Himriyah, and Umm al Quwain; furnishing doctors, needed technicians, medicines, and equipment for the functioning of these clinics; and finally, sending some 31 teachers for adult education in literacy. In the few years of its existence, GUPAC efforts have been successful, if modest. By 1965 Kuwait was fully operating some 32 schools, two hospitals, and seven clinics in the area, at no cost to the population. The Permanent Committee has also financed, since its first program, the construction of four general hospital buildings, two sanatoriums, 12 new school buildings, and about 50 housing units to accommodate the persons engaged in the social services.[41] GUPAC has extended aid to Yemen along the same lines through the construction of school and hospital buildings. About 20 schools, a teachers' college, and 7 clinics and hospitals are to be built at a cost of about $4.2 million. However, the actual operation of these facilities will be the responsibility of the Yemeni government. GUPAC's budgetary share has increased from $2.8 million in 1964/65 to $6.1 million in 1966/67.[42] About one-half of one per cent of Kuwait's national income is earmarked for assistance in the form of grants.

In June, 1966, GUPAC was replaced by the General Authority for South Arabian and Gulf States, composed of the undersecretaries from various concerned ministries and chaired by the Foreign Minister. The Board will assume the same responsibilities of the

[41] During the 1964–65 school year enrollment reached 5,000 boys and 2,300 girls, with a teaching staff of about 300. The teachers are largely provided on a grant basis by the U.A.R., Qatar, and Bahrain, but Kuwait is financially and administratively responsible for the operation of the schools.

[42] Kuwait also contributed $700,000 to the Arab League Fund for the Arabian Gulf Sheikhdoms in 1966/67.

Permanent Committee but is to enjoy a greater degree of administrative freedom. The smallness and isolation of the Trucial states
have been serious obstacles to development and higher standards
of living. Any evaluation of the effectiveness of Kuwait's aid to the
Gulf states must recognize the qualitative factors inherent in breaking
down the deeply fixed isolation of the area, assisting in the establishment of a credit rating for most of the recipients and thereby
enhancing the possibility of attracting outside investment and aid.

THE ARAB-AFRICAN BANK

Although Kuwait's interest has been concentrated upon the Arab
states, it has not restricted its lending activities to the Middle East
only. The fact that six Arab countries are located in Africa provides
a natural link between Kuwait and the rest of that continent. In
1964 the governments of Kuwait and the United Arab Republic
concluded an agreement whereby the Arab-African Bank was
created with the objective of supporting the economic development
of Arab and African economies.[43] It is chartered as an Egyptian
joint-stock company with a capitalization of 10 million sterling
pounds ($28 million) on a subscription basis of one million shares
at 10 pounds per share.[44] Kuwait and the U.A.R. subscribed to
slightly over one-third each (335,000 by the respective governments),
and the remaining 330,000 shares are to be floated for public
subscription by governments and nationals of Arab and African
states other than Kuwait and the U.A.R. If this portion is not
covered, it is to be equally covered by the two founders. The
original duration of the Bank is set at 50 years, which is extendable,
with its headquarters in Cairo.

Of the utmost importance is the relationship between the Arab-
African Bank and the financial laws of the U.A.R. The Charter
provides for exemptions from the general income tax of funds
acquired by individual shareholders as the yield of their shares
in the Bank's capital. Tax exemption is also provided, for a period

[43] *Arab-African Bank: Acts and Statutes* (Cairo: C.B.E. Printing Press, 1964), p. 2.
[44] The Kuwaiti Ministry of Finance and Oil is the actual co-founder of the
Bank and it may put a portion of its 335,000 shares on the market for subscription
by Kuwaiti citizens or by joint-stock companies owned exclusively by Kuwaitis.
The contracting U.A.R. agency in the establishment of the Bank was the Egyptian
Public Organization of Banks which in April 1964 was abolished with the Central
Bank of Egypt taking over the former institution's functions.

of seven years, on profits, dividends, and distributions of the Bank as well as on the interest on deposits. As the activities of the Arab-African Bank are, as stipulated in the Charter, to be outside the U.A.R., neither the Bank revenues accruing from operations outside the United Arab Republic nor the distribution of profits resulting from its operations are to fall under any Egyptian taxes. Finally, the Arab-African Bank is to be exempted from the "nationalization laws, the laws of joint stock companies, the laws . . . regulating exchange control, the Bank and credit laws, [and] the control of the State Audit Department. . . ."[45] Within the U.A.R. this institution can carry out any banking operations through banks existing in that country with the exception of the free zone areas, such as Port Said, where the Bank can function directly.

The Bank is to be managed by a Board of Directors, with the Ministry of Finance and Oil of Kuwait and the Central Bank of Egypt each appointing one-third of the membership and the remaining third elected by the other shareholders. In addition to carrying out its major objective of investment in development projects, the Arab-African Bank has been designed to pursue all regular banking and commercial operations including (1) the acceptance of deposits and the advancement of loans; (2) organizing public subscriptions in shares and bonds and carrying out all operations connected with securities; (3) the right to issue, handle, and discount bonds, bills, and promissory notes; (4) the undertaking of foreign exchange transactions; and (5) to carry out the functions of investment trusts on behalf of others.

The Arab-African Bank is in its formative stage. By early 1966, however, this institution's total invested funds were estimated at over $30 million.[46] It has already established a branch office in Beirut. The first project receiving support from the Bank was for the creation of the Industrial Development Bank of Jordan. Possibilities for cooperation between the Bank and African countries are being appraised by staff missions to Uganda, Kenya, Tanzania, Somalia, Nigeria, Dahomey, Niger, Ivory Coast, and Senegal.

Although the Arab-African Bank is still in its infancy, and it is far too early to assess the ultimate impact and importance of its

---

[45] *Arab-African Bank: Acts and Statutes*, Article 15, Provisional Title Deed of a Company, p. 31.

[46] Intra-Bank, *Monthly Bulletin*, March, 1966, p. 1.

role in African and the Middle Eastern developmental efforts, its existence has set a pattern for further cooperation between Kuwait and other nations. If a functioning arrangement between a state with a proportionately large public sector, such as the U.A.R., and a country such as Kuwait can be worked out, then the differences among the economic makeups of nations need not be an insurmountable obstacle to cooperation. By opening its subscription to the governments and individual investors alike, by guaranteeing against nationalization and presenting a healthy investment climate, the Bank has taken a step toward bridging the gap between the public and private sectors.

Apart from Kuwait's position as a founder of the Arab-African Bank, some mention should be made of the Government's interest in Africa. In 1965 Kuwait subscribed to 70 per cent of the $14 million capital of a newly formed Kuwait-Northern Nigeria Company Limited, a corporation established under Nigerian law for investment in development projects within that country.

CREDITS FROM THE STATE RESERVES

Aside from the activities of the Permanent Committee, the KFAED, and the Arab-African Bank, the Kuwaiti government has followed a policy of extending substantial loans from the state reserves. By August, 1966, the total amount committed was $348.74 million, or about two and a half times the sum lent by the Fund. The nine recipients of the state reserves loans include Algeria, Iraq, Jordan, Lebanon, Morocco, Sudan, Tunisia, the U.A.R., and the Trucial state of Dubai. Aid extended from this source has been distinguished by program rather than project lending with fairly liberal terms, occasionally interest-free as in the cases of Algeria and Iraq. One of the first sources of aid to independent Algeria, and coming at a critical time, was a Kuwaiti credit from the reserves of $28 million, without interest and carrying a 12-year maturity period. (This loan accompanied the KFAED credit in support of the pipeline construction from the Hassi Messaoud field.) The terms of maturity generally range from 5 to 25 years, the latter amortization in the large loan to Iraq, with interest never exceeding 4 per cent. Table 4 gives a breakdown of state reserves credits.

It will be noticed from this table that, as with the KFAED loans, the state reserves credits are widely spread throughout the Arab world. The recipients vary from a relatively large nation, the U.A.R., to small countries such as Jordan and Dubai. These loans have been largely for balance-of-payments requirements and are designed to assist in meeting the pressing capital needs in the area.

TABLE 4

STATE RESERVES LOANS TO ARAB COUNTRIES RANKED BY AMOUNT BORROWED TO
AUGUST, 1966
(IN MILLION DOLLARS)

	Amount	No. of Loans
United Arab Republic	94.50	4[a]
Iraq	84.00	1
Algeria	70.00	2
Lebanon	28.00	2[b]
Morocco	28.00	1
Jordan	16.80	2
Sudan	14.00	1
Tunisia	11.20	1
Dubai	2.24	1
Total	348.74	15

SOURCE: The Planning Board, *Kuwait—Economic Survey 1965/66* (mimeographed, July, 1966), p. 12.

[a] The U.A.R. has concluded agreements for $70 million, $14 million, and $8.4 million to assist in the preservation of the Abu Simbel antiquities and $2.1 million for residential facilities for the armed forces.

[b] One loan of $14 million was extended to the municipality of Beirut.

The National Assembly must ratify all state reserves loan agreements, though not KFAED commitments; thus political considerations are prominent. Because of the obvious political element in these credits, the National Assembly in 1965 voted to halt this form of aid, and since that time ratification has been voted only for those arrangements concluded prior to the cutoff date. The question which remains is whether the Kuwaiti government will expand KFAED's operations to include an agency for program lending which will ultimately culminate in budgetary support specifically in foreign exchange needs, or if considerations within the region will bring a reestablishment of assistance through the state reserves. The doubling of KFAED's capitalization in mid-1966 indicates that the former policy may be encouraged.

The political elements in Kuwaiti aid, whether real or imagined, can be summed up in four major points. (1) National security is an internationally accepted reason for aid. This element was brought home to Kuwait during the territorial threat by Kassem of Iraq. By spreading its aid among many recipients, it could be thought that Kuwait is now in a position such that no single country would threaten its independence without having to provoke those other states which benefit from Kuwaiti aid and/or investment. (2) As a small country in the Arab League, Kuwait desires recognition and acceptance as an equal within the region. This situation implies a "good will policy" which also acts as a positive form of public relations. It could be viewed as a move toward minimizing the jealousies between the oil "haves" and "have nots". (3) Kuwait thrives on stability because of its dependence on the oil industry and international trade. Hence, Kuwaiti economic assistance is a palliative means of shoring up and strengthening the area's stability. (4) The makeup of the population, in which non-Kuwaitis, the majority coming from Arab countries, account for over 50 per cent of the total inhabitants, presents an obvious political element.

As with the United States Congress, the Kuwaiti National Assembly has its opponents of foreign aid, particularly loans from the state reserves. Their arguments are that a political rather than economic *raison d'être* underlies the aid program, that funds earmarked for assistance could be spent at home, specifically in such projects as low-income housing. Those opposing Kuwait's aid, however, have been deprived of two contentions, first, that of a balance-of-payments problem, and second, that with reference to KFAED loans waste is minimized by project lending, although this charge might be more applicable to credits from the state reserves. Nonetheless, the political content of Kuwaiti aid should not be overexaggerated. Kuwait is not ambitious territorially. It is something of a neutral island in the Arab currents of what are commonly labeled "conservative" versus "progressive" and widely oversimplified and equated with monarchy versus nonmonarchy. Because of its prosperity, fewer economic problems and pressures are engendered and Kuwait is domestically fortunate in being relatively removed from deep political disturbances. Its interests for expanded economic well-being are served by regional continuity, gradualism in change, and reduced political instability.

Finally, reference should be made to program as contrasted to project lending, the latter being less likely to fall subject to political pressure from either donor or recipient. To achieve efficiency in the allocation of aid, economic standards could be more easily assessed in project rather than program lending. Admittedly, all aid in general has political content; the objective is to minimize this content and maximize the economic aspects. In most cases aid is given for three purposes: (1) economic development of the recipient, (2) support of political stability in countries having special ties with the donor, and (3) export promotion.[47] Kuwait's assistance policies thus far have been conditioned by the first two elements but not by the third—export promotion—as the country has not yet achieved an industrial export sector requiring aid support. This does not mean, however, that aid-supported exports will not become a factor in the future. A fourth facet, which does not assume the same magnitude or proportion in other donor countries, yet exists in the Kuwaiti case, is the drive for financial diversification. Considering this condition, selectivity is an important element and efficient aid allocation is stimulated by the set of controls inherent in project lending. Included are bases for the determination of the amount to be lent, specification of resources to be used, and a system of evaluation and technical appraisal of the efficiency with which the credit is being utilized. Perhaps the most obvious value of project lending is the ability to curb waste of capital aid which otherwise might be used for increased consumption. This does not mean that program lending per se is wasteful.[48]

Aid and investment are closely linked in Kuwait's economic international relations. Not only are the loans to Arab states a form of diversification of investment of surplus capital, but quasi-public and often completely private concerns, under government auspices and/or guarantees, participate in the transfer of funds designated for developmental purposes in numerous developing countries. The loan arrangement concluded in February, 1966, between Kuwait and the U.A.R. involves the provision by Kuwaiti banks of credit facilities totaling $42 million to the Central Bank of Egypt under guarantees from both governments.[49] Included in this agreement was the participation of the Kuwait Company for Foreign Trade, Contracts and Investments in specific projects in

[47] These motives for extension of aid are given by Chenery and Strout, "Foreign Assistance and Economic Development," p. 726.

[48] *Ibid.*, pp. 726–29.

[49] The details and implications of this agreement have been discussed under "Bilateral Arrangements" in the preceding chapter.

the United Arab Republic. In 1965 this company was established, its subscription in an 80 : 20 government–private framework and its functions those defined in its name. Four years earlier the Kuwait Investment Company had been created as an institution which would be capable of attracting private capital for investment domestically and abroad. Its original capitalization was set at $21 million on a 50 : 50 government and private basis.[50] Recently the K.I.C. has participated in the creation of a Kuwaiti bank in London. This should not be confused with Kuwait's investment office in England, which does not make public any accounts of the extent of its operations. The investment angle of Kuwaiti aid will be pursued later in this chapter with greater detail.

THE LEVEL OF ECONOMIC ASSISTANCE

We have examined thus far the structural and qualitative aspects of Kuwaiti assistance, its terms of amortization and interest, its concentrated impact on a selected region (yet its spread of recipients within the area), the facility with which loans can be acted upon, and finally, the predominance of economic factors in the institutionalization of its aid programs. In completing the total appraisal of the economic foreign aid of Kuwait, an assessment of the level of its assistance effort involves a dual measurement. The first is to relate the extent of its assistance to its national income. Second, we can compare the Kuwaiti program quantitatively with that of other aid-extending nations.

In 1964 the United Nations Conference on Trade and Development meeting in Geneva adopted the following recommendation, which has since been dubbed the "1 per cent formula."

> Each economically advanced country should endeavor to supply . . .
> financial resources to the developing countries of a minimum net amount
> approaching as nearly as possible to one per cent of its national
> income . . . .[51]

---

[50] The Company's assets by early 1965 were some $43.92 million while there was an increased drive to attract additional savings to be invested. This corporation is also involved in feasibility studies on industrial development. Kuwait Chamber of Commerce and Industry, *Survey of Kuwait* (Kuwait, 1965), p. 422.

[51] United Nations, Conference on Trade and Development, *Final Act*, E/CONF.46/L.28, Annex A. IV.2, p. 86.

Parenthetically, Kuwait was designated as belonging to the developing country grouping at this Conference.

While this recommendation was specifically understood not to be interpreted as either a ceiling or a rigid yardstick for assessment, the D.A.C. members, despite its shortcomings as a comparison base and the difficulties involved in heterogeneity, concurred in its passage as offering a target for their aid efforts. Considering only official net disbursements, and thereby avoiding the pitfalls of estimated net private assistance, the ranking, as shown in Table 5, may be assigned.

TABLE 5

DISBURSEMENTS OF ASSISTANCE AS PERCENTAGE OF NATIONAL INCOME OF MAJOR
CONTRIBUTORS, 1964

	Total Official Net Assistance as Per Cent of National Income	National Income (In Billion Dollars)
Kuwait	9.61	1.439
Portugal	2.24	2.8
France	1.26	66.5
United States	0.70	506.1
United Kingdom	0.67	73.1
Belgium	0.67	12.0
Germany	0.58	79.2
Canada	0.39	32.8
Netherlands	0.37	13.2
Norway	0.35	4.8
Japan	0.33	53.9

SOURCE: *Development Assistance Efforts and Policies, 1965*, p. 55.

In light of the one per cent formula, Kuwait's official net flow alone places that nation first. Even if one takes into account the net private flow, the total effort of the D.A.C. members averages 0.96 per cent of their combined national incomes for 1964. And if loans and credits of five years' maturity or less on private net are included rather than the five-year cutoff point used in Table 5, still the overall percentage for official net disbursement would be only one per cent.[52] All Kuwaiti loans are developmental credits and none falls below the five-year maturity level.

With respect to a ranking simply by the amount of official bilateral lending, the United States stands far above any donors, extending almost eight times that of the United Kingdom, which is second among D.A.C., that is, non-Soviet lenders. As seen in

[52] *Development Assistance Efforts and Policies, 1965*, p. 137.

Table 6, Germany, Japan, and France follow closely. Kuwait, in sixth place, extends more than half that of the United Kingdom.

TABLE 6

RANKING BY OFFICIAL BILATERAL LENDING COMMITMENTS, 1964
(IN MILLION DOLLARS)

United States	2,373.0
United Kingdom	298.9
Germany	279.2
Japan	252.2
France	210.8
Kuwait	151.8
Italy	131.5
Canada	84.2
Portugal	35.5
Netherlands	16.4

SOURCE: *Development Assistance Efforts and Policies, 1965,* p. 137.

Quantitatively, Kuwaiti bilateral lending in 1964 was almost one-quarter of total U.S.S.R. assistance in the same year. Yet the 1964 aid figure of the Soviet Union was exceptionally high, the largest amount to be extended in a single year throughout the first half of the 1960's.[53] A more appropriate comparison can be made for the 1962–65 period, covering the time during which Kuwait has been formally extending aid. Using such a basis, total Kuwaiti assistance averages one-third of the total aid of the U.S.S.R. Moreover, these Soviet aid figures include economic and non-economic types of assistance, while Kuwaiti official bilateral aid has been strictly for developmental purposes. Finally, in comparing the lending level of Kuwait with those of the Development Assistance Committee and the Sino-Soviet commitments, it should be reiterated that Kuwaiti loans are not tied.

In just half a decade Kuwait has emerged as the only major bilateral aid-extender apart from the bipolarized sources, the industrialized nations of the "West" (the D.A.C.), and the Communist bloc. We have tried to assess Kuwait's position through the use of various criteria—its assistance as a share of its national income and the level of its total lending on an international

[53] The amounts committed in loans by the U.S.S.R. for those years are (in millions of dollars): 1960—$582; 1961—$302; 1962—$214; 1963—$203; 1964—$618; 1965—$369. *Middle East and African Economist,* September, 1966, p. 119.

comparative base. Yet Kuwaiti lending has not been distributed on a worldwide basis, but directed toward regional destinations. Thus, the impact of Kuwait's assistance programs is restricted in geographical scope but increased by its depth. The Arab Middle East and Africa has long straddled a seesaw of Soviet and U.S. aid. The evolution of a middle force has been a positive factor toward greater balance in the region. Even though 1963 was not a heavy year in Kuwaiti lending, still its net flow through KFAED and the state reserves credits to certain Arab countries was greater than the net flow of lending by the OECD members (D.A.C.) to those nations. The extent of the gap is apparent in Table 7.

TABLE 7

NET FLOW OF LENDING FROM THE OECD AND KUWAIT[a] TO SELECTED ARAB COUNTRIES, 1963
(IN MILLION DOLLARS)

	OECD	Kuwait
Sudan	1.460	11.838
Jordan	3.680	5.057
Iraq	2.970	84.000
Lebanon	1.100	5.600

SOURCES: Ministry of Finance and Oil; KFAED, *Second Annual Report 1963–1964*; OECD, *The Flow of Financial Resources to Less-Developed Countries 1956–1963* (Paris, 1964), pp. 172–73, 176.

[a] Actual drawings on the state reserves and KFAED loans.

Kuwaiti aid to the U.A.R. and Jordan in relation to their size and population has been substantial. In Jordan's 1965/66 budget of $163.862 million, development loans totaled about $29.173 million. Of this sum, Kuwait is the second bilateral lender, extending $8.252 million, surpassed only by the U.S. Agency for International Development with $10 million. The third largest lender is a multilateral agency, the I.D.A., affiliate of the World Bank ($6.331 million). German development loans accounted for $2.634 million, and England, formerly the major source of assistance to Jordan, ranked fourth with $1.96 million. In 1964 the foreign exchange shortage of the U.A.R. was eased considerably by loans from the state reserves and the KFAED credit to the Suez Canal Authority. These commitments totaled more than the assistance delivered by either the U.S. or the Soviet Union.[54]

[54] *New York Times*, August 29, 1965.

For the Arab world, Kuwaiti aid for developmental purposes has earned, without doubt, a place among the top three bilateral lending powers. Within the context of the level of its overall aid programs, Kuwaiti economic assistance does not play a mere supplementary role but rather is an active catalyst, enhancing the credit ratings of the recipients and supplying initial support through KFAED for technically and economically feasible projects to which additional private and foreign investment can be drawn. Nor should Kuwait's assistance remain confined to the Arab world alone. Diversification of aid-investment is already underway in Africa. As Kuwait industrializes a new set of conditions will be added to the milieu of the aid programs, linking trade prospects to the assistance patterns of the country.

AID, TRADE, AND DEVELOPMENT

Tying Aid

While the tying of aid has not been considered yet by Kuwait, it is likely to become a major area of discussion as industrialization proceeds and the country not only has surplus capital but an export surplus. Tied aid is the newest mode in economic assistance. This system of linking aid to a nation's export promotion has been adopted increasingly by all major assistance-extending nations, with the purpose of mitigating some of the negative effect on the international accounts of these donors. Employment also enters the picture. It has been estimated that in the U.S. economy more than half a million people are directly employed in aid-supported industries.[55] Those countries which suffer from balance-of-payments deficits, such as the United States and Great Britain, have found the aid-tying method particularly attractive. Among the D.A.C. members' assistance, about two-thirds of gross bilateral aid are contractually tied or otherwise limited. Canadian, Japanese, and Danish aid today is almost 100 per cent tied; the U.S. and Italy require from 85 to 90 per cent of their aid funds to be spent in purchasing their respective products. In France and England about one-third of their aid funds are formally tied, but this latter percentage has only a very limited significance as French and

[55] Ragaei El Mallakh, "Foreign Aid," *Challenge*, December, 1964, p. 13.

English aid can be tied, in fact, without being so by contract or regulation.[56]

To Kuwait the system of tied aid might appear appealing as Kuwait has a limited domestic market for locally produced industrial items and possesses the means to support and even subsidize exports. Yet, is such a method the most suitable for the Kuwaiti economy, at present or in the future? A closer look at the Kuwaiti economic structure shows that Kuwait is not and cannot be for some time a supplier of the types of goods most urgently needed by the borrowing countries for developmental purposes, that is, capital goods such as hydroelectric turbines, cranes, and heavy machinery. Furthermore, Kuwait is in no way pressured by balance-of-payments difficulties, as many developed lenders have been. Perhaps more important is the strong possibility of creating inefficiency of resource use through heavy subsidization of exports. The temptation is great indeed to pursue such a policy where there there is no capital shortage to finance export-oriented industries.

Just how beneficial would such an approach prove for Kuwait? Kuwait must find a way of broadening its market, either through a widened "domestic" market via regional cooperation and/or through a deliberate policy of export support. One element must be kept in mind: that Kuwait's capital surplus is based upon the exploitation of a wasting asset which is also a primary commodity; hence, there are factors of price fluctuations, and ultimately the quantity of oil can be a restrictor of capital accumulation. In such a case a supplementary sector such as industry is not only required but it must be, in the final analysis, profitable, competitive, and self-supporting. Thus efficiency in the use of resources in industry, while not an important factor in the immediate future, may prove decisive later. Such reasons would call for caution in grasping the system of tied aid as a cure-all for industrialization and export trade. Still, selective and temporary tying might be used to advantage in breaking into markets for certain products (e.g., petrochemicals, specifically fertilizers), where the would-be consumer nations lack financing.

[56] *Development Assistance Efforts and Policies, 1965*, p. 90. This is particularly the case where commercial and social links and contact remain between the donor and recipient, as between France and the members of the French franc area and between England and the sterling bloc members. For example, the value of the trade surplus of France with the French franc area, plus the value of services, tends to be almost equal to the monetary evaluation of French aid.

The economic by-products of aid tying include negative effects to both recipient and donor, and the principle of freedom in international trade from which Kuwait has traditionally benefited. The most obvious regressive aspect of tied aid for the recipient is the possible waste through restricted procurement, which can disregard or minimize differences in quality and actual cost. It can also play havoc with the successful and timely completion of the supported projects by relegating the project priorities through supply to the prevailing economic conditions in the donor country. Since the emphasis in Kuwaiti aid is moving toward greater project rather than program lending, efficient implementation, including meeting schedules, is basic to sound lending and investment.

There is a definite movement among major donors who presently follow a tied aid policy, more specifically the D.A.C., to minimize the negative effects while, at the same time, maintaining the objectives of improvement in and safeguarding the balance-of-payments position. Measures which could be utilized include the encouragement of domestic competition, a flexible policy of waivers to offset substantial cost differential, and sub-contracting to third countries when economically advantageous.[57] Should Kuwait ever employ tied aid to any degree, the above liberalizing conditions would be compatible with the peculiarities of Kuwait's economic structure. Kuwaiti assistance is characterized by a high investment content and businesslike practices, hence, the economic use of resources resulting in a high rate of return from a supported project is a predominant factor. If and when Kuwait finds itself with industrial products needing export markets, then a separate agency, quite apart from its established aid programs, patterned after the U.S. or Japanese export-import banks, could offer the necessary boost into international markets. Because of the KFAED's experience in appraisal and technical assessment, such an institution could function under the auspices of or in affiliation with the Fund to benefit from its mechanism.

Kuwaiti Aid in Perspective

Kuwaiti aid does not function within a vacuum but rather within the worldwide framework of assistance. Comparison must not

[57] Recommendations along this line were adopted by the D.A.C. at its Paris meeting in July, 1965. See *Development Assistance Efforts and Policies, 1965*, Annex B, pp. 117–22, for all the recommendations, including terms.

distort the true perspective of Kuwaiti aid. Kuwaiti lending terms of KFAED and the state reserves can be compared favorably with the rates of the members of the D.A.C. and are almost in line with the medium terms of the United States A.I.D. (see Chart 1). The quality of aid has been relatively high, based upon lenient but not concessional terms. We have noted that Kuwait stood far above any other country in bilateral disbursements as a percentage of its national income in 1964. This share has always hovered between 9 and 10 per cent annually. Yet Kuwait's national income is only slightly more than half that of Portugal, the D.A.C. member with the smallest national income. In this manner, the total amount of Kuwaiti aid is limited by the approximately $1.5 billion base. So while Kuwait ranks as sixth among the official bilateral lenders in 1964 in comparison with the D.A.C. countries, its level has probably peaked. Kuwait could not meet the total capital requirements of the region even if it so desired; its lending should be viewed in terms of the strategic impact in selective areas.

Functioning within the context of such limitations, the aid policy of Kuwait, particularly through the KFAED, attempts to minimize the noneconomic elements which attend assistance programs. This is not a unique problem for Kuwait alone but extends to other donors in general.

> The present distribution of world flows of aid is more easily explained along historical and political lines than according to any obvious economic or ethical criterion.[58]

Yet with no colonial or former colonial ties with its borrowers, and being free from military commitments abroad, Kuwait can concentrate more on the economic rationale in extending aid than those other donor nations whose programs more nearly fit the description above. Because of a new slant to Kuwaiti aid, that of investment orientation, the weight of political motives, specifically in the Fund's activities, has been reduced.

Because Kuwait has fulfilled most of its local social overhead and economic infrastructure, and has attained a high standard of living, domestic opportunities, even with the demands of industrialization, need not alter radically the aid component of the national income.

[58] I. M. D. Little and J. M. Clifford, *International Aid* (Chicago: Aldine Publishing Company, 1966), p. 71. Although this is a very recent study, the authors fail to even mention Kuwait or its aid programs.

What could be a more serious alternative to economic assistance is investment abroad in long-established industrial projects and in advanced nations. However, certain considerations ameliorate this possible clash. (1) At present Kuwait manages to "invest" through investment and "invest" through aid with a balance which has remained fairly stable. (2) Aid may be considered a source of income and a method of diversifying the use of surplus capital. (3) Kuwaiti entrepreneurs and industries can benefit from the development processes in neighboring countries and through export possibilities. (4) Kuwait has a regional mentality cognizant of the larger geographical entity of which it is a part, owing to its long history of trading, the admixture of its population, and sharing in common the experience of post-World War II nationalism and independence. Its policy decision as a prosperous nation to participate in the development of the surrounding capital-deficit area could be seen within this context.

Kuwaiti aid can also be weighed within the framework of its economic development, which has been derived from a combination of natural resource exploitation and the importation of skills and labor, generally from regional sources. Kuwait's specialty of capital dictates its role as a lender. Unlike other nations, such as Formosa and Japan, the former considered developing, Kuwait could not launch a technical-assistance-based program from its own resources as it still has a shortage in this sector. However, it can and does finance technical aid. This has been facilitated through Kuwait's close cooperation with international, regional, and United Nations agencies. One can point to the possibility of mutual assistance and exchange among the developing nations which have surpluses and deficits in various factors, whether capital, management or labor. Such intra-help among developing countries, based on specialty, is an element to be reckoned with in putting Kuwaiti assistance in perspective.

A New Dimension for Economic Aid

As a developing country Kuwait has to concern itself concurrently with the impact of aid not only on the recipient country but also on the rate of growth of its own economy. Economically Kuwait is preoccupied, and rightly so, with diversification both in sources of income, through expansion of the non-oil sector, and in spreading the investment of its capital. Assistance performs here wearing a new face as investment, and it should be designed to facilitate and encourage private investment to accompany or follow the public funds. An example is the growing and healthy shift of capital funds from real estate to support of industrial and agricultural projects. In the realm of private investment in foreign enterprises, a national or regional institution similar to the International Finance Corporation (IFC), an affiliate of the World Bank, comes to mind. The IFC raises money by floating bonds and selling participation in its projects to private and official investors. The Kuwait Company for Foreign Trade, Contracts and Investments (KCFTCI) offers a nucleus for the development of a national version of an IFC type of organization, provided that its main emphasis would be placed on the promotion of private enterprise at home and abroad.[59] At present the public-private mix of this company leans heavily toward government participation and might require greater concentration on one specific activity, i.e., investment, and a larger share of private backing. Such an instrument could tap and channel the often dormant though sizeable reservoir of entrepreneurial ability and private savings.

Private investment in development projects usually accompanies or follows foreign aid. But this has not reached an adequate level in the Kuwaiti case, and thus a new dimension should be sought. Whether the Kuwait Company for Foreign Trade, Contracts and Investments can be adapted, or a new agency created, such an institution could be supplementary to the KFAED as the IFC is to the World Bank on an international level. It should be recalled that the KFAED is closely constructed on the IBRD pattern of project lending on the basis of creditworthiness and efficiency of operations. An IFC-modeled agency would create investment opportunities by drawing together domestic and foreign investors and experienced management. The operational guidelines of the IFC which could be modified for a national investment institution include the maintenance of a reasonable diversification in investments, consideration of predominantly industrial proposals and those agricultural and service projects connected with manufacturing ventures, and the avoidance of participation in schemes for re-

---

[59] The Kuwait Investment Company described earlier in this chapter has centered its investing activities primarily in Kuwait. Changing its emphasis would probably be more difficult than for the KCFTCI, as the former company was established four years before the latter.

financing, direct financing of exports and imports, or real estate development.[60]

In conclusion, investment is an additional dimension to those established motives for the extension of aid—the economic development of the recipients, their political stability, and the support of exports—and is of the utmost importance to the Kuwaiti economy, being closely related to the rate of economic growth. Thus Kuwait's total aid program could be moulded to meet its specific objectives through the use of agencies concerned with separate areas such as supporting trade and/or encouraging private investment in small industries. If the stress is to remain on the capital investment diversification through aid, then the KFAED would continue as the dominant institution under which other agencies could function and be coordinated. It appears that the drive for investment is an established trend, with the discontinuation of the state reserves loans and program lending. Although it has been argued that greater total resource utilization by the recipient can be achieved on a program basis, project lending is to the investment dimension in assistance as tying aid is to the support of trade expansion.

[60] The International Bank for Reconstruction and Development, *The World Bank, IFC and IDA: Policies and Operations* (Washington, D.C., 1962), pp. 95–102. The IFC has the enviable record that for every IFC dollar invested, some three or four more dollars from private channels have flowed into the supported projects.

Maintaining Development: A Summing-Up

7

THE ECONOMICS AND CONSTRAINTS OF A WASTING ASSET

Kuwait's economic growth to date has been premised upon a sharp imbalance in the economy, but maintaining growth will be linked increasingly with efforts toward balance. This situation evolves from the fact that the economy is overwhelmingly dependent upon the exploitation and gradual exhaustion of a single wasting asset, crude oil. Throughout this study it has been emphasized that in addition to the sectoral imbalances frequently found in many developing countries, predominantly in raw material producing economies, Kuwait evidences factoral inbalance. This factoral distortion is staggering.

The availability of capital looms far above the other three factors of production—land, labor, and management. The abundance of capital, however, has allowed for substitution from nondomestic sources of the other factors. Yet the questions to be faced are how long can and should this factoral substitution take place? Given the projection that reserves of crude oil are sufficient for 80 or more years at the present level of output, and given the maximum and minimum guidelines of such elements as price and demand, then adequate capital could allow the substitution to go on for quite some time. But would the economic cost be too high?

Alternatives to the factoral disparity are to be discerned in the overlapping approaches of balancing, conserving, and replacement. Considering the fluctuations and limitations of oil as a primary commodity, Kuwait can be said to have a lump sum of capital, realized and potential, which is, by its source, nonrenewable. Thus the disposal of oil-generated funds must be of maximized

227

economic efficiency. Capital may be used to achieve greater balance by developing the lagging factors of land, labor, and management. While the latter two apparently are of unlimited absorptive capacity and infinite economic possibilities, their development faces very real restrictors in (1) the time lag in acquiring skills and education, and (2) the problem of inadequate entrepreneurial ability and attitudes toward specific employment opportunities.

The former problem has been sidestepped by immigration and by attracting from abroad manpower and skilled personnel to fill positions temporarily. The latter limitation, a qualitative one, is a by-product of affluence. The phenomenon is similar to the differing attitudes of the "Great Depression" generation in the United States and its successors which were spared deprivation and hardship. The older generations in Kuwait, which have spanned the period from poverty to prosperity, exhibit conservative economic attitudes and a hardy native entrepreneurship of a dominantly mercantile type. It is difficult to redirect such individuals into a managerial class geared toward industry. In the younger generation a weakening of the relationship between effort and reward is noticeable, nor has it been strengthened by the government's practice of overstaffing, which reinforces the Kuwaiti preference for civil service employment. Moreover, the heavy reliance on the land purchase program seriously undermined economic incentive. On the other hand, there is a growing awareness of the Kuwaiti's need to attach his own economic well-being to the steady and continued growth of the national economy. Education is the principal factor in this process which will enable the weaving of economic principles into the fabric of national thinking and policy.

The affluence of the last twenty years has spawned two extreme attitudes toward continued growth. One is a near-obsessive fear that the affluence could drastically and abruptly end because of radical changes in the oil economy. The economics of the oil industry is not widely understood by this grouping, which is specifically pessimistic over what is believed to be the imminent depletion. Little reassurance for such thinking is forthcoming from the industry itself, which tends to be conservative and cautious in estimates, the companies hesitating to publish exact reserve figures. This is further aggravated by the widespread transit mentality attributable to the high percentage of temporary non-Kuwaiti residents. The second attitude is of complacency, that Kuwait can simply purchase anything it needs, be it a skill, commodity, or experience, rather than developing the requirement at home. Such a view is basically isolationist and noncreative. In maintaining economic growth the former attitude would appear to be the greater deterrent. Although both attitudes are dangerous, they are also diminishing and neither has enjoyed any sustained dominance. Nonetheless, when mild business slumps occur, as in 1963–65, the economically conservative outlook surfaces quickly. Entrepreneurial ability and the development of an indigenous managerial class have been hampered by such economic behavior. The elements of time, education, and experience should ameliorate these dual problems of fear and overconfidence as related to incentive.

The remaining two approaches, other than factoral balance, are of conserving and replacing the capital funds to better insure a continued rise in the economy's potential, and largely involve deferment and investment. By deferring the immediate use of funds through lending and saving, the goal of conservation is achieved with a modest increment resulting from interest charges and earnings. It will be recalled that while in Kuwait the savings rate is extremely high, reaching in general about 44 per cent of the GNP, domestic investment has absorbed but 41 per cent of the total savings. This deferment can be traced to three causes: (1) the high per capita income, reaching over $3,500 in 1966, and the low marginal propensity to consume in the high-income brackets, which have reached or are near to reaching the saturation point in consumption; (2) the cautious attitude which has led to saving and hoarding rather than investment; and (3) a monetary mechanism inadequate for encouraging and channelling the transfer of private funds into productive investment opportunities at home and abroad. The government has likewise mainly followed a policy of accumulating and banking reserves (discussed in chapter 3).

Finally, replacement here refers to the investment of funds derived from the nonrenewable oil source in capital-generating and reproducing ventures in industry, maritime activities, and agriculture. It is at this juncture that the sectoral imbalance and narrowness of the domestic market constrict the opportunities for investment within Kuwait. This is evident in the fact that while domestic investment is on the increase, up from the relative slump years of 1963/64 and 1964/65 from 19 per cent of the GNP to 21 per cent in 1965/66, the area of concentration has been the traditional activity, private construction, which had received impetus earlier from the government's land purchase scheme. The Kuwaiti government recently adopted the policy of attempting to restrict the overinvestment tendencies in this sector by limiting the number of construction permits. Yet the major problem still remains one of luring private investment toward industry, which to date has been accomplished for the most part through government participation, support, or subsidy. Private investment in the usual forms of agriculture is almost nil as most work in this sector is experimental, backed by government financing. Economic attitudes can be noted in the willingness to invest in certain enterprises. Since agriculture, especially to the younger generation, is foreign, there is a lack of readiness to risk investment, but in maritime ventures, where the Kuwaiti has a background of experience on which to draw, transport and fishing have received ample private funds.[1]

The problem of maintaining development in Kuwait has received attention only in recent years. In the initial flush of capital accumulation, the overriding concern was to broaden the economic base by dispersing funds through the land purchase program and to provide a modern social infrastructure. With the growing level of affluence, a self-motivated drive evolved to maintain this level. Included was a greater attachment to and interest in the source of original wealth, oil.

The basic elements which are the center of Kuwaiti attention, both public and private, are the amount of production and price stability. The stance of Kuwait regarding the former concern is that the output of crude oil should continue to rise in view of the vast reserves and the low production costs, thereby giving the economy a base upon which government revenues can depend and be estimated. Because of the constant threat of competitive energy sources to oil, the prevailing notion is that little can be gained from excessive deferment of exploitation. Deferment and conservation represent two different issues vis-à-vis petroleum. The Kuwaiti push for conservation has been aimed, for the most part, at the

---

[1] The author experienced personally this "agricultureless" viewpoint when addressing the United Nations Institute for Social and Economic Planning on the topic of Kuwait's capital-surplus economy and aspects of potential growth. In the discussions which followed it was clear that to many Kuwaitis agriculture is truly an unknown quantity and one which they find difficult to assess. The near-total dependence on imported foodstuffs in the last two decades has become firmly established.

minimization of natural gas waste and has been actuated through reinjection, wider utilization of this product as an energy base, and its vital role in the rapidly developing petrochemical industry. In the drive to receive the highest return for the exploitation of its wasting resource, the price level is a matter of consuming involvment. To increase its bargaining power, and in an attempt to influence the underlying factors in pricing such as the total crude oil output of producing nations, Kuwait has joined with other major exporters in multilateral efforts to program production and present the operating companies with a common policy on royalties and taxes.

Another facet of the concern for the continued growth of the national economy is the initiation of economic planning, with the final version of the First Five Year Plan published in April, 1967, and yet to be implemented. The essence of the Plan (described in chapter 4) is the long-range development of a self-sustaining economy, with diversification as a major objective as well as modifications in the population mix of Kuwaiti and non-Kuwaiti and the trend toward Arab economic complementarity and integration. As to the immediate goals of the Plan, an increase of 48 per cent of the GNP from 1967/68 to 1971/72 is projected. In addition, the short-run targets include the lessening of the economy's reliance on such activities as residential construction and the trade sector.

But the effectiveness and performance of the Five Year Plan will be contingent upon the fluctuations in capital supply directly emanating from the level of oil revenues, which is part and parcel of the worldwide petroleum industry's supply and demand functions. The Plan's viability will lie in its responsiveness and ability to incorporate any changes in governmental revenues available for developmental purposes, and in its effectiveness in selling the program to the private Kuwaiti investor. The Central Bank may be able to assist in reaching the targets of the Plan by its role in creating economic stability through the regulation of monetary policies and the adjustment of interest and rediscount rates. Perhaps, however, the Bank's major contribution will be its research and collection of economic data. By keeping its finger on the pulse of the economy, it can better advise governmental planners and private entrepreneurs, actual and potential, of trends which would indicate the need for modifications in development goals. Only with the passage of time and as economic repercussions of the Plan roll in can one assess how suited the Plan is to the Kuwaiti requirements and how well readjustments are being made.

It has been argued that planning in developing countries should be formulated from the present and projected by a short period into the future, "optimizing as one goes along," rather than shaped from a status in the future backward to the contemporary exingencies.[2] While such a practical approach is valid in general, particularly in countries where data are scarce and poorly assembled, and although it would keep planning in touch with the current economic realities, in the case of Kuwait there can and should be some planning from the future to the present. This position can be supported by the basis which oil, as a wasting asset and, within margins, a gaugeable total resource, gives the Kuwaiti economy. Lest one assumes that such possibilities of two-way planning are peculiar to Kuwait, it should be recalled that any country which depends heavily on the exploitation of an exhaustible natural resource shares the characteristic, for example copper in Zambia and Chile, tin in Bolivia, or oil in Libya, Iran, Iraq, Saudi Arabia, and Venezuela. Admittedly, Kuwait stands out as an extreme example because of the degree of its reliance on a single primary commodity.

DEVELOPMENT THROUGH COOPERATION:
REGIONAL LINKAGES

The domestic problems of the economics of rapid development have become inextricably interwoven with the expanding role Kuwait plays in regional and international finance. The sensitivity of this relationship is particularly clear in Kuwait's activities in foreign trade, investment, aid, and its human resource demands. A dominant thread which runs through the Kuwaiti international outlook is the country's physical size and the overall natural resource restrictions, including climate. Not only is Kuwait small, with a population of less than half a million, it has no natural fresh water and is, for all practical purposes now, 100 per cent desert. We have seen that the Kuwaiti influence regionally is far

---

[2] Wolfgang F. Stolper, *Planning Without Facts* (Cambridge: Harvard University Press, 1966), p. 4.

greater than can normally be expected of a state with such restrictions of size and lack of varied resources, this an effect of the economic power it exerts through the movement of its capital in a capital-deficit area. This impact has led to a national pride and image, illusive but real elements which make it difficult for the Kuwaiti to see his nation as one small and not especially significant part in the total regional picture, since this is not the case today. But what of the future?

As other Middle Eastern countries develop, the economic consequences of size should prevail eventually unless the base of the Kuwaiti economy can be broadened. Such expansion can take place through industrialization, but the domestic market offers an immediate limitation. Hence, sectoral development and balance of a magnitude to continue the rate of growth experienced to date would necessarily be export-oriented. The details of the need to link industrialization to foreign trade have been studied in chapter 4, and the direction of present and potential trade examined in the subsequent chapter. In the Five Year Plan the long-term target of increasing economic complementarity on a regional basis was enunciated.

Concrete steps, however, must be initiated if this objective is to be more than a mere wish. Certain of the fields of industrial development are reasonable possibilities for many of the economies in the area. One of the more fundamental means of keeping wasteful competition in check is by not allowing it to begin. Any decisions for the creation or expansion of specific industries should be implemented without excessive delay as (1) Kuwait has the necessary capital for investment, particularly in capital-intensive industries, without the pressure of an either-or choice between operational costs and, for example, those of research, and (2) getting in on the ground floor is a positive factor in which time works to the advantage of the established industry. If Kuwaiti industrial products can secure markets in other countries before investment has been laid out for national development in the same enterprises in those economies, the complementarity would be beneficial to Kuwait, lessening the difficulties of competition by Kuwaiti commodities with domestically produced items.

Meanwhile, Kuwait's position as a free trader and middle man in the Mideast is well entrenched and can be expanded, particularly if the policy of negligible tariffs and absence of importation restrictions is continued. Transit trade accounts for the greatest non-oil share of exports in the sector. Apparently this activity is to go on without interruption as there is no mention otherwise in the 1967/68—1971/72 economic plan. The patterns of trade show that a high degree of reciprocity exists regionally since Kuwait utilizes these sources for imports of foodstuffs and light manufactured goods.

The region in general and Arab countries more specifically have served as an outlet for Kuwaiti investment. Most private entrepreneurs have preferred to invest in the long-accepted mode of real estate development in such Arab cities as Beirut, Cairo, and Ramallah. In order to break out of this narrow use of capital funds and to diversify investment, the government has taken the lead in moving to support selected industrial projects throughout the Middle East. The government is enticing private funds into these ventures by its participation in mixed enterprises, an example being the Kuwait Company for Foreign Trade, Contracts and Investments (KCFTCI). The process has not met with unqualified success; instead the response from the private sector has been weak in comparison with the share of government outlay. The KCFTCI has been on an 80–20 per cent public–private subscription basis.

Multilateral efforts through the Arab League to facilitate the movement of commodities and capital among the member states, while impressive on paper, have a dismal record in implementation. Obstructions to collective actions for greater mobility of trade and investment have more often been political and administrative than economic. Thus, attempts to fill this implementation gap are devolving upon the individual nations in bilateral arrangements.

Closely allied to investment and sharing certain of the same economic features is the relatively large-scale aid program undertaken by Kuwait. The first impetus in development lending to Arab nations took the form of strongly politically motivated credits extended from the state reserves. In less than five years more than one-third billion dollars was loaned for general programs in the recipient countries. There was a marked undercurrent of "crisis" lending as the funds were often used for compelling foreign exchange and balance-of-payments requirements. Despite the obvious pressures to continue this type of assistance financing, the Kuwaiti government seemingly has recognized the weak economic returns to Kuwait from this program with the decision to restrict state reserves credits. One might also assume that Kuwait was chafing under the persistent demands of the recipients for such loosely tied loans, frequently with long maturities and little or no interest. The massive government lending has drawn down the accumulated capital reserves. Future extensions of credits must come increasingly from current surpluses and returns on investment and earlier lending. Thus, although Kuwait will undoubtedly continue some "crisis" financing, as in the summer of 1967, it will concern itself more with loans of a greater economically productive and development-inducing nature.[3] To carry out the objective within a disciplined framework the Kuwait Fund for Arab Economic Development offers a viable means.

The Fund and its operations must stand as one of the major Kuwaiti achievements in its development process. The KFAED's principal contributions have been in reducing the political content of aid and in maximizing the businesslike handling of development lending. With a potential capital of $1.68 billion, it stands as one of the largest such national assistance agencies in the world. The terms of KFAED credits as noted in the preceding chapter, compare favorably with such institutions as the World Bank, the United States Export-Import Bank, and the average of the Development Assistance Commitee of the O.E.C.D. The impact of Kuwaiti aid on the region has been substantial and is likely to continue and rise, particularly as some adverse trends have appeared in international development finance.

The total flow of capital resources, public and private, from the D.A.C. members to all recipient nations in 1966 actually fell to $9.9 billion from the 1965 level of $10.3 billion, this despite the expansion in the national incomes of the donors. Moreover, the debt burden of the developing countries in 1966 leaped ahead by 10 per cent over the 1965 estimate of $40 billion.[4] The Arab aid recipients in the Middle East offer no exception to the general pattern of rising debt burden and the decline in total assistance and investment from the D.A.C. to the development countries.

---

[3] On October 15, 1967, aid contribution payments began to the U.A.R. and Jordan from Kuwait, Saudi Arabia, and Libya. Kuwait's share is the largest, $109.2 million of the total $266 million promised Egypt, and $44.8 million of the three-nation contribution of $112 million to Jordan. *Middle East Economic Survey*, October 20, 1967, p. 4.

[4] *Survey of International Development*, August 15, 1967, p. 1.

Furthermore, the United States aid authorization for 1967/68 has suffered major cuts. Multilateral capital assistance has bogged down because of the disinclination of developed nations to channel additional funds through international institutions. Specifically, the International Development Association, the soft-loan affiliate of the World Bank, has been facing a critical slowdown in financing from the developed member countries. Finally, there was a definite probability of an increase in World Bank rates to 6 per cent or more by the autumn of 1967 as the spread between the Bank's borrowing and lending rates narrowed.

As the need for assistance funds for the region is growing in line with the requirements of the developing countries as a whole, and as the sources for such financing have been unable to keep pace with demand, what then are some possible alternatives open to the KFAED? The Fund could raise its interest rates to that of the world market for capital funds and benefit accordingly. Second, the KFAED could continue and intensify the selectivity it follows in determining which projects to support. The latter alternative might prove more advantageous to pursue for the long run. This is true if one weighs the investment element inherent in aid itself, i.e., the chances of default are lessened by a reduced debt burden pressure and emphasis on project efficacy in the process of selection. Involved as well are the cumulative processes of investment, where public and private funds tend to follow in the wake and take advantage of development loans as a recipient's creditworthiness increases. The population mix in Kuwait reinforces this tendency as the non-Kuwaitis offer a source of knowledge and contacts throughout the region.

With all the surplus Kuwait has and is likely to accumulate in the future, it will not be able to meet the total capital requirements of the area. At best, its aid program can act as a catalyst to attract additional assistance and investment from developed countries and multilateral agencies. It can, as well, give a boost to the credit rating of the Arab nations and thereby facilitate borrowing from varied sources. Nor are Kuwaiti's lending and investment activities confined to the Arab world. Its historical ties with the Gulf and the Indian subcontinent make investment there a natural activity. Africa is also coming in for its share of attention in Kuwaiti capital movement through direct investment and development lending from the newly established Arab-African Bank. As a result of the multiple aid efforts, Kuwait ranks seventh among all assistance-extenders. That Kuwait, as a country in the process of development itself, has undertaken a capital-aid program of such magnitude gives it a unique place in international development. It provides a prototype of the methods and benefits to both donor and recipient which can accrue in capital movement. Nations such as Libya, Saudi Arabia, and Venezuela which are experiencing a capital surplus may borrow from the Kuwaiti experience to simultaneously undertake a role in the development of their regional milieu and diversify their investment possibilities.

AFFLUENCE VERSUS DEVELOPMENT

The economic aspects of affluence and development are not synonymous nor are they necessarily complementary. While Kuwaiti society can most certainly be defined as affluent, its economy cannot be strictly classified as developed. The economy of Kuwait is highly transitional, in something of a limbo between the underdeveloped and developed. By per capita income, growth rate of the GNP, capital surplus, favorable balance of payments, the high level of employment, availability of social services, the extraordinarily high savings rate, and the widespread distribution of income among the indigenous Kuwaitis, the economy falls into the developed category.

Symptoms of underdevelopment exist in the sectoral and factoral imbalance, the narrowness of the domestic market, an investment bottleneck, and an unfavorable balance of trade if oil exports are excluded, thus laying bare the dependence on a single commodity with its attendant vulnerability. Unemployment is nonexistent, but this condition can be traced to the non-Kuwaiti immigration system, with admission to the country based upon the availability of jobs and required departure when employment terminates. Such regulations also have helped to stabilize the wage level. Underemployment, nonetheless, is widespread, and the degree of productivity in the services sector has fallen far behind the level of industrial productivity. Additionally, Kuwait is spared the tensions and pressures to increase savings and limit imports which face the mass of developing countries, yet at the same time it must recognize the need of raising the level of indigenous skills and diffusing the sources of income and investment.

Affluence as manifested in high incomes and capital surplus can be a dual-edged sword either to dampen economic development through diminishing the strict necessity of priority decisions or to spur on development through the presence of savings for channeling into profitable and productive investment. Here we find that although development requires a commitment, affluence may not. Affluence can be plotted by rises and changes in habits of consumption; development usually refers to the combination of methods used to raise the level of production and individual productivity as well as consumption. For Kuwait, indications are that because of the long-standing isolation of the majority of the population from the output and processing of oil, the development of habits and techniques of indigenous production are likely to be more exacting and difficult than the adoption of consumption habits. Filling the gap between the aspects of development and underdevelopment will require deliberate efforts by both the public and private sectors.

The positive use of affluence, that is the surplus capital, in productive investment internally and externally furnishes a key to maintaining growth. Development is essentially an educational process of economic choice; affluence can widen the range of such choice but not delete the necessity of it to minimize waste which usually accompanies a capital-surplus situation. The two main obstacles to the Kuwaiti economy's continued growth, however, are the narrowness of the domestic market and fuller utilization of the human resources. The first stumbling block can be circumvented through regionalism. The second presents a greater challenge: the development of Kuwait into a research and technological core within the area, a time-consuming yet valid objective. Unlike other developing nations, Kuwait can provide the required capital outlays for such a program without burdening the economy. Despite the concentration on social services, little attention has been devoted to research possibilities. Fields in which Kuwait might innovate are research concerning the economic utilization of arid lands, weather modification, petro-chemistry, desalination, and hydroponics. Although heavily capital-intensive, the long-range economic returns may be considerable and might prove a cushion for sustained economic growth in the future. New ventures could be opened for Kuwaiti development. It is possible that Kuwait could convert from an importer to an exporter of technical skills and could specialize in other exports with a high content of research.

The economic development of Kuwait has proceeded with unprecedented rapidity, free from distorting stops and starts. The growing concern to maintain this development has crystallized in regional activities of lending and investment and in the finalization of the first Five Year Development Plan. The architects of this development program are spared the tensions of capital scarcity, deficits in balance of payments, and overpopulation, but in the final analysis their task is a complicated one of balancing capital with the ability and willingness to innovate. Finally, in the process of planning there is no pressure to sacrifice some of the needs of the present generation for the future. Quite to the contrary, the essence of and drive toward maintaining development in Kuwait today is to insure a sustained rate of growth so that the needs of future generations will not suffer from the present prosperity.

Selected Bibliography

OFFICIAL SOURCES, GOVERNMENT, INTERNATIONAL AGENCIES, COMPANY REPORTS

Agency for International Development, United States Department of State. *A Study on Loan Terms, Debt Burden and Development*. April, 1965.

Arab Petroleum Congress. *First* through *Fifth*. Papers and Discussions. Organized by the Secretariat General of the League of Arab States. (In English and Arabic.) Vol. 1: *Economics*; Vol. 2: *Production*; Vol. 3: *Processing of Petroleum*.

British Petroleum Company, Ltd. *Annual Report and Accounts, 1958* to *1966*.

————. *Statistical Review of the World Oil Industry, 1959* to *1966*.

European Coal and Steel Community. *Étude sur les perspectives énergétiques à long terme de la Communauté européenne*. Luxembourg, 1964.

————. *La conjoncture énergétique dans la Communauté européenne*. Luxembourg, April, 1965.

Al-Kuwait Al-Youm. Official Gazette. Kuwait: Government Printing Office. (In Arabic.)

Kuwait Currency Board. *Annual Reports, One* through *Five*.

Kuwait Fund for Arab Economic Development. *Annual Reports*.

————. *Fund Press Releases*.

Kuwait, The Planning Board. *The First Five Year Plan for Economic and Social Development, 1966/67—1970/71*. Kuwait: Government Printing Press, December, 1965. (In Arabic.)

————. *The First Five Year Plan for Economic and Social Development, 1967/68—1971/72*. Kuwait: Government Printing Press, April, 1967. (In Arabic.)

————. *Annual Surveys*. (Mimeographed.)

The Planning Board. Central Office of Statistics. *Yearly Summary Foreign Trade Statistics*.

The Planning Board. Central Office of Statistics. *Monthly Bulletins of Foreign Trade Statistics.*

———. *Annual Abstract for 1966.*

Kuwait, Ministry of Commerce. *Law No. 2 of 1961* (promulgating Law of Commerce). Kuwait: Government Printing Press, 1961.

Kuwait, Ministry of Finance and Oil. *General Budget of the State of Kuwait, 1962/63 to 1966/67.* (In Arabic.)

———. *The Oil of Kuwait, Facts and Figures.* Ist ed., 1964; 2d ed., 1965.

Kuwait Oil Company, Ltd. *Annual Review of Operations, 1960 to 1965.*

Organization for Economic Co-operation and Development. *The Flow of Financial Resources to Less-Developed Countries 1956–1963.* Paris, 1964.

———. *Development Assistance Efforts and Policies: 1964 Review* and *1965 Review.* Paris, 1965 and 1966.

Organization of the Petroleum Exporting Countries. *Elasticity of Demand for Crude Oil; Its Implications for Exporting Countries.* (Based on a talk given by Isam K. Kabbani, at a seminar on the International Oil Industry, held by the London School of Economics and Political Science, London, May 7, 1964.) EC/64/II.

———. *The Oil Industry's Organisation in the Middle East and Some of Its Fiscal Consequences.* (Based on a talk given by Franciso R. Parra at a Business Administration Seminar at the American University of Beirut, November 13, 1963.)

———. *OPEC and the Oil Industry in the Middle East.* (Based on a talk given by Franciso R. Parra at a Seminar on the Middle East held by the School of Advanced International Studies of the Johns Hopkins University in Washington, D.C., October 22, 1962.)

———. *Statute of the OPEC Economic Commission.*

———. *Exporting Countries and International Oil.* (Based on a talk given by Franciso R. Parra at the Imperial Defence College, London, May 8, 1964). EC/64/I.

———. *Offshore Oil Concession Agreements in OPEC Member Countries.* (Presented by E. A. Mabruk at the First International Congress on "Petroleum and the Sea," organized by the Centre International de Documentation et d'Etudes Petrolières, Monaco, May 12–20, 1965.) EF/65/I.

———. *Cheap Energy, Diversification of Sources and Security of Supply.* (Based on a talk given by Nameer A. Jawdat at the Loughborough College of Technology, November 24, 1965.) PR/66/I.

———. *Note on Resolution IX.61.*

———. *The Statute of the Organization of the Petroleum Exporting Countries.*

———. *Pricing Problems: Further Considerations.* Geneva, 1963.

Organization of the Petroleum Exporting Countries. *Explanatory Memoranda on the OPEC Resolutions: IV.32, IV.33, IV.34 of the Fourth Conference Held in Geneva—April–June, 1962.*

———. *Resolutions Adopted at the Conference of the Organization of the Petroleum Exporting Countries.*

———. *The Development of Petroleum Resources Under the Concession System in Non-Industrialized Countries.* (Based on a talk given by Francisco R. Parra at the invitation of the Iraqi Engineers' Association and the Iraqi Economists' Society in Baghdad, June 2, 1964.) EC/64/III.

———. *Data Required For Hydrocarbon Reservoir Analysis and an Effective Programme of Conservation.* (Presented at the Vth Arab Petroleum Congress, Organized by the Secretariat General of the League of Arab States, Cairo, March 16–23, 1965; paper no. 62 [B-1].)

———. *OPEC and the Principle of Negotiation.* (Presented at the Vth Arab Petroleum Congress . . . ; paper no. 20 [A-2].)

———. *From Concessions to Contracts.* (Presented to the Vth Arab Petroleum Congress . . . ; paper no. 19 [A-2].)

———. *Taxation Economics in Crude Production.* (Presented at the Vth Arab Petroleum Congress . . . ; paper no. 18 [A-2].)

United Nations. *Economic Developments in the Middle East: 1959–60; 1960–61; 1961–63.* New York.

———. Conference on Trade and Development. *Final Act.* E/CONF. 46/L.28.

United Nations Economic and Social Council. *International Symposium on Industrial Development.* Held in Kuwait, March, 1966. E/C.5/35/Add.4.

Individual Papers presented to the Arab Industrial Development Conference held in March 1966. (In Arabic.)

BOOKS

Basch, Antonin. *Financing Economic Development.* New York: Macmillan Co., 1964.

Belassa, Bela. *The Theory of Economic Integration.* Homewood, Ill.: Richard D. Irwin, Inc., 1961.

———. *Trade Prospects for Developing Countries.* Homewood, Ill.: Richard D. Irwin, Inc., 1964. A publication of the Economic Growth Center, Yale University.

Black, Eugene R. *The Diplomacy of Economic Development.* Cambridge: Harvard University Press, 1960.

Chamberlain, Neil W. *Private and Public Planning.* New York: McGraw-Hill Book Co., 1965.

Clawson, Marion, ed. *Natural Resources and International Development.* Baltimore: Johns Hopkins Press for Resources for the Future, Inc., 1964. ("The World Oil Outlook," M. A. Adelman, pp. 27–125.)

Diab, Muhammad A. *Inter-Arab Economic Cooperation, 1951–1960.* Beirut: Economic Research Institute, American University of Beirut, 1963.

Frank, Helmut J. *Crude Oil Prices in the Middle East.* New York: Frederick A. Praeger; Praeger Special Studies in International Economics and Development, 1966.

Hartshorn, J. E. *Oil Companies and Governments.* London: Faber & Faber, Ltd., 1962.

Hicks, Ursula K. *Development Finance: Planning and Control.* New York: Oxford University Press, 1965.

Hirschman, A. O. *The Strategy of Economic Development.* New Haven, Conn.: Yale University Press, 1958.

Hirst, David. *Oil and Public Opinion in the Middle East.* London: Faber & Faber, Ltd., 1966.

The International Bank for Reconstruction and Development. *The Economic Development of Kuwait.* Baltimore: Johns Hopkins University Press, 1965.

Issawi, Charles, and Yeganeh, Mohammed. *The Economics of Middle Eastern Oil.* New York: Frederick A. Praeger, 1962.

Kuznets, Simon. *Economic Growth and Structure.* New York: W. W. Norton & Co., 1965.

Lenczowski, George. *Oil and State in the Middle East.* Ithaca: Cornell University Press, 1960.

Lewis, W. Arthur. *The Theory of Economic Growth.* Homewood, Ill.: Richard D. Irwin, Inc., 1955.

Little, I. M. D., and Clifford, J. M. *International Aid.* Chicago: Aldine Publishing Co., 1966.

Longrigg, Stephen H. *Oil in the Middle East.* London: Oxford University Press, 1961.

Lutfi, Ashraf. *Arab Oil: A Plan for the Future.* Beirut, Lebanon: The Middle East Research and Publishing Center, 1960. Middle East Oil Monographs: No. 3.

Mason, Edward S. *Economic Planning in Underdeveloped Areas.* New York: Fordham University Press, 1958.

———. *Foreign Aid and Foreign Policy.* New York: Harper & Row, 1964.

Meyer, A. J. *Middle East Capitalism.* Cambridge: Harvard University Press, 1959.

Mikdashi, Zuhayr. *A Financial Analysis of Middle Eastern Oil Concessions: 1901–65.* New York: Frederick A. Praeger, 1966.

Mikesell, Raymond F. *Public International Lending for Development.* New York: Random House, 1966.

Nurkse, Ragnar. *Problems of Capital Formation in Underdeveloped Countries.* New York: Oxford University Press, 1953.

Polk, William R. *The Developmental Revolution: North Africa, Middle East, South Asia.* Washington, D.C.: The Middle East Institute, 1963.

Robinson, E. A. G., ed. *Economic Consequences of the Size of Nations.* Proceedings of a Conference held by the International Economic Association London: Macmillan & Co., Ltd., 1960.

Shamma, Samir. *The Oil of Kuwait.* Beirut, Lebanon: The Middle East Research and Publishing Center, 1959. Middle East Oil Monographs: No. 1.

Singer, Hans W. *International Development: Growth and Change.* New York: McGraw-Hill, 1964.

Stevens, Georgiana G. *The United States and the Middle East.* Englewood Cliffs, N. J.: Prentice-Hall, Inc., 1964.

Survey of Kuwait. Kuwait: Kuwait Chamber of Commerce and Industry, 1965. (In Arabic.)

Timbergen, Jan. *International Economic Integration.* Amsterdam: Elsevier, 1954.

———. *Shaping The World Economy.* New York: The Twentieth Century Fund, 1962.

ARTICLES, JOURNALS, BULLETINS

Adelman, M. "Efficiency in Resource Use in Crude Petroleum." *Southern Economic Journal,* October, 1964.

———. "Oil Prices in the Long Run." *Journal of Business,* April, 1964.

Allen, Robert L. "Integration in Less Developed Areas." *Kyklos* 14, no. 3 (1961).

Belassa, Bela. "Towards a Theory of Economic Integration." *Kyklos* 14, no. 1. (1961).

The Chase Manhattan Bank. *Capital Investments by the World Petroleum Industry, 1961, 1962,* and *November 1962.*

———. *The Petroleum Situation.* Monthly review from the Petroleum Department.

El Mallakh, Ragaei. "Economic Development Through Cooperation: The Kuwait Fund." *Middle East Journal,* Autumn, 1964.

———. "Kuwait's Foreign Aid." *International Development Review,* December, 1965.

El Mallakh, Ragaei. "Kuwait's Economic Development and Her Foreign Aid Programmes." *The World Today*, January, 1966.

———. "Planning in a Capital Surplus Economy." *Land Economics*, November, 1966.

———. "Foreign Aid." *Challenge*, December, 1964.

Emergent Nations. New York, Autumn, 1965. Issue on "Modern Kuwait."

First National City Bank. *Financing Oil Expansion in the Development Decade*, by Edward Symonds. New York, 1963.

———. *Eastern Hemisphere Petroleum—Another Year's Progress Analyzed*, by Edward Symonds. New York, 1963.

———. *Oil Advances in the Eastern Hemisphere*, by E. Symonds. New York, 1962.

———. *Oil in the National Balance*, by E. Symonds. New York, 1965.

First National City Bank, Petroleum Department. *Energy Memo*. Quarterly memo.

Fox, A. F. "The Development of the South Kuwait Oilfields." *Institute of Petroleum Review* [*London*] 15 (1961).

Intra-Bank S.A.L. [Beirut]. *Monthly Bulletin*.

Kuwait Chamber of Commerce and Industry. *Kuwait Chamber of Commerce and Industry Bulletin*. (In Arabic.)

The Middle East Economic Survey. Beirut, Lebanon: The Middle East Research and Publishing Center. Weekly.

Penrose, E. T. "Profit Sharing Between Producing Countries and Oil Companies in the Middle East." *Economics Journal* [*London*], June, 1959.

———. "Middle East Oil; The International Distribution of Profits and Income Taxes." *Economica* [*London*], August, 1960.

Shehab, Fakhri. "Kuwait: A Super-Affluent Society." *Foreign Affairs*, April, 1964.

Waterston, Albert. "A Hard Look at Development Planning." *Finance and Development*, June, 1966. Quarterly publication of the International Monetary Fund and the International Bank for Reconstruction and Development. Washington, D.C.

Index

Abdullah al-Salem al-Sabah (1950–65), 12
Absorptive capacity, 2, 23, 97, 103, 128, 129, 229
  regional, 103
Abu Dhabi, 165
  immigration from, 173
Aden, immigration from, 173
Affluence, versus development, 237–39
  benefits of, 238
  and negative economic attitudes, 228–29, 230, 238
Afghanistan, aid (Sino-Soviet) to, 206
Africa, 1, 4, 26, 87, 112, 139, 159, 198, 206
  Arab-African Bank. *See* Arab-African Bank
  authors, 160
  Kuwaiti investment in, 159
  non-oil exports to, 164
  oil, production and reserves in, 58, 68
  See also North Africa; under names of individual countries
African Development Bank, 186
Agriculture, 5, 8, 116–19, 230
  aid to, 203–4
  hydroponics, 118, 238
  labor force in, 16–17
  and land reform, 75
  and Plan, GDP contribution and investment, 127
  private investment in, 118, 230

Agriculture—continued
  role in economic development, 5, 81, 104, 117
  Savings and Credit Bank support of, 93, 94
  subsidies for, 118
  See also Hydroponics
Ahmad al-Jabir al-Sabah (1921–50), 11
Ahmadi, 8, 31
Airline, airport, 79. *See also* Kuwait Airways
Algeria, and North African regionalism, 153, 205
  Haoud El Hamra-Arzew pipeline project, 198–99
  KFAED loans to, 198–99, 204, 207, 208
  labor force in, 145
  oil of, 62
  oil production and/or reserves, 55–56, 65, 148
  and OPEC, 65
  natural gas production, 148
  sectoral distribution in GDP of, 143
  state reserves loans to, 212, 213
Allocation of financial resources, 120
Al-Sabah family, 11
Aminoil (American Independent Oil Company), concession of, 43–44
  production of, 32
  refining by, 38

247

Anglo-Iranian Oil Company, 40.
  See British Petroleum Company,
  Ltd.
Arab-African Bank, 183, 210–12,
    236
  capitalization, 210
  functions of, 211
  incentives, 210–11
  missions of, 211
  See also individual African and
    Arab countries
Arab Common Market, 27, 155,
    166–72
  balance of payments, 169
  common tariffs, 168
  competitiveness within, 170–71
  complementarity, 170
  duplication, 170–71
  and EEC, 169
  industrialization, 168, 169–70
  investment, 153
  Kuwait's position, 166–69, 170,
    171, 172
  membership in, 153, 166
  mobility of labor, 153, 171
  population and market, 169
  trade, 153, 166–67
Arab Gulf, 8, 17, 21, 45, 112, 119,
    148, 164, 172, 236
Arabian Gulf States. *See* Trucial
    States
Arabian Oil Company, concession
    of, 44–45
  production of, 32
  refining by, 38
Arab League. *See* League of Arab
    States
Arab Petroleum Congress, 29, 70–
    71, 72
  multilateralism and oil producers,
    69–70, 72–73
  petrochemicals coordination, 72
Arab world:
  and agriculture, 144–45, 154
  balanced development, 142–46
  complementarity in, 139, 170
  economic linkages in, 140
  economies of scale in, 141, 149

Arab world—continued
  and employment, 143
  factoral imbalance, 4, 233
  financial planning in, 206
  foreign aid to. *See* Foreign aid
  foreign exchange, 147
  and industry, 141, 142–44, 205
  integration, 156–58
  Kuwaiti aid to, 183
  labor force, 145
  markets in and of, 138–39, 149,
    205
  and oil, 145–46, 149, 151–52
  per capita income, 137
  petrochemicals, 106, 144, 148, 152
  and productivity, 145
  publishing in, 159–60
  sectoral imbalance, 141, 142–43
  trade, 154, 155
  See also Crisis assistance; General
    Authority for South Arabian
    and Arabian Gulf States; Ku-
    wait Fund for Arab Economic
    Development; State reserves
    loans
Argentina, wages in national in-
    come, 109
Aridity studies, 18, 238
Asia, 112
  imports from, 25, 161, 162
  non-oil exports to, 164
  oil exports to, 61
Atomic power. *See* Energy sources
    and competition
Australia, 133
  wages in national income, 109
Austria, aid from, 190
Average propensity to consume, 130

Bahrain, 11
  fertilizers to, 115
  immigration from, 173
  non-oil exports to, 164, 165
  oil production and/or reserves, 63
Bain, Joe S., 141–42
Balance of payments, 1, 26, 76, 82–
    83, 92, 134, 136, 193, 195, 199,
    214

Balassa, Bela, 50
Banking, 2, 89–94
    balance sheets of commercial banks, 89–90
    British Bank of the Middle East, 89
    Central Bank, 82, 92, 127, 231
    Commercial Bank of Kuwait, 89
    credit policies in, 90, 91
    Gulf Bank, 89
    interest rates, 90–91
    Kuwaiti Bank in London, 87
    National Bank, 89
    original stock issues sales, 91
    Savings and Credit Bank, 21, 84, 92–94
    and trade, 90, 91
    See also Interest rates; Kuwait Investment Company; Savings and Credit Bank
Belgium, 133
    aid from, 190
    aid share of national income, 217
    energy policy of, 58
    wages in national income, 109
Berlin-Baghdad railway, 10
Bilateral agreements, 158–61
    with Iraq, 160, 161
    with U.A.R., 158–60, 161
Birth rate, 13
Black, Eugene R., 132
Bolivia, 232
Brazil, 133
    aid (Sino-Soviet) to, 206
    wages in national income, 109
Britain. *See* United Kingdom
British Petroleum Company, Ltd., 20, 39–40, 43, 68, 87
    long-term supply contracts of, 40, 68
Bubiyan, 10
Budgets, 77, 80
    independent, 83–84
    and public investment program, 80
    review of, 81
    See also Higher education; Kuwait Airways; Kuwait Currency

Budgets—continued
    Board; Kuwait Fund for Arab Economic Development; Savings and Credit Bank; the Shuaiba Board
Burgan oil field, 3, 30
    injection plant, 36
Burma, exports of, 99

Canada, 133
    aid from, 181, 189–90, 218
    aid share in national income, 217
    and Arab Petroleum Congress, 151
    tying aid, 220
    wages in national income, 109
Capital, 2, 4, 96, 101, 106, 227–28
    conserving, 229
    deepening investment, 99
    -output ratio, 129–30
    regional deficit in, 4, 233
    "replacement" of, 229–30
    surplus, 4, 6, 19, 76–77, 81, 82–83, 86, 91, 103, 132, 134, 145, 230, 233, 235, 237, 238
    widening investment, 99
Caustic soda production, 19, 108, 111
Cement production, 20, 85, 106
Central Bank, 82, 92, 127, 231
Central government organization, 11
Chemicals, production of. *See* Petrochemicals; Sea water, chemicals from
Chile, 232
    wages in national income, 109
Choice, problem of, 3, 120, 132, 233
City planning, 75
Civil service, 16, 78–79, 228
    efficiency in, 85, 99, 122
    Kuwaiti workers, 16
    non-Kuwaiti workers, 16
    number of workers in, 16, 79
    overstaffing in, 78–79, 85, 99
Climate, 8, 232
Colombia, exports of, 99
    wages in national income, 109

Commerce:
  historical attachment to, 12
  labor force in, 16–17
  and Plan, contribution in GDP
    and investment, 127
Commercial Law of 1961, 91
Common market, 156, 157
Communications, Plan contribution
  in GDP and investment, 127
Company Law (Article 120), 88–89
Constitution, promulgation of, 11
  provisions in, 11
Construction industry, 6, 22, 75, 83,
    85, 116, 229–30, 231
  demand for building materials, 19
  expenditures on, 79
  labor force in, 17
  and Plan, contribution in GDP
    and investment, 126, 127, 231
  school construction program, 79
Consumption, 126, 168–69. *See also*
  Average propensity to consume;
  Marginal propensity to con-
  sume; Propensity to consume
Crisis assistance (1967), 234, 235
Customs union, 156, 157
Cyprus, fertilizers to, 115
  wages in national income, 109

Dahomey, Arab–African Bank mission to, 211
Debt burden, 182, 187, 235
  of Arab countries, 187–88 235–36
Defense, expenditures in Plan, 127
Denmark, aid from, 190
  tying aid, 220
  wages in national income, 109
Desalination of water, 19, 117, 238
Developing nations:
  and agriculture, 116–17
  aid requirements of, 181–82, 235
  energy requirements of, 52–53
  infrastructure needs, 100–101
  and oil utilization, 59, 61
  and planning, 4, 100–101
Development Assistance Committee.
  See Foreign aid; Organization

Development Assistance
  Committee—continued
  for Economic Co-operation and
  Development
Diesel oil, prices of, 48–49
Directly productive activities, 101,
  120
Distillation, 19, 36, 108, 110–11,
  117–18
Domestic industries, 19–20. *See also*
  Industries
Domestic market, narrowness of, 81,
  103, 106, 109, 138–39, 233, 238
Dubai, grants to, 208–9
  state reserves loan to, 212, 213
  See also General Authority for
  Arabian and Arabian Gulf
  States
Duties, on imports, 22

East India Company, 10
Economic aid (Kuwait), 4, 12, 26,
  27, 66–67, 68, 71, 181, 183–84,
  224–26, 234–35; 236–37
  Arab–African Bank, 183, 210–12,
  236
  comparative analysis of, 216–19
  creditworthiness, 185, 193, 235
  crisis assistance in Middle East
  (1967), 234, 235
  economic content of, 223–24
  General Authority for South
  Arabian and Arabian Gulf
  States (Gulf Permanent Assistance Committee), 183, 208–10
  grants. *See* General Authority for
  South Arabian and Arabian
  Gulf States
  as investment, 26, 27, 132, 215–16,
  223–24, 236
  Kuwait Fund for Arab Economic
  Development (KFAED), 184–
  208, 235, 236
  political content in, 212, 215, 223,
  234–35
  program lending, 184, 214–15
  project lending, 193, 214–15
  quality of aid,182,188–90,192,217

Economic Aid (Kuwait)—continued
quantitative level of aid, 217–18,
223, 237
regional impact of, 219–20, 236
share of national income, 183, 216,
217, 223
state reserves loans, 183–84, 212–
16
"tied," 191–93, 221–22
See also Algeria; Dubai; Iraq;
Jordan; Lebanon; Morocco;
Sudan; Tunisia; Trucial
States; U.A.R.; Yemen
Economic cooperation, 135–36, 137,
148–49, 156–58, 232–37
Common market. *See* Arab Common Market
and implementation gap, 155,
157–58
Middle East (Arab world), 26–
27, 125, 232–37
trade-creation and diversion, 155–
56
Economic development, measurement of, 1–2
and change, 5
through cooperation, 232, 237
and growth, 125, 142–46
Economic growth, 3, 6, 96–97, 100–
104, 124, 227, 238
balanced, 6, 26, 97, 100–102,
103–4, 120, 123–24, 142–46
diversification, 6, 19–20, 21–22,
25, 26, 37, 108–9, 124, 126, 140,
149
unbalanced, 17–19, 101, 102–3,
227
Economic linkages, horizontal, 140
vertical, 140–41
Economics of size, 133–39, 233
and competition, 135, 137
economies of scale. *See* Economies
of scale
and efficiency, 135
technological aspects of, 134
and vulnerability, 135
Economics of a wasting asset, 227–
32

Economics of a wasting
asset—continued
and special demands on capital,
227–28
Economies of scale, 27, 135–36, 137,
140–42, 149
Economy, 74–83, 97, 138, 160
competition, 139
domestic market. *See* Domestic
market
enclave pattern in, 85, 102
government role in, 81, 84–85, 116
gross national product (GNP), 7,
8, 9, 81, 125, 229, 231, 237
growth rate, 3, 7, 18, 126, 137–38
labor force. *See* Labor force
legislation affecting, 21, 77–78
national income, 98
non-oil resources, 3, 4, 81, 103
oil sector. *See* Oil industry
per capita income, 1, 6, 134, 161,
168, 237
private sector. *See* Private sector
savings rate, 1, 8, 81, 229
sectoral balance. *See* Sectoral
balance
transportation, 75, 81
water and electric power, 82
See also Absorptive capacity;
Industries; Public sector investment
Education, 14, 16–17, 120–22, 123–
24, 125
construction program, 79
expenditures for, 77, 78, 120–21
goals of, 17, 123–24
higher education, 17, 84, 121–22
independent budget, higher education, 84
number of students, 120
of women, 121
petroleum institute, 70
planning and research in, 122,
233
primary and secondary schools,
120
scholarship students, 17, 121, 122
secondary education, 121

Education—continued
  teachers, 120
  United Nations Center for Economic and Social Planning in the Middle East, 122
  university, 17, 125
  See also University of Kuwait
Effort and reward relationship, 4, 26, 76, 109, 121–22, 228–29
Energy sources and competition, 28, 46, 55, 59–61, 73, 98, 230
  coal, 60–61
  hydroelectric, 61
  natural gas (North Sea, European), 57–58, 62
  nuclear power (atomic energy), 55, 59–60, 61, 98, 118
England. *See* United Kingdom
Entrepreneurial ability, 5, 80
  development requirements in, 26, 105, 106, 232
  indigenous, 5, 12, 80, 106, 134, 165, 173, 224, 228, 229
Ethiopia, fertilizers to, 115
Europe (Western), 47, 112, 116
  aid from, 181, 189–90
  energy consumption in, 50, 52
  energy sources of, 60–61
  imports from, 25, 161
  non-oil exports to, 164
  oil exports to, 29, 58, 61, 160, 161
  tax policies on oil products, 48–49, 57–58
European Economic Community (EEC), 29, 139, 146, 169
  energy consumption of, 51
  energy policy of, 57
  natural gas production, 57–58
Expenditures by government:
  airport, 79
  construction, 79
  capital, 76, 77, 79, 80, 81
  current, 77, 79, 81
  defense, 77
  education, 77, 78
  foreign investment, 80, 81
  health, 77, 78
  housing, 79

Expenditures by government—continued
  labor, 78–79
  land purchases, 76, 77, 79, 83
  mixed joint-stock companies. *See* Mixed joint-stock companies
  ports, 77, 79
  public utilities, 77, 79
  public works, 77
  roads, 77, 79
  water supply, 77
Exports, 24–25, 83, 99
  duty on, 77, 78
  non-oil (reexports), 23–24, 25
  non-oil to Africa, 164
  non-oil to Arab world, 163, 164, 165
  non-oil to Asia, 164
  non-oil to Europe, 164
  non-oil to U.S. (Western hemisphere), 164
  of oil, 24–25, 160, 161
  of oil, destination of, 25, 161
  prospects for, 160–61

Factors of production:
  capital. *See* Capital
  domestic imbalance of, 5–6, 227–28, 229, 237
  labor. *See* Labor force
  land. *See* Agriculture; Land
  management, 105, 227, 228, 229
  See also Entrepreneurial ability
Failakah, 10
Fertilizer production, 20, 114, 115–16, 160–61
  and marketing, 115
  See also Kuwait Chemical Fertilizers Company
Financial institutions. *See* Banking
First Five Year Plan for Economic and Social Development, 1967/68—1971/72, 124–32, 231–32, 234, 239
  Arab complementarity and cooperation, 125, 231, 233
  Central Bank, 127, 231

First Five Year Plan—continued
diversification, 124, 126
foreign investment, 128–29, 132
gross domestic product, 125, 129
gross national product, 231
growth rate, 124, 126
human resource development, 124, 126
infrastructure development, 127
labor force, 124–25, 125–26
mixed enterprise investment, 128, 129
oil revenue base, 125, 126
Plan draft alterations and implications, 130–31
population, 124, 125–26, 231
private investment, 128, 129
public investment, 128, 129
public receipts, 130, 131
redistribution of income, 127
savings, 128–29, 130
sectoral contribution in GDP, 126, 127, 128
sectoral investment goals, 127, 128, 129, 131–32
urban balance, 126
See also Urbanization
First National City Bank, Petroleum Department of, 50
Fishing industry, 20, 110, 119
labor force in, 17, 119
and Plan, GDP contribution and investment, 127
Food processing, 108, 119. *See also* Agriculture; Fishing; Kuwait Flour Mills Company
Foreign aid, 235
Agency for International Development, U.S. (A.I.D.), 192, 195, 207, 219, 223
to agriculture, 203–4
and Arab world, 219
comparative analysis of, 216–19
Development Assistance Committee, OECD, (D.A.C.), 4, 181, 189–90, 191, 192, 217, 218, 219, 220, 222, 223, 235

Foreign aid—continued
Export-Import Bank, U.S., 189, 190–91, 192, 194, 222, 235
forms of, 182
International Bank for Reconstruction and Development (IBRD), 183, 185, 192, 194, 200, 207, 225
International Development Association (IDA), 192, 219, 236
International Finance Corporation (IFC), 225
and needs of developing nations, 181–83, 235
political content of, 223
quality of, 182–88, 189–91, 192
quantitative level of, 217–18
"tied" loans, 193, 220–21, 222
See also Economic aid; Organization for Economic Co-operation and Development (OECD); under individual countries
Foreign contacts. *See* International contacts and outlook
Foreign exchange income, 23
Foreign investments, 23, 76, 160
advising for, 12, 132
and budget, 77, 81
expenditures for, 81
income from, 8, 23, 77
office in England, 216
private, 76, 81
Foreign-owned business, taxes on, 21
France, aid from, 4, 190, 218
aid share of national income, 217
Compagnie française des Petroles, 68
energy consumption of, 49
energy policy of, 55, 57, 58
oil exports to, 25
tying aid, 220–21
wages in national income, 109
Free trade area, 141, 156, 157
Fuel oil, 25, 49

Gas, natural. *See* Natural gas
Gas oil, 37, 48–49

Gasoline, cost of, 48
  natural, 38
General Authority for South Arab-
    ian and Arabian Gulf States
    (Gulf Permanent Assistance
    Committee), 183, 208–9, 209–
    10
  allocations to, 209
  economic surveys, 208–9
  social overhead, 208, 209
  See also Economic aid
Geography of Kuwait, 8, 10
Germany (Western), aid from, 4,
    190, 218, 219
  aid share of national income, 217
  energy policy of, 55, 58
  refining in, 58
  wages in national income, 109
Ghana, wages in national income,
    109
Glass manufacturing, 20, 110, 111
Government:
  budget of. *See* Budgets
  civil service. *See* Civil service
  expenditures of. *See* Expenditures
  investments in private sector, 20
  land purchases. *See* Land purchase
    program
  role in economic life, 26, 116
  See also Public sector investments
Greece, wages in national income,
    109
Gross domestic product, 3, 16, 18,
    99, 106, 125, 129
Gross national product, 5, 7, 9, 229,
    231, 237
  expenditure (1962/63—1965/66),
    9
  and Plan, 125
  savings rate of, 1, 8, 81
  See also Economy
Gulf Bank, 89
Gulf Fisheries, 119
Gulf Oil Corporation, 20, 39–40,
    43, 56, 68, 87
  long-term supply contract of, 40,
    68
  tankers, 176

Gulf Permanent Assistance Com-
    mittee. *See* General Authority
    for South Arabian and Arabian
    Gulf States

Harrod-Domar model, 97
Health services, 123, 125
  expenditures for, 77, 78, 120
  facilities, 79, 123
  statistics of, 123
Hirschman, A. O., 102–3
History of Kuwait, 10–12
Housing, expenditures on, 79
  low-income program of, 87
  and Plan, investment for, 126
  Savings and Credit Bank support
    of, 92, 93
  See also Kuwait Investment Com-
    pany; Kuwait Prefabricated
    Building Company
Human resource development, 26,
    120–24, 125. *See also* Education,
    Health services; Labor; Popu-
    lation
Hydroponics, 118, 238

Illiteracy, 16–17
Immigration, 5–6, 13, 14–17, 123
  control of, 123, 125
  economic significance of, 123
  and naturalization policy, 123
  and regionalism, 17
Import trade, 22–23, 25, 83, 108
  with Africa, 161, 162
  with Arab world, 161, 162
  with Asia, 161, 162
  duties on, 22, 77, 78
  with Europe, 161, 162
  per capita imports, 22
  propensity to import, 82, 83
  -substitution, 109
  with U.S. (Western hemisphere),
    161–62
Income distribution, 5, 85, 230
  and land purchase program, 75–
    76, 230
Income tax, 75

India, 12, 133
  aid (Sino-Soviet) to, 206
  and Arab Petroleum Congress, 151
  fertilizer requirements of, 113
  immigration from, 172–73
  Kuwaiti investment in, 236
  and oil utilization, 59
Indonesia, and Arab Petroleum Congress, 151
  oil production and reserves, 33, 67, 68
  and OPEC, 65, 67
Industries, 5, 19, 81–82, 139, 141, 142
  chemicals. *See* Petrochemicals; Sea water, chemicals from
  capital-intensive, 238
  construction, 19
  domestically oriented, 106, 108, 109–11
  export oriented, 25, 95, 106, 111–16, 136, 140, 233
  financing required for exports, 22, 225–26
  food processing, 20, 108, 110
  infant-industry argument, 109–10
  investment in, 108, 127
  labor force in, 17, 85, 106–8
  mixed enterprises, 20–21
  and Plan, contribution to GDP and investment, 127, 128
  potential projects, 20, 110
  protectionism, 109
  Savings and Credit Bank support of, 21, 93–94
  share companies, 91
  share in GDP, 106, 127
  See also Petrochemicals; Refining
Inflation, 95, 100, 109, 132
Interdependence, 172–78
  and population, 172–74
  water and waterways, 174–78
  See also Labor force; Population of Kuwait; Shatt-el-Arab project; Suez Canal; Suez Canal pipeline project

Interest rates, in Kuwait, 82, 90–91
  Commercial Law of 1961, 91
  other nations, 82
International Bank for Reconstruction and Development (World Bank), missions of, 80, 110. *See also* Foreign aid
International contacts and outlook, 12, 19, 174, 224, 232. *See also* Exports; Foreign investment; Import trade; Regionalism
International Development Association. *See* Foreign aid
International Finance Corporation. *See* Foreign aid
International Fisheries Company, 119
International Monetary Fund, 92, 187, 188
Intra-help (intra-aid), 4, 27
Investment, 4, 5, 7, 149, 150
  Advisory committee on, 12, 132
  as capital "replacement," 229–30
  diversification of, 97
  domestic, 8, 229–30
  foreign. *See* Foreign investment
  guarantees, 161
  by private sector. *See* Private sector
  in private sector, by government, 8
  in public sector. *See* Public sector investment
  regional, 149–50, 174
  See also Economic aid; Regionalism
Investment companies, 85, 86, 87, 89. *See also* Kuwait Foreign Trade, Contracts and Investment Company; Kuwait Investment Company
Italy, aid from, 190, 218
  energy policy of, 57, 58
  oil exports to, 25, 58
  tying aid, 220
Iran (Persia), 12, 45, 69
  Consortium, 68
  immigration from, 172–73
  nationalization of oil in, 55, 58, 62

Iran (Persia)—continued
  and oil, 40, 41
  oil production and/or reserves, 31,
    33, 55, 63, 64, 68
  and OPEC, 65, 71
Iraq, 45, 69, 152, 153
  and Arab Common Market, 153,
    166
  economic cooperation with Ku-
    wait, 160
  exports of, 99
  exports to, 87
  fertilizers to, 115
  gold tranche position of, 188
  immigration from, 172, 173
  imports from, 162, 163, 166
  inter-Arab trade, 154
  labor force in, 145
  and natural gas, 148
  non-oil exports to, 163, 165
  and oil, 40, 41
  oil production and/or reserves, 31,
    33, 62, 63, 68, 148
  OECD-Kuwaiti aid to, 219
  and OPEC, 65, 71
  petrochemicals, 160, 170
  state reserves loans to, 212,
    213
  water from, 117, 177–78
  See also Shatt-el-Arab project
Ivory Coast, Arab-African Bank
    mission to, 211

Jabir al-Ahmad al-Sabah, 167
Japan, 12, 119, 140
  aid from, 4, 181, 190, 218
  aid share of national income, 217
  energy consumption of, 51, 52
  energy policy of, 52
  fertilizer consumption, 113
  imports from, 161, 164
  oil exports to, 26, 44, 61, 160, 161
  tying aid, 220
  wages in national income, 109
  See also Arabian Oil Company
Jordan, 138, 170
  and Arab Common Market, 153,
    166, 170

Jordan—continued
  Arab-African Bank support, 211
  fertilizers to, 115
  gold tranche position of, 188
  immigration from, 172, 173
  imports from, 162, 163, 166
  Industrial Development Organi-
    zation, 189
  inter-Arab trade, 154
  KFAED loans to, 189, 194–95,
    195–96, 196–97, 204, 207
  labor force in, 145
  non-oil exports to, 163–64, 165
  OECD-Kuwaiti aid to, 219
  sectoral distribution of GDP, 143
  state reserves loans to, 212, 213
  Yarmouk River project, 195–96

Kenya, Arab-African Bank mission
    to, 211
Kerosine, production of, 37, 48
  prices of, 48
Khafji refinery, 38
Kuber, 44
Kuwait Airways, budget of, 84
Kuwait Asbestos Industries Com-
    pany, 86, 88
Kuwait Aviation Fueling Company,
    87
Kuwait Chemical Fertilizers Com-
    pany, 20, 86, 87, 115–16
Kuwait City, 5, 10, 75, 134
Kuwait Currency Board, budget of,
    84
  functions of, 92
  See also Central Bank
Kuwait Flour Mills Company, 86
Kuwait Foreign Trade, Contracts
    and Investment Company, 86,
    216, 225
  projects of, 87, 159, 216
Kuwait Fund for Arab Economic
    Development, 6, 184–208, 225,
    226, 235–36
  amount extended, 204
  budget of, 84
  capital of, 184, 185
  as catalyst, 207

Kuwait Fund—continued
development lending and creditworthiness, 184, 186
feasibility requirements, 185–86
impact of, 203–8
loan to Lebanon, 201–2, 204, 208
loan to U.A.R., 175, 199–200,
204, 207, 208
loans to Algeria, 198–99, 204, 207,
208
loans to Jordan, 189, 194–95,
195–96, 196–97, 204, 207
loans to Morocco, 200–201, 204,
207, 208
loans to Sudan, 194, 200, 204, 207
loans to Tunisia, 197, 197–98,
204, 208
objectives of, 185
operations of, 193–202
and other agencies, 207
and Plan, 129
quality of aid of, 186–93
regional implications of, 207–8,
218–19, 220
repayment to, 191
restrictions on, 185, 191, 193
sectoral support by, 203–5
terms of, 188–89, 223
and U.A.R. projects, 159
and Yemen, 202, 206
Kuwait Hotels Company, 86
Kuwait Investment Company, 86, 88
projects of, 87, 216
Kuwait National Fisheries, 119
Kuwait National Petroleum Company, 20, 21, 38, 87, 111–12
all-hydrogen refinery (Shuaiba),
38, 46, 111, 112
concession of, 46, 87
government equity in, 86
government loan to, 88
marketing operations of, 112
refining by, 24, 46, 87, 111–12
See also Kuwait Aviation Fueling
Company
Kuwait Oil Company, 25, 36, 38,
68, 77, 82, 87
concession of, 39–42

Kuwait Oil Company—continued
injection plant, 24
production of, 32, 39, 58
refining by, 37
royalty expensing issue, 42–43
special payments of, 77
Kuwait Oil Tanker Company, 88,
176
loan from government, 88
Kuwait Prefabricated Building
Company, 87, 88
Kuwait Shell Petroleum Development Company, Ltd., con-
cession, 45–46
Kuwait Transport Company, 86, 88
regional basis of, 88

Labor force, 5–6, 14–17, 74, 97,
105–6, 106–8, 227, 228
in construction industry, 16–17
employment opportunities, 85,
98, 125
expenditures for, 78–79
Kuwaiti workers, 14–17, 97, 124–
25, 125–26
non-Kuwaiti workers, 5–6, 14–17,
172–74
in oil industry, 16–17, 78, 99,
145
in services, 17–18, 99
share in national income, 108
sources of, 13, 17, 172–74
wages of, 81
See also Civil service; Wages
Land, 227, 228
price of, 76
Land purchase program by government, 6, 75–76, 80–81, 228, 230
expenditures for, 77, 79, 81, 83, 85
Law of National Industries, 21
Law No. 49 of 1966, 89
League of Arab States, 70, 234
Arab airline, 152, 153
Arab Financial Institution for
Economic Development, 152,
155, 186
Arab Navigation Company, 152–
53, 155

League of Arab States—continued
    Arab Oil Company, 153, 155
    Arab Oil Tankers Company, 152, 155
    Arab Petroleum Congress, 70–71, 151–52
    collective measures of, 150–54, 158, 161
    Convention for Facilitating Trade Exchange and Regulating Transit Trade, 150, 154
    Convention for Settlement of Payments of Current Transactions and the Transfer of Capital, 150–51
    Economic Council of, 150, 151, 152, 153, 155
    implementation gap, 154–55, 158, 161, 179
    Joint Arab Potash Company, 152, 154–55
    Kuwaiti membership and participation in, 11–12, 149–50, 152, 153
    Petroleum Committee of, 151
Lebanon, 138
    Arab-African Bank branch in, 211
    gold tranche position of, 188
    immigration from, 172, 173
    imports from, 162, 163
    inter-Arab trade, 154
    KFAED loan to, 201–2, 204, 208
    Kuwaiti investment in, 87
    Litani River project, 201–2
    non-oil exports to, 163–64, 165
    OECD-Kuwaiti aid to, 219
    sectoral distribution of GDP, 143
    state reserves loan, 212, 213
Legislation affecting economy, 21, 89, 91
Lewis, W. Arthur, 3, 10
Libya, 1, 4, 118, 138, 207, 237
    capital surplus, 145, 207
    crisis assistance by, 235
    gold tranche position of, 188
    natural gas, 148
    and North African regionalism, 153, 205

Libya—continued
    oil production and/or reserves, 31, 33, 55, 64, 67, 148
    and OPEC, 64, 65, 67
Loombe, Claude, 132

Maintenance, labor force in, 108
Manufacturing industries, 106
    labor force in, 17, 107
    share in GDP, 18
    See also Industries; Sectoral balance
Marginal propensity to consume, 95, 130, 229
Marginal propensity to save, 134
Marine products, 19
Maritime, background, 12, 16
    industries, 12, 17, 110–11, 230
Medical care. See Health services
Mercantile attitude of Kuwaitis, 12, 25, 85, 168, 228
Metallurgy, aluminum and steel, 20
Mexico, 151
Middle East, 14, 122, 136, 159
    consumption of petrochemical products, 114, 148
    fertilizer needs, 113–14
    oil, production and/or reserves. See individual countries
    per capita income, 137
    and regionalism, 87
    See also Arab world
Mill, John Stuart, 101
Minagish injection plant, 36
Mixed joint-stock companies (public and private), 20–21, 80, 84–89. See also Kuwait Flour Mills Company; Kuwait Foreign Trade, Contracts and Investment Company; Kuwait Hotels Company; Kuwait Investment Company; Kuwait National Petroleum Company; National Industries Company; Petrochemicals Industries Company
Monetary developments, currency, 92

Monetary developments—continued
supply of money, 91–92
See also Banking; Kuwait Currency Board
Morocco, and North African regionalism, 153, 205
gold tranche position of, 188
immigration from, 172
KFAED loans to, 200–201, 204, 207, 208
sectoral distribution in GDP, 143
Muskat, immigration from, 172, 173

Naphtha, 37–38
National Assembly, 20, 153, 184, 213, 214
National Bank of Kuwait, 89
National income, 7
and the Plan, 125
share generated by labor force in, 108, 109
National Industries Company, The, 85, 86, 88
National Industries Law, 21
Natural gas, 34–36, 46, 230–31
analysis of, 35
as a by-product of oil, 36
European sources (North Sea) and production, 57–58, 62
flaring off of, 35, 148
injection of, 36
LPG (liquid petroleum gas), 34, 35, 36
production of, 34–35, 148
utilization of, 20, 34–36, 71, 230–31
Netherlands, aid from, 190, 218
aid share of national income, 217
Economic Institute, 202
oil exports to, 25
wages in national income, 109
Neutral zone, 68
administration of, 8
oil companies in. *See* Aminoil; Arabian Oil Company
Nigeria, 69
Arab-African Bank mission to, 211
Kuwaiti investment in, 212

Nigeria—continued
oil production and/or reserves, 53, 55–56, 62, 65
and OPEC, 65
North Africa (Maghreb), 136
economic cooperation among nations of, 153–54
immigration from, 173
oil of, 53, 58, 60, 61
non-oil exports to, 164
Norway, aid from, 190
aid share of national income, 217
wages in national income, 109
Nuclear power. *See* Energy sources and competition
Nurkse, Ragnar, 101–2
Nursing, Institute, 123

Oil industry, 19, 26, 29–73, 160, 161
analysis of gas, 35
concessions, 39–42, 43–46, 68
consumer-producer dialogue, 28
contribution to GDP, 127
demand for oil, 49–53
destination of exports of, 25
effects on economy of, 3, 74, 97–98
elasticity of demand for, 46–49, 59
exports of, 3, 29, 98
foreign exchange income from, 24, 98
"heavy" crude and ramifications, 38, 48, 52, 54–55, 58, 59
income tax payments, 41
labor in, 16, 17, 18, 99, 108
national energy policies, 29
natural gas production. *See* Natural gas
petroleum institute, 70
pipelines, 53, 152, 176–77
price elasticity of refined products, 47–48
price of oil, 33, 41–42, 47, 54–55, 98, 231
price stabilization, 26, 53–61, 98
production (Kuwait), 3, 32, 62, 63, 64, 65–66, 67, 68, 98, 125, 230–31

Oil industry—continued
  production costs of non-Kuwaiti oil, 31, 62
  production costs of oil (Kuwait), 30–31, 62, 230
  production of other nations, 62, 63, 98
  production programming, 62–69
  product mix flexibility, 111–12
  refining operations, 24, 128
  reserve-production ratio, 32–33, 34, 65–66, 230
  reserves of, 3, 98, 230
  revenues from, 3, 77, 97–98, 131
  royalties and royalty expensing, 42–43, 231
  security of supply, 46, 58, 68, 69
  tankers for, 53
  tonnage royalty, 40–41
  vertical integration of, 28, 39–40
  as wasting asset, 2, 53, 98, 227, 228
  See also Aminoil; Arabian Oil Company; British Petroleum Company, Ltd.; Gulf Oil Company; Kuwait National Petroleum Company; Kuwait Oil Company; Kuwait Shell Petroleum Development Company; individual exporting and importing countries
Oman, immigration from, 172, 173
  non-oil exports to, 164, 165
Organization for Economic Co-operation and Development (OECD), 181, 189, 235. *See also* Development Assistance Committee; Foreign aid
Organization of the Petroleum Exporting Countries (OPEC), 26, 29
  establishment of, 54, 71
  multilateralism in oil production, 69–70, 72–73, 231
  objectives of, 71–73
  petrochemicals coordination, 72
  price stabilization, 55, 66, 71–72

OPEC—continued
  and production programming, 64–69
  royalty expensing, 42–43, 72

Pakistan, immigration from, 172–73
  fertilizer needs of, 113, 115
  Kuwaiti investment in, 174
Palgrave, William, 10
Pearling industry, 12, 88, 119
Persian Gulf. *See* Arab Gulf
Personnel. *See* Labor force
Peru, wages in national income, 109
Petrochemical industry, 38, 85, 86
  coordination of, 71, 159, 160
  domestic, 20, 21, 112–16, 170, 231, 238
  ethylene, 114
  intermediates in, 115
  and marketing, 113, 114
  regional, 114, 148, 159
  synthetic rubber, 114
  See also Kuwait Chemical Fertilizers Company; Petrochemicals Industries Company
Petrochemicals Industries Company, 20, 86, 87. *See also* Kuwait Chemical Fertilizers Company
Petroleum. *See* Oil industry
Philippines, wages in national income, 109
Planning, 4–5, 96, 97, 122, 157, 158, 232, 239
  in capital-surplus economy, 97, 239
  First Five Year Plan for Economic and Social Development, 1967/68—1971/72, 69, 124, 132
  regional, 146–50, 157–58
  in relation to resources, 96, 232
  See also First Five Year Plan for Economic and Social Development; Regional sectoral planning
Planning Board, functions of, 79. *See also* First Five Year Plan for Economic and Social Development

Population of Kuwait, 6–7, 13, 15, 74, 124, 134, 173, 236
  age-distribution, 13–15
  in civil service, 16
  immigration and control, 5–6, 13, 74, 123, 125, 172–74, 237
  and labor force. *See* Labor force
  naturalization policy, 13, 123
  non-Kuwaiti residents, 13–16, 116, 125, 172–74
  and the Plan, 124–25, 126
  in schools, 18
  transit mentality in, 118–19, 123
Ports, 79
  revenues from, 77, 78
Portugal, aid from, 190, 218, 223
  share of aid in national income, 217, 223
Power, expenditures for, 77
  labor force in, 17, 108
  and Plan, contribution in GDP and investment, 127
Prebisch, Raul, 169
Prices, 25–26
  of oil. *See* Oil industry
Private sector:
  and agriculture, 94
  and domestic investment, 87–88, 92–93, 94, 95, 229
  external investment of, 26, 81, 83, 92, 174
  flow of funds through, 91–92
  government investment in, 95
  loan capital for, 90–92
  regional investment of, 174
  share companies, 91
  stock exchange, 91
  See also Agriculture; Industries
Productivity, 99, 104
  in agriculture, 117
  and education, 123–24
  and labor force, 108
  See also Civil service; Industries; Labor force
Public finance. *See* Budgets; Taxes
Public sector investment:
  domestic expenditures, 77, 79, 83

Public sector investment—continued
  expenditures for external, 26, 67–68, 80, 81, 83
  housing. *See* Housing
  loans to companies, 88, 89
  planning. *See* Planning
  ports. *See* Ports
  roads. *See* Roads
  water. *See* Water supply
  See also Education; Health services
Public utilities, expenditures for, 77, 79
  revenue from, 77

Qaru, 44
Qatar, immigration from, 173
  capital surplus, 145
  fertilizers to, 115
  non-oil exports to, 164, 165
  oil production and/or reserves, 33, 63
  and OPEC, 65

Rainfall. *See* Climate
Raudhatain, gas injection plant, 36
  oil field, 36
  water from, 117–18
Real estate, 5, 85, 87, 109
  Savings and Credit Bank support of, 93, 94
Regional sectoral planning, 146–50
  and agriculture, 146–47, 149
  for expanded markets, 147, 149
  and industry, 147–48
  petrochemicals, 148
  and safeguarding capital movement, 148, 149
  steel, 147–48
  supply and demand, 146
  and technical skills, 147, 149
  textiles, 147, 149
Regionalism, 26–27, 87, 104, 122, 150–54
  benefits of, 135, 148–49
  bilateral measures for, 158–61
  and coordination, 144, 149, 157
  and economic cooperation, 26–27, 133–80

Regionalism—continued
  and human resources, 17, 138, 153, 172–74
  and industrialization, 139
  in investment, 4, 6, 26, 27, 67–68, 104, 154, 174, 234
  motivations for, 233–34
  multilateral measures for, 149–54
  and trade, 12, 25, 136–37, 138–39, 154–55, 156, 161–66
  See also Arab world; Economic aid; the Kuwait Fund for Arab Economic Development; Middle East
Remittances of non-Kuwaitis, 173
Research, 238
  and innovation, 19
  See also Education
Revenues, 74, 76–77
  allocations of, 77
  assistance programs, 66–67
  development requirements, 65, 66–67, 67–68
  foreign exchange, 23
  foreign investment, 76, 77, 82, 83
  import duties, 76, 77, 83
  oil, 63, 74, 75, 82, 83
  and Plan, 130–32
  public utilities, 76, 77
  resale of land, 76, 77
  sources of, 77, 82, 83
  taxes. *See* Taxes
Roads, 76
Royal Dutch/Shell, 68
  long-term supply contract of, 40
Royal family. *See* Al-Sabah family
Rumania, 151

Salaries. *See* Wages
Saudi Arabia, 4, 69, 207, 237
  capital surplus, 145, 207
  crisis assistance by, 235
  fertilizers to, 115
  gold tranche position of, 188
  immigration from, 173
  imports from, 163
  inter-Arab trade, 154

Saudi Arabia—continued
  labor force in, 145
  natural gas, 148
  non-oil exports to, 163, 165
  and oil, 41, 152, 153
  oil production and/or reserves, 30–31, 33, 62, 63,64,67,68, 148
  and OPEC, 64, 65, 67, 71
Savings, 76, 81, 82, 97, 102, 128
  -investment bottleneck, 102, 103, 106, 229
  and Plan, 128–29
  private, 85
  public, disposition of, 81
Savings and Credit Bank, 92–94
  capitalization of, 93, 94
  independent budget of, 84
Schools. *See* Education
Schumpeter, Joseph, 101
Schweizer, Dr. Samuel, 132
Sea water, chemicals from, 19, 108, 110–11
Sectoral balance, 5, 99–100, 124, 230
  agriculturalization, 100, 104, 116–19, 127
  commerce, 108, 127
  domestic, 17–22, 97, 143, 229–30, 237
  industrialization, 21–22, 100, 104–16, 127, 233
  leading sector, 18, 101
  oil, 18–19, 98–99, 104, 105, 127
  and Plan, contribution to GDP and investment, 126, 127
  region. *See* Regional sectoral planning
  services, 85, 99, 104, 108
  See also Agriculture; Civil service; Commerce; Industries; Trade
Senegal, Arab-African Bank mission to, 211
Services, 85, 99, 104, 108
  and Plan, contribution in GDP and investment, 127
  labor force in, 143
  See also Civil service
Shale oil, 59, 66
Shatt-el-Arab project, 117, 177–78

Shipyards, shipbuilding, 12, 88, 108
Shuaiba, industrial complex in, 20,
    21, 36, 79, 87, 111
  all-hydrogen refinery at, 111, 112
  independent budget for, 84
  See also Kuwait Chemical Ferti-
    lizers Company; Kuwait Na-
    tional Petroleum Company
Singer, Hans W., 102
Single-product economy, 2–3, 7, 29,
    97–99, 103, 130, 144
  effect of, 95, 97–99
Sino-Soviet aid, 193, 206, 218
Smith, Adam, 101
Social overhead capital, 101, 104,
    120, 127
Socony-Mobil (Socony-Vacuum Oil
    Company), 68
  long-term supply contract of, 40
Somalia (Somaliland), Arab-African
    Bank mission to, 211
  fertilizers to, 115
Standard Oil Company (New Jer-
    sey), 68
  long-term supply contract of, 40
Standard Oil of California, 68
State reserves loans, 183–84, 212–16,
    234–35
  to Algeria, 212, 213
  amount extended, 212
  curtailment of, 213
  to Dubai, 212, 213
  to Jordan, 212, 213
  to Lebanon, 212, 213
  to Morocco, 212, 213
  political content of, 213–14
  program lending of, 214–15
  regional implications of, 218–20
  to Sudan, 212, 213
  terms of, 212, 223
  to Tunisia, 212, 213
  to U.A.R., 212, 213
Sudan, 144
  fertilizers to, 115
  gold tranche position of, 188
  immigration from, 172, 173
  KFAED loans to, 194, 200, 204,
    207

Sudan—continued
  non-oil exports to, 164
  OECD-Kuwaiti aid to, 219
  railroads, modernization scheme,
    207
  sectoral distribution of GDP, 143,
    144
  state reserves loan to, 212, 213
Suez Canal, 174–75, 207
  loan from KFAED, 175
Suez Canal pipeline project, 175–77
Suez crisis (1956), 58
Supply and demand, 100, 101, 102,
    105
Sweden, 18
  wages in national income, 109
Switzerland, 133
  interest rate in, 82
  wages in national income, 109
Syria, 153
  and Arab Common Market, 153,
    170–71
  exports of, 170–71
  gold tranche position of, 188
  immigration from, 173
  imports from, 162, 163, 165,
    166
  inter-Arab trade, 154, 166
  labor force in, 145
  non-oil exports to, 164
  sectoral distribution in GDP, 143,
    144

Tankers, oil, 88
  supertankers, 176
Tanzania, Arab-African Bank mis-
    sion to, 211
  fertilizers to, 115
Tar sands, 59, 66
Tariffs and customs, 157, 233
  rates of, 22
  receipts from, 131
Tax policy, 75, 76, 77–78
  See also Income tax
Technical aid, 224
Temperature. *See* Climate
Texaco, 68
Total economic integration, 156–57

Trade, 12, 22–26, 82, 88, 136, 137, 161–66, 168, 233, 234
with Arab Common Market, 166, 168–69
balance of, 23–24, 82, 165–66
composition of, 24, 164–65
-creation, 136, 156
direction of Kuwaiti, 161–66
-diversion, 136–37, 156
international, 25–26, 161–62, 163–64
and Plan, contribution to GDP and investment, 126, 234
regional, 25, 136–37, 141, 161, 162–63
terms of, 33, 53, 55, 102, 189
Transport, transportation, 85, 86
and Plan, contribution in GDP and investment, 127
See also Airport; Kuwait Airways; Kuwait Navigation Company; Kuwait Oil Tankers Company; Kuwait Transport Company; Ports; Roads
Trucial States (Arabian Gulf States), immigration from, 173
agricultural imports, 146
capital surplus, 1, 145
Kuwaiti aid to, 208–10
non-oil exports to, 164
oil production and/or reserves, 55
See also General Authority for South Arabian and Arabian Gulf States
Tunisia, and North African regionalism, 153
gold tranche position of, 188
KFAED loans to, 197, 198, 204, 208
La Goulette II Power project, 197
Medjerda Valley project, 197–98
sectoral distribution in GDP, 143
Soviet aid to, 198
Turkey, fertilizers to, 115

Uganda, Arab-African Bank mission to, 211
wages in national income, 109

Union of Soviet Socialist Republics (USSR, Soviet Union), 133
aid from, 193, 198, 206, 218
and Arab Petroleum Congress, 151
oil production and/or reserves, 31, 33, 47, 55, 56
trade with, 164
United Arab Republic (U.A.R., Egypt), 153
aid (Sino-Soviet) to, 206, 219
Arab-African Bank, 210–11, 212
and Arab Common Market, 153
Aswan High Dam, 200
bilateral arrangements with Kuwait, 87, 158–60, 215–16
Central Bank of, 159
exports of, 99, 170–71
fertilizers, 114, 159
gold tranche position of, 188
immigration from, 173
impact of Kuwaiti aid compared, 219
imports from, 155, 162–63
inter-Arab trade, 154, 166
Kuwait Foreign Trade, Contracts and Investment Company, 87, 159, 215–16
Kuwaiti investment in, 159
labor force in, 145
loans from KFAED, 159, 175, 219
natural gas production, 148
non-oil exports to, 164, 165
oil production, 148
petrochemicals, 159, 160
Port Said free zone, 159
sectoral distribution of GDP, 143, 144
state reserves loans to, 212, 213, 219
Suez Canal, 174–75, 219
Suez Canal pipeline project, 175–77
wages in national income, 109
United Kingdom, 119
agriculture of, 117
aid from, 4, 182, 190, 217, 218, 219, 236

United Kingdom—continued
  aid share in national income, 217
  British Foreign Office, 11
  British Petroleum Company. *See*
    British Petroleum Company,
    Ltd.
  energy consumption of, 49, 51
  energy policy of, 55, 57, 58
  foreign investment in. *See* Foreign
    investment; Kuwait Invest-
    ment Company
  imports from, 25, 164
  oil exports to, 25
  treaty with, 10–11
  tying aid, 220
  wages in national income, 109
United Nations, 133
  Conference on Trade and Devel-
    opment (UNCTAD), 53–54,
    72, 216
  Food and Agricultural Organi-
    zation, 119, 202, 207
  Institute for Economic and Social
    Planning in the Middle East, 122
  Kuwait's membership in, 12
  Special Fund, 122, 202, 207
  Trade and Development Board,
    72–73
United States, 116, 123, 133, 140
  Agency for International Devel-
    opment. *See* Foreign aid
  aid from, 181, 182–83, 189–90,
    192, 198, 206, 217–18, 236
  aid share of national income, 217
  American Independent Oil Com-
    pany. *See* Aminoil
  and Arab Petroleum Congress, 151
  coal production of, 60
  Congress of, 214
  distillation in, 117, 118
  energy consumption of, 49, 50,
    51, 52, 53
  energy policy of, 55, 56–57
  Export-Import Bank. *See* Foreign
    aid
  and Great Depression, 228
  imports from, 25, 161–62, 164
  non-oil exports to, 119

United States—continued
  nuclear energy in, 60
  oil exports to, 25, 56
  oil production and/or reserves,
    31, 33, 34, 66
  tying aid, 220
  wages in national income, 109
University of Kuwait, establishment
    of, 17, 121
  enrollment in, 121–22
Urbanism and urbanization, 5, 75,
    124
  Kuwaiti preference for, 116, 118,
    134
  sociological aspect, 116

Venezuela, 4, 99, 232, 237
  and Arab Petroleum Congress, 151
  oil production and/or reserves, 31,
    33, 34, 57, 67, 68, 99
  and OPEC, 65, 67, 71

Wages, 81, 108
  in national income, 109
Wallenburg, Dr. Marcus, 132
Water supply, 19, 232
  and agriculture, 81–82, 117, 118
  chemicals from sea water. *See*
    Sea water, chemicals from
  cost of distilled water, 117, 118
  desalination, 19, 117, 238
  and industry, 81–82, 118
  labor force in, 17
  and Plan, contribution in GDP
    and investment, 127
  Raudhatain source, 117–18
  Shatt-el-Arab. *See* Shatt-el-Arab
    project
Wheeler, General Raymond, 177
World Bank. *See* Foreign aid; Inter-
    national Bank for Reconstruc-
    tion and Development

Yemen, 208
  General Authority for South
    Arabian and Arabian Gulf
    States, 208–9
  immigration from, 172, 173
  and KFAED, 202
Yugoslavia, 151